Political Ideologies

This is a completely new edition of a widely used, concise and readable text.

Political Ideologies contains chapters on liberalism, conservatism, social-ism, democracy, nationalism, fascism, feminism and ecologism. It also includes a wide-ranging introduction looking at the role of ideology from Bacon to Fukuyama.

Each chapter:

- Analyses the principal ideas and concepts of each ideology, dis-tinguishing it from rival doctrines
- Sets each ideology clearly within the historical and political context
- Provides an annotated guide to further reading

This book is written in a clear and accessible style, introducing students to the complexities of political ideas. Those approaching the subject for the first time will find *Political Ideologies* an informative and engaging introduction.

Robert Eccleshall, Vincent Geoghegan, Richard Jay, Iain MacKenzie and **Rick Wilford** are all members of the Politics Department at the Queen's University of Belfast, and **Michael Kenny** lectures in Politics at Sheffield University.

Political Ideologies:
An Introduction

Second edition

Robert Eccleshall, Vincent Geoghegan,
Richard Jay, Michael Kenny,
Iain MacKenzie and Rick Wilford

London and New York

First published by Unwin Hyman, 1984

Second edition published 1994
by Routledge
11 New Fetter Lane, London EC4P 4EE

Simultaneously published in the USA and Canada
by Routledge
29 West 35th Street, New York, NY 10001

Typeset in 10/13pt Palatino by
Ponting–Green Publishing Services, Chesham, Bucks
Printed and bound in Great Britain by
TJ Press (Padstow) Ltd, Padstow, Cornwall

British Library Cataloguing in Publication Data
A catalogue record for this book is available from the
British Library

Library of Congress Cataloging in Publication Data
    Political ideologies / Robert Eccleshall . . . [et al.]. – 2nd ed.
        p.   c.m.
    Includes bibliographical references and index.
    ISBN 0–415–09982–X
    1. Political science.   2. Ideology.   I. Eccleshall, Robert.
    JA74.P63   1994
    320.5–dc20   94–21697
                                                        CIP

ISBN 0–415–09982–X

Contents

Chapter 1

Introduction

The arena of ideology

Iain MacKenzie

> An ideology really succeeds when even the facts which at first
> sight contradict it start to function as arguments in its favour.
>
> Slavoj Zizek, *The Sublime Object of Ideology,*
> London, Verso, 1989, 49

Ideologies help us to make sense of the complex social world in which
we live. They do this by providing a description of society, an intellectual map, which enables us to position ourselves in the social
landscape. Yet, in providing a description of social reality, ideologies
also embody a set of political ideas that detail the best possible form of
social organisation. Along with a map of reality comes a picture of an
ideal society. An ideology, then, provides both an account of existing
social and political relations and a blueprint of how these relations
ought to be organised. Beyond this general definition, however, the
concept of ideology is notoriously difficult to get to grips with. It is
loaded with a wide range of possible meanings, many of which are
contradictory. In one survey twenty-seven different senses of the term
were identified.[1] The development of some of these competing definitions will be looked at below. For the present, it is enough to recognise
that the concept of ideology has many different elements to it but a few
key ideas at its centre.

Given that it is possible to highlight the central features of the
concept of ideology, we must further recognise that there are many
different kinds of question we can then pursue. As with the study of a
particular ideology, we can examine the history of the term 'ideology',
the ideas that give it a distinctive character, alternative traditions within
it and so forth. It is impossible, however, to present a full discussion of
all such topics within the scope of this introduction. The focus shall be

on a specific issue, namely, what is involved in assessing ideologies? Can we find a way of critically comparing the ideologies discussed in this book? If so, on what grounds? If not, what are the implications of this? The importance of this kind of investigation is twofold. First, it strikes at the theoretical heart of the concept of ideology. Secondly, it stresses the need to think about the practical implications of ideologies in 'the real world'. As discussed in the following chapters this is particularly relevant when addressing, for example, the collapse of the Soviet bloc, the rising tide of fascism and nationalism in Europe and the growing importance of 'new' ideologies like feminism and ecologism throughout the world. Such developments require that we not only assess the particular features of these ideologies but also that we examine the concept of ideology in general in order to gain insight into ways of evaluating ideological conflict. For example, to understand the 'Thatcherite project', discussed by Robert Eccleshall in his chapter on conservatism, we may wish to examine it in terms of the effect it had on traditional conservative ideology. Yet, in doing so we are also drawn to evaluate the claims upon which Thatcherism rests; for instance, is it true, as Mrs Thatcher pronounced, that 'there is no such thing as society'? To do this, however, requires an understanding of the wider concerns raised in the study of ideology. These concerns will be mapped out in the remainder of the introduction and illustrated with reference to the chapters that follow.

IDEOLOGY: THE CLASSICAL CONCEPTION FROM BACON TO MARX

The concept of ideology has many precursors. The most notable is in the writings of Francis Bacon (1561–1626). In his book *Novum Organon* (1620) he argued for a rigorous scientific approach to the world that would dispel the 'idols' and 'phantoms' that he believed had held human thought captive since antiquity. The idols, he argued, were the trappings of the Aristotelian–Christian approach to the world that dominated his era. They were based on religious revelation and other-worldly myths, on superstition and prejudice, enshrined in tradition and upheld by feudal lords and masters; 'from ambition and in a dogmatic manner, these men have done the greatest damage to philosophy and the sciences'.[2] Crucially, Bacon saw that the beliefs they advanced were 'deeply rooted' in people's minds. Yet as the world became increasingly secular and modern, by way of burgeoning indus-trialisation for example, the ability of these old forms of knowledge and authority to hold sway in the minds of the populace began to wane. The attempt to find ways of providing a foundation of knowledge on an empirical, 'this-worldly' and human basis was the motivation of Bacon's book.

In this early attempt to extricate human thought from the grip of 'phantoms' we can discern a feature of ideology that recurs throughout its history. Ideology implies distinguishing false ideas from true ones. The study of ideology is concerned with how we know the difference between 'idols' and reality, and the philosophical foundations of knowledge in general. Ideology, to put it another way, has a close relationship with epistemology. Karl Mannheim, in his influential work *Ideology and Utopia* (1936), suggests that 'it is only when the distrust of man toward man, which is more or less evident at every stage of human history, *becomes explicit and is methodologically recognised*, that we prop-erly speak of an ideological taint in the utterances of others'.[3]

The processes of secularisation and growing dissent with traditional sources of authority and knowledge came to their most dramatic outpouring in the great upheaval of the French Revolution. It was in the midst of this attempt to overthrow the *ancien régime* and replace it with a new rational system of government based on the universal principles of liberty, equality and fraternity, that the term 'ideology' emerged. Antoine Destutt de Tracy (1754–1836), in whose writings it first appears, had been a key player in the revolution, only to find himself imprisoned with the onset of the Terror in 1793–4. It was in his cell, however, that he began to formulate an approach to the rational study of ideas that he called ideology (from idea/ology). As Eagleton has put it, 'the notion of ideology was thus brought to birth in thoroughly ideological conditions'.[4] De Tracy sought a way of objec-tively showing that the *false* ideas of the Terror contravened the *true* principles that had motivated the revolution. He sought to elaborate a science of ideas that would enable this distinction to be made, basing his work on what would now be called a behaviourist approach to psychology. If Newton had discovered the laws of gravity, thought de Tracy, why would it not be possible to discover the laws that govern the thought of humans? What was required was a 'Newton of the science of thought', and it was in this role that he saw himself. Upon his release from prison he pursued his work as a member of the *Institut*

Nationale, attempting to create a liberal system of national education that would put into practice his science of ideas.

However, as Napoleon came to power and a new nobility emerged in France, the overtly rationalistic approach of de Tracy did not find favour with the increasingly autocratic regime. Napoleon saw in the thought of de Tracy, and those who sympathised with him in the *Institut Nationale*, a threat to his authority. Their liberal and republican political ideas were to become for Napoleon, the source of 'all the misfortunes that have befallen our beloved France', and he dismissively labelled these thinkers 'the ideologues'. Thus, at the very birth of the term we find that ideology has assumed two contrasting meanings: ideology as a science of ideas (de Tracy) and ideology as a set of false, even subversive, ideas (Napoleon). This opposition sets the tone for the classical approach to ideology. In the thought of Karl Marx and Friedrich Engels, however, this approach was given a new twist.

The novel approach Marx and Engels took to the concept of ideology was to prove a definitive moment in the history of the concept. As we shall see in the next section, when people refer to ideology in the twentieth century they tend to assume the Marx–Engels definition. Despite the importance of this new examination, the work of Marx and Engels on ideology was destined to the same fate as de Tracy's; from being proposed as a scientific account of the generation of ideas in respect to material conditions, their work on ideology was soon to become criticised as containing dangerous abstractions. In his book *Alien Powers* Kenneth Minogue, for example, displays a similar attitude to the Marx–Engels conception as Napoleon had taken against de Tracy.[5] Minogue views ideologies as reductionist, that is they distil the 'perpetual and never resolved crisis' of life into 'a single governing mechanism', and Marxism, in his view, represents the paradigmatic ideology. Ideologies, for Minogue, create the false expectation in people's minds that a perfect world is ultimately attainable. In opposition to this view, many socialists argue that Minogue's position is the dangerous one because his analysis justifies the inequality of the *status quo* by denying that real advancement can be made towards an equal distribution of goods and powers. It is, they claim, Minogue's account of the imperfectibility of human beings that represents the ideological point of view. To get a clearer picture of the issues raised we must turn to examine Marx and Engels' account of ideology.

Although they never published an explicit and systematic discussion of the term in their life-time, we can look to their early collaboration,

The German Ideology (1846), for an initial appreciation of what they meant by ideology:

> Men are the producers of their conceptions, ideas, etc. – real active men, as they are conditioned by a definite development of their productive forces and of the intercourse corresponding to these, up to its furthest forms. Consciousness can never be anything else than conscious existence, and the existence of men is their actual life-process. If in all ideology men and their circumstances appear upside-down as in a camera-obscura, this phenomenon arises just as much from their historical life-process as the inversion of objects on the retina does from their physical life-process.[6]

It is not the case that false ideas can be overcome through the application of timeless truths generated by abstract reason, as it was for the Enlightenment thinkers of the French Revolution. Rather, for Marx and Engels, it is the role of changing historical conditions that is fundamental to the formation of ideas. The novelty of their inter-pretation lies in the way they link these concerns to the 'actual life-process' of human beings. It is in the actual world of human relations, principally our economic transactions, that ideas come into being, and as the biologist can study the inverted image on our retina (even though we may not be aware of it), Marx and Engels detail a method to study the 'inverted' forms of thinking that have arisen out of the real world. Yet this raises the question of how they conceived of the processes that generate our ideological conceptions. What is it in our 'real life' transactions that causes false ideas to come about?

The answer, famously, is that it is class interests that give rise to false ideas. As Robert Eccleshall and Richard Jay discuss, liberal democracy, for example, is often justified by appeal to ideas of individuality and the neutrality of the state. For Marx and Engels, such justifications are an expression of the dominant class interests of the industrial bour-geoisie; far from being true descriptions of the way the world is, they protect the interests of the ruling class. Such attempts at upholding liberal democracy, therefore, rest on a set of ideas that serve particular and biased class interests rather than reflect the truth of the whole situation. They constitute a false set of ideas, an ideology. To take another example, John Major's crusade in 1994 to get 'back to basics', to re-establish 'traditional British values', is for Marxists a way of justifying the values of the ruling class. In the name of 'universal truths' – that the nuclear family is better than the single parent family, for instance – the Conservatives are actually peddling the particular perspective of the class whose interests they represent; that is the bourgeoisie or ruling class.

The importance of this Marxist view of ideology can once again be examined in contrast to the Enlightenment view. Where de Tracy had conceived of combating a false system of ideas with another system of ideas, Marx and Engels argue that the only way to remove the ideological frameworks of society is to remove the contradictions of particular class interests inherent in the economic and social realms. As the Marxist critic Istvan Meszaros puts it, ideology is 'insurmountable in class societies' and theoretical reason alone cannot solve the problem of ideology.[7] Of course, much could be said about the intricacies of Marx and Engels' theory of ideology.[8] The important point is that, in grounding a theory of ideology in social and historical conditions, Marx and Engels combined the earlier notions of a science of the way ideas come into being (de Tracy) with the calling to account of false ideas (Napoleon). Moreover, by arguing that the real source of false ideas was to be found in the 'actual life-process' of human beings, their theory implied that false ideas could only be overthrown by revolutionary action in the real world. Finally then, overcoming real material contradictions in the class structure of society would inevitably lead, they argued, to the coming into consciousness of true understanding. A classless society would be devoid of ideology.

Immediately, though, a problem arises with this view of ideology. If it is claimed that social conditions generate false ideas through class conflict, how is it possible to know that this proposition itself is not a product of these same contradictions? What gives Marx and Engels access to the truth that is denied to the ideologically tainted majority? As Eagleton puts it, 'the critique of ideology . . . is at the same moment the critique of the critique of ideology'.[9] Taking two recent examples we can explain this paradox further. Meszaros, in a broad-side against free-market liberalism, claims that John Maynard Keynes, whom he views as one of its chief proponents (though this itself is debatable), 'assumed a highly partisan ideological position towards everything'. By way of numerous examples, Meszaros goes on to show that this ideological position as a defender of the industrial bourgeoisie 'underlines the total unreality of his [Keynes's] "scientific" diagnosis'.[10] In contrast, Richard Ebeling argues that 'collectivism' in the economic, social and political spheres is a dangerous 'fantasy'. He concludes that 'the only rational political-economic alternative' to it is free-market-based liberal society.[11] The profound, ideological difference of these two outlooks is a familiar aspect of political debate, one that we can see on the world stage of politics and, to a lesser degree, on the floor of the House of Commons. Both sides think they are right and the other mistaken. It is also a feature of debates within particular political ideologies. As Rick Wilford shows in his chapter on feminism, the 'crisis of identity' in feminist thought brought about by whether or not women and men are essentially the same *or* different in important respects involves two incompatible positions. No matter how hard we try to resolve the disputes, there will always be the chance for each side to label the other ideological. As Boudon puts it, 'what is knowledge for one person is ideology for another, and vice versa'.[12] Thus, the Marx–Engels approach to ideology can itself be viewed as ideological.

This paradox of the concept of ideology arises from the difficulty in defining concepts like freedom, equality, justice and so on. All the ideologies discussed below claim, to varying degrees, to offer the correct definition of these concepts. We are familiar with the debates around the concept of freedom, for example, between conservatives and socialists; freedom from the state in a market framework vs. freedom to fulfil one's creative capacities in a collective setting. This is a staple of British party politics. Are taxes, for instance, an infringement of personal liberty in that they remove the right of the individual to spend their money in the way they see fit? Or, are taxes an important form of redistribution that enables people to fulfil their potential as free and equal human beings? Interestingly, a new twist was given to these debates with the success of the Green Party at the European elections of 1989 where it gained 15 per cent of the vote. The two main parties in Britain immediately began to reassess their conceptual frameworks in light of the green definition of freedom – freedom in a global environmental context of sustainability and ecological awareness. There thus ensued the spectacle of conservatives and socialists presenting their views of freedom as the one that was 'most green'. Conservatives appealed to the free market as the most appropriate and effective mechanism for ensuring ecological goals. Unrestrained competition, they argued, would provide a way of accurately assessing the 'value' people placed on the environment. In such a way we could compare this with the value we place on other goods and make judgements accordingly. The Labour Party, in contrast, emphasised the need for a collective approach towards the environment. The free market, they claimed, was the cause of the problem, not the solution. As the ecological crisis demonstrates, the source of freedom is in co-operation rather than competition. Alternatively, and as some green theorists argue, an ecological conception of freedom may be impossible to incorporate into conservative or socialist ideologies (see Michael Kenny's chapter on ecologism).

This illustrates the way in which ideologies seek to claim a limited number of contestable concepts as their own. It also gives rise to the ultimate intractability of ideological debate as there is no one true definition of freedom against which we can judge ideologies. It is precisely this kind of paradox that has led some thinkers to jettison the classical understanding of ideology on which we have concentrated so far. Before exploring this further, it is worth specifying in more detail some features of the classical conception. It may appear odd at first, but we can do this by discussing the possibility that 'the age of ideology' is over. As Vincent Geoghegan suggests at the end of his chapter on socialism, it is often the claim that a set of beliefs is 'dead' that raises the interesting questions.

THE END OF IDEOLOGY: BELL AND FUKUYAMA

The American sociologist Daniel Bell, whose book *The End of Ideology* (1960)[13] was to prove enormously influential in debates concerning this difficult term, did much to popularise the 'end of ideology' argument. His work, though, did not exist in a vacuum. Notably, Raymond Aron, in a book entitled *The Opium of the Intellectual* (1957), declared that the 'conditions of ideological debate' could no longer be found in advanced countries like America and those of western Europe. Similarly, Seymour Martin Lipset claimed that 'democracy in the Western world' represents 'the good society itself in operation' and that large-scale ideological battles were a thing of the past.[14] Recently this theme has been given a new and interesting twist by Francis Fukuyama in *The End of History and the Last Man* (1992)[15]. Drawing upon a contentious interpretation of the German philosopher G.W.F. Hegel (1770–1831), Fukuyama presents us with a view of the world ultimately devoid of ideological concerns. Fukuyama's is a world where the destiny of humans has been realised in the structures of liberal democracy. In the following brief discussion the focus will be on Bell and Fukuyama.

The context of Bell's analysis is given in the subtitle of his book, *On the Exhaustion of Political Ideas in the Fifties.* This historical context is further narrowed geographically as we realise that the bulk of the essays that make up the volume are specifically concerned with America. Thus, we must be cautious of taking the grandiose title, *The End of Ideology,* at face value. This is also evident from the 'Epilogue' where Bell distinguishes 'the old ideologies' which have become exhausted and 'the new ideologies' emerging in Asia and Africa.[16] All this alerts us to the fact that it is a quite specific conception of ideology that Bell believes has ended, and it is the nature of this notion that I shall presently explore.

In his essay 'The End of Ideology Revisited', Bell laments that 'ideology has come to designate almost any creed held with the will to believe' and this entails that the 'historicity of the term has lost its context' to the extent that ideology 'has become an irretrievably fallen word'.[17] The proliferation of usage's surrounding ideology, claims Bell, makes it an unworkable concept. This gives us the first clue to his understanding of the term. Bell, a sociologist, is primarily concerned to assess the worth of ideology as a conceptual tool for the comprehension of society. Does ideology, in 1950s America, serve as a workable model for understanding social formations, or is it prey to 'the falsity of simplification'?[18] This general methodological question, of course, presupposes an account of what ideology is and how it operates in any particular study of society.

The essence of Bell's approach can be found in a crucial paragraph in response to his critics, where he states that '[w]hat is striking is that none of the criticisms challenged the substantive analyses of structural changes which cut at the heart of classical Marxism'. Indeed, he applauds one commentator for recognising that this is his 'central argument'.[19] Not only does this confirm the claim that Bell is primarily interested in ideology as a descriptive tool but it also tells us that it is the 'classical Marxist' version that he has in his sights. Essentially his argument is that whether or not Marxist accounts of the social and historical foundations of ideological belief were at one time correct, in 1950s America they simply did not apply. The 'structural changes' in society, which led Bell to an awareness of 'the *particular and crucial* differences between societies', meant that a simple class analysis of the kind offered by traditional left-wing scholars had become invalid. Ideology as a part of the Marxist tool-bag of concepts slung over the shoulder of the 'radical intellectual' could no longer be considered relevant. The generalised claim it implied, that every society could be thought to generate ideological frameworks in the same way (through class conflict), was inappropriate to the particular instance Bell studied. The exception, in this case, *dis*proved the rule.

It is from this position that Bell makes his larger claims about 'the end of ideology in the West'. For our purposes it is important to understand that Bell is criticising the role of ideology, as a limited Marxist concept, in terms of the claims it makes about reality; 'few issues can be formulated any more, intellectually, in ideological terms'.[20] This explains Bell's account of the emergence of 'new ideologies' in a book entitled *The End of Ideology*. These new ideologies pay heed to specific and local issues typically regarding national economic interests. The claim inherent in the classical Marxist conception of ideology, that social relations can only truthfully be discerned in terms of class analysis, is replaced by Bell with the claim that prudent 'problem-solving' in a liberal framework accounts for the actual generation of ideas in society.[21] Bell recognises, however, that this does little to affect the possible moral worth of Marxism; the 'commitment to ideology – the yearning for a "cause", or the satisfaction of deep moral feelings – is not necessarily the reflection of interests in the shape of ideas'.[22] Marxism, then, may provide a way of thinking about a better future and as such be an ideology *in the sense of offering a political alternative*. It may in this sense be very much alive. On Fukuyama's account, though, even this aspect of Marxism has come to an end.

The response generated by Fukuyama's essay 'The End of History?', published in the small American journal *The National Interest*,[23] was quite remarkable and very reminiscent of the furore sparked off by Bell's book. Fukuyama has now published a book-length defence of the thesis presented in that essay, *The End of History and the Last Man*, and it is on this that I shall concentrate.

Fukuyama's central claim, that there is 'only one competitor standing in the ring as an ideology of potentially universal validity: liberal democracy',[24] rests on a two-pronged argument. The first proposition is that the natural sciences are 'both cumulative and directional' and they have thus had a 'uniform effect on all societies that have experienced' their 'unfolding'.[25] The 'ever expanding set of human desires' requires the growth of technology to satisfy these desires, and because of the uniform effect of science this points to an increasing homogenisation of cultures. One of the pressures that started the process of 'democratisation' in Eastern Europe, he claims, was the desire to own Western goods. Yet this is only possible, he goes on, with Western technology and work practices. Therefore, there is a 'direction towards' common technological advancement and the regimes that accompany such practices. However, Fukuyama is quick to recognise that, as technologically advanced countries need not necessarily be pluralist and open, this alone 'is not sufficient to account for the phenomenon of democracy'.[26] A similar point is suggested by Rick Wilford's discussion of the connections between technological 'self-sufficiency' and fascism.

In order to make the link between 'directionality' in the natural sciences and democracy Fukuyama introduces a second line of argument. It relies, though, on a much-contested interpretation of the German philosopher Hegel.[27] Hegel viewed history as a process that was progressing towards a goal. Over time the tensions, or contradictions, in society, like those between master and slave or feudal lord and serf, would be overcome. As history progressed, a rational social order would become reality. This would ultimately be achieved in a state that perfectly harmonised everybody's individual liberty together with their character as a social being. For Fukuyama, this end-point is the liberal-democratic state (though whether or not Hegel held this to be true is a matter for discussion). Broadly speaking, Fukuyama asserts that 'the motor of history' has been the 'struggle for recognition', recognition that can only be fully achieved in terms of the liberal logic of equal rights and freedoms. The quintessential fact about humanity, argues Fukuyama, is that we long to be recognised as humans by our fellow humans. This recognition is not possible in tyrannical or autocratic regimes (and he cites the former Soviet Union and China among many examples) because such forms of government fundamentally treat people as parts of a higher good, thus not as fully recognised people in themselves. The only form of political association that recognises people as the individuals that they really are is liberal democracy. It is these beliefs, which he argues are empirically proven by world events like the collapse of communism in Eastern Europe, that lead Fukuyama to make the claim that there exists 'a Universal History of mankind in the direction of liberal democracy'.[28] In the terms of the present discussion, the 'end of history' means the success of a single ideology, liberal democracy, thus effectively signalling the 'end of ideology'. The lack of a viable alternative to liberal democracy negates the reasons for ideological contestation.

Where Bell disputed the validity of ideology as a narrowly defined tool of analysis, Fukuyama paints the picture of ideologies as alternatives to liberal democracy becoming exhausted. There is, he states, 'a complete absence of coherent theoretical alternatives to liberal democracy' to the extent that the era of 'large political struggles' is over.[29] Thus, the end of ideology for Fukuyama is essentially not a question of conflicting claims about the reality of social structures (as with Bell) but about conflicting claims regarding the best way to live. This would appear to answer the problem left by Bell that Marxism may have a source of moral value, if not descriptive value. Taken together, the two end-of-ideology theorists represent an attack on the two strands implicit in the classical Marxist formulation – that it is a tool for the analysis of existing societies together with an alternative political programme. In the next section the possibility that the end-of-ideology thesis overcomes the central paradox of ideology – that one person's knowledge is another person's ideology – shall be discussed through the criticisms levelled against Bell and Fukuyama.

DEBATING THE END OF IDEOLOGY

The strengths of the arguments put forward by Bell and Fukuyama rest in large measure on the historical context in which each was writing. In the case of Bell, it was the purported lack of strongly held ideological beliefs in 1950s America (and the West in general). Edward Shils, describing the events of a major conference held in Milan in 1955, pointed to the fact that ideology had 'lost its appeal to the intellectuals'. The horrors of fascism, totalitarianism and communism had undermined the roots of any possible radical perspective among those who sought to discuss society. 'Grandiose visions', he maintained, were being, and had to be, abandoned.[30] Moreover, post-war Britain appeared to back up Bell's thesis. From 1945 to the second half of the 1960s, there existed a broad ideological consensus. There was agreement on many issues, that there be a mixed economy, state welfare provision and the enhancement of individual liberty within this framework. While disagreement about specific policy issues still occurred, there did, nevertheless, appear to be no serious ideological disputes remaining.

Fukuyama similarly draws widely upon his knowledge of world affairs (gained while working for the American government), pointing to the collapse of the Berlin wall, the opening up of eastern Europe, the reform process in China and the increasing number of democratic regimes around the world (to name a few) in order to establish the truth of his claim that liberal democracies represent the final form of political association. As totalitarian, fascist and communist regimes topple, the number of alternative ways of organising a political association does indeed seem to be dwindling.

However, the reliance upon empirical examples to back up their arguments has also been viewed as a weakness in their respective positions. C. Wright Mills in his 'Letter to the New Left' (1960) claimed that 'facts of a displeasing kind are simply ignored' by Bell.[31] Towards the end of his letter he cites several contemporary occasions of uprisings, including those in Cuba, Turkey, South Korea and Taiwan, where the end of ideology seemed patently false. In Britain, the United States and France ideological conflict took new forms and seemed to refute Bell's theory. The growing feminist, student and anti-Vietnam movements brought ideological issues back to the fore. This was backed by the 'New Left', centred around *The New Left Review*, who emphasised the revolutionary potential of such movements and the ways in which they challenged the cultural assumptions of capitalist society.[32]

Alan Ryan, reviewing Fukuyama's book, claims that the factual basis of his theory is 'incoherent'. Fukuyama, argues Ryan, relies on an analysis of world politics 'that rarely rises above the banal'. By way of example he ridicules Fukuyama's 'chart of liberal democracies' that cites both Singapore and Japan as democracies while in the text these countries are treated as illiberal and non-democratic. Such incoherence, suggests Ryan, springs from the fact that Fukuyama 'does not know what he really believes'.[33]

The lists could be endless. It seems strange indeed to talk of the end of ideology when ideological conflicts appear to be surrounding us every day. Yet, both Bell and Fukuyama reject this insistence on alternative examples. Bell argues that such struggles are only 'small-scale' and uses the events since the publication of his original thesis (which he calls 'the upsurge of radicalism', citing the student protests of the 1960s and 'third-world liberation movements' as examples) to 'prove' his point.[34] Fukuyama is even applauded by one of his critics (Anderson) for his 'coolly judicious treatment' of current events that are wrongly construed as ideological, for example, the rise of nationalism.[35] Both recognise the existence of protest movements but point to two 'facts'. First, such movements have, they believe, died out. Secondly, these protest groups merely 'meddle' with the system rather than try to challenge the underlying assumptions of liberal democracies.

This kind of debate over empirical examples is, I would argue, futile. Minogue's conviction that at this stage of the argument 'academics' need only ask 'who is telling the truth?' thoroughly misses the target.[36] The issue at stake is precisely how everyone (not just academics) can tell what amounts to a true claim? What is it that guides Bell and Fukuyama to see the facts in the way they do? This leads to a second line of criticism brought against their approach. Simply, it is claimed that both Bell and Fukuyama are engaged in ideological projects. In regard to Bell, and others who talked of the end of ideology in the 1950s and 1960s, Mills labels them 'the NATO Intellectuals', arguing that they are an almost direct parallel to the Soviet propagandists of the period. Their aim, whether they know it or not, is the defence of the American way of life rather than an 'objective' analysis of the character of ideology. They are pursuing an ideological project that biases their approach. Fukuyama's arguments have come under fire on the same grounds. Christopher Norris, in a wide-ranging article detailing the lack of response of sections of the contemporary intelligentsia in regard to the Gulf War, accuses Fukuyama of 'rationalisations of the ideological *status quo*'.[37] It is not difficult to see the strength of this argument. Fukuyama's article in *The Guardian* on the Gulf War drew upon the idea that the war represented 'a throwback to the geopolitics of the 19th century', going on to state that 'we will ultimately have to make our home' in 'democratic and capitalist' countries.[38] As Norris puts it, '[t]his analysis is nothing short of breathtaking in its placid acceptance of the US state-sponsored line'.[39]

SUMMARY

It is worth reviewing the argument as it stands. Examining ideology as a concept that is intimately connected with epistemology (what we know to be true, how we know it to be true, etc.) has brought the discussion to an impasse. The possibility of distinguishing false ideological views of society from true ones seems to be fading into the distance. A number of alternatives are available at this point. Firstly, ideology as a conceptual tool to understand the fabric of ideas in society, could be redefined. Ideology, as a Marxist concept, may be false but perhaps it can be salvaged as a descriptive tool if we define it more analytically, that is, give it a meaning within the bounds of traditional empirical social science. Hamilton attempts this and argues that he has reached a definition that operates 'to meet the requirements of empirical application and research'.[40] Without going into his definition, though, we can see immediately that this approach presupposes the very question at issue. For many Marxists and feminists, for example, it is the traditional social scientific approach that is the problem as it is premissed on class or gender interests. Again, one person's knowledge appears to be another's ideology.

Secondly, we may follow Minogue and attempt to appeal to 'the truth' of the matter. For Minogue, the truth is that Marxism is paradigmatic of the ideological approach and, as the collapse of communism has illustrated, ideological attempts at forging the perfect society are bankrupt and clearly false. This argument, though, leads us back into the quagmire we are trying to avoid. The response to Minogue by the Marxist critic Alex Callinicos illustrates this clearly. Callinicos claims that 'whether Minogue likes it or not, he seems to be engaged in the same kind of intellectual project as that undertaken by the classical theorists of ideology.'[41] In other words, he claims to be unmasking falsehood to proclaim his version of the truth. Is it Minogue who is the 'ideologue'? When it is truth that is at stake, when people disagree about what the truth of a situation really is, this approach is likely to dig us deeper into the mud.

Thirdly, it may be contended that the paradox implicit in ideology (that one person's knowledge is another person's ideology) is precisely its essential character. As Andrew Vincent puts it, we can accept the paradox and use the tensions inherent in the concept to theorise 'self-consciously' about the role of ideology. This common approach tries to straddle the problems inherent in the concept of ideology by relying on the possibility of gaining a 'distance' from ideological positions: we are 'sufferers' of ideology, 'but not complete sufferers'.[42] However, it is often left unclear how exactly this 'distancing' is possible. How is it possible to criticise ideological frameworks, given the impasse this leads us into every time we try? This is a particularly pertinent question when dealing with political ideologies. All the ideologies represented in this book claim to be based on a truth (or truths) about the social world. How can we distance ourselves from the ideological assumptions of one position (say, conservatism) in order to comment on another particular ideology (say, socialism)? In the next section we shall look at some alternative approaches to ideology as a way of beginning to map out the 'distancing' implicit in the ideological arena.

IDEOLOGY: AN ALTERNATIVE

So far the discussion has concentrated on ideology as a science of true ideas, a set of false ideas and the problems raised by these concerns. Yet there is another way of looking at ideology which side-steps this approach. That is, one that relates ideology to human action: putting it simply, ideology as doing rather than as knowing. Although this approach has different strands to it, we shall focus on the versions that came out of the Marxist tradition.

V.I. Lenin, in *What is to be Done?* (1902), talked of *socialism* as 'the ideology of struggle of the proletarian class'. Breaking from the classical conception of Marx and Engels, ideology no longer represents the ideas of the ruling class. It has become, in this sense, a framework for political action. The crucial factor now is not the extent to which ideology masks the true consciousness of the proletarian class, but the extent to which it is an effective weapon in the class war (whether true or not). As Boudon puts it, the salient fact about Lenin's approach is that, regardless of whether ideologies are true or false, they are 'useful'.[43] This undermining of the classical Marxist conception of ideology (which relies upon the revelation of 'false consciousness') opens the way for a conception of ideology that portrays all forms of action as, in some sense, ideological. Truth and falsity fall out of the equation if every position is accepted as ideological. Indeed, if it is impossible to escape ideology, the question becomes 'which one most usefully suits my purposes?'. Yet this raises two problems. First, how are we to conceive of all forms of action as being ideological? What is involved in making this claim? Secondly, how are we to adjudicate between different forms of ideology if we accept this approach? If everything is ideological, then how can we say that one ideology is more ideological than the next? This, as we shall see, raises doubts about this alternative perspective.

A possible answer to the first problem can be found in the writings of the French neo-Marxist philosopher Louis Althusser. Althusser insists upon the strict separation of ideology and science. Arguing against the traditional relationship between ideology and truth, he claims that ideology is the 'cement' that binds human societies together. Therefore, it makes no sense to talk of an ideology being true or false: 'ideology is . . . an organic part . . . of every social totality'. Or again: 'human societies secrete ideology as the very element and atmosphere indispensable to their historical respiration and life'.[44] The 'ideology of the school', for instance, provides one of the limits of our social interaction. Schools become one medium through which we are social-ised into deference towards our 'superiors', in which we are taught to compete against each other and ultimately moulded into the 'good citizens' required by a capitalist society. In this way ideologies bond society together. Ideology, in this formulation, is the 'indispensable' framework for every action we carry out; it makes social life possible. Importantly, ideology would not disappear in a post-capitalist society – the ideology of the school would still exist but in a form that sought to bolster the bonds of post-capitalist society.

For Althusser, what he calls the 'practico-social function' of ideology, its function as the bond of all societies, is more important than its 'theoretical function', its function as knowledge. For example, under-standing an ideology like conservatism requires that one examine the ways in which it binds social structures like schools, churches, trade unions and the family together (structures that Althusser calls 'Ideo-logical State Apparatuses'). It thus makes no sense to talk of ideology ever coming to an end. If ideology functions as a framework of social activity then this requires that it must always be present. Although Althusser's theory of ideology takes on board many subtleties which we cannot cover at present, the central point remains: ideology must be viewed as functioning outside the quagmire of the traditional con-ception if its relevance is to be maintained.

While this view of ideology may help to broaden the scope of the debate, it is not without difficulties. The possibility of denouncing a point of view because it is ideological seems to have disappeared. How are we to criticise an ideological position, like fascism for example, if ideology no longer refers to standards of truth? Althusser's approach, it is argued, leads to a 'labyrinth of relativism',[45] and 'political bleak-ness'.[46] We appear to be back at the beginning, requiring a concept of ideology that can retain the idea that some ideologies are better or worse than others. This is the crux of the 'problem of ideologies': if ideologies are concerned with truth, then how do we tell which ones are actually true (given that they can't all be), but if they are not concerned with truth, then how do we judge between them? Is there a way of salvaging the concept so that we may get to grips *in a critical manner* with the competing claims represented by the particular ideo-logies in this volume?

In the concluding section it will be argued that by way of this diversion into an alternative notion of ideology the possibility of gaining a critical distance can now be more adequately assessed. The arena of ideologies does allow for the 'self-conscious' theorising discussed by Vincent, only now we are in a position to appreciate why this is the case.

ASSESSING IDEOLOGIES

In a useful essay on Marx's concept of ideology, Stuart Hall argues that the 'problem' of truth and falsity in the classical conception can be abated by refusing to think in such 'all-or-nothing' terms.[47] He suggests that in place of these we refer to ideologies as being 'partial' and 'adequate', for example. In a similar fashion, McLellan believes we must hold on to the idea that 'some views are more ideological than others'.[48] He admits that this necessitates an acceptance that ideology may end, though this 'is certainly nowhere in sight – not even on the horizon'.[49] Boudon suggests that the criterion relevant to passing judgements on ideologies is that of 'soundness'. It is impossible to prove the truth of an ideology, he argues, but we may assess the soundness of its principles.[50] All these authors, therefore, recognise the need to avoid the strong connection between ideology and knowledge, yet ultimately see the requirement of a weak conception of the relationship in order to maintain the idea that ideologies represent oppressive structures of thought. Bacon's 'idols' and 'phantoms' must, by some means, be vanquished.

In response to these approaches the temptation is to suggest that any account of, for example, an 'inadequate ideology' simply serves to mask the claim that it is false. If I were to label any of the ideologies in this book 'inadequate' it would surely cause its proponents to rebuff the charge with the claim that I was deluded by other (inadequate) ideologies. To solve the problem by muddying the waters doesn't seem very satisfactory. Is there any way we may see the patterns in the ideological pool?

Ideologies arise through our need to make sense of the world around us. They make the seemingly incomprehensible appear intelligible to us. For example, Richard Jay illustrates how nationalism can provide a coherent focus for disparate peoples through the idea of the nation-state. Similarly, Michael Kenny demonstrates how the ideology of ecologism raises key issues relating to a 'green' perspective on the world's problems; it puts the local in a global perspective. This is the way ideologies can function as a system of knowledge. Importantly though, as all the chapters also demonstrate, ideologies have to change with the times, they have to keep up with new situations, new technologies, new forms of social relations and so on. Of course so far, this would all seem to imply that ideologies can be judged by their ability to keep up with changing social structures and technologies – that is, how well they accurately reflect social reality. This argument has been aired many times especially since the collapse of communism in Eastern Europe – the changing social formations of the former Soviet countries eventually meant that communism could no longer sustain its claim to truth (if indeed it was ever deemed to have had one).

However, new relations, new ways of organising society, new technologies and the like do not come out of thin air. They are only possible from within the frame of already existing ideological perspectives (whether they are coherently expressed or not). This brings us back closer to the conception of ideology proposed by Althusser – ideology as the 'atmosphere' essential for social activity. Ideologies, therefore, help us to make sense of the world by providing the framework through which we act in the world. If we accept the conservative 'New Right' idea of individual responsibility, for example, this means that we view criminals as responsible for the crimes they commit and punish them accordingly. Yet through our everyday transactions, conversations and actions we may find ourselves in situations that challenge our ideological assumptions. Thus, for whatever reason (political, economic, social, personal) we may come to question whether or not social factors, such as unemployment and poverty, are more important than individual responsibility in levels of crime. In this way we may re-examine the original New Right assumptions that guided our actions and refine (or even redefine) what we take to be the most salient factors regarding the social world. If this feeling is mobilised in a political form then ideologies mutate to accommodate our changing perceptions of the world. Importantly, though, this is an on-going process. Ideologies shape our actions while we, through our actions, also shape ideologies. This creates a 'feedback' relationship in all ideologies that is impossible to disentangle. Criteria of truth or falsity become unrealisable because there is no original, non-ideological moment against which to judge them.

We can clarify this by way of another example. The call for female emancipation, as Rick Wilford argues, was intimately entwined with the way other ideologies – Marxism, socialism and liberalism, for instance – conceived of the role of women. In this way, from the very outset 'the dividing lines among feminists were derived from their association with one or other of these ideologies'. As feminist movements flourished and began to formulate their own perspectives on political issues (indeed, redefining what is meant by the term 'political') they forged new spaces in the ideological arena. In this way, they have created new sets of possible human relations, providing an atmosphere in which 'non-patriarchal' associations may hold sway. Yet in pursuing this, new problems have emerged as social relations and other ideologies change and mutate, changes brought about in many ways by the feminist movement. Feminists, therefore, must refine what they mean by feminism; witness Rick Wilford's discussion of 'the politics of identity' which strikes at the heart of 'mainstream feminism'. The feedback loop has been completed. The problem becomes, therefore, where we direct a question that seeks to determine the truth or falsity of feminist ideologies. How can we sort out the reality of women's relations to the social world from those expressions of the feminist movement that may be construed as ideological? In short, I don't believe it can be done. Yet does this not leave us once again in a position of crippling relativism? A further couple of examples from the chapters below reveal why this is not the case.

In critically assessing conservatism Robert Eccleshall shows how those who espouse it have tried to mask the fact that it has always 'been awash with abstractions and convictions' they have sought to deny. To bring this to the surface is to reveal the way conservatism tries to obscure one of the key functions of an ideology, namely to provide a model through which people view the social world. It is not necessarily to proclaim conservatism as false, but it is none the less to make a valid criticism of it as an ideology. Similarly, Michael Kenny argues that the 'next stage in the development of ecologism lies in the articulation of a body of hard-headed political ideas'. Again, this highlights the manner in which ecologism fails to fulfil another of the key elements of an ideology, that of providing a framework for political action. In both cases the particular ideology is judged in relation to the way it manages to 'fit' with the core features of *the general concept of ideology*. In this way we can adopt a political and critical attitude to ideologies that does not rely upon appeals to an external reality (which, after all, is itself in dispute). It is not that we can step out of our ideological shoes via an act of 'self-consciousness', as if we can somehow suspend the operation of ideologies. Rather, critical perspectives emerge by exposing the features of the general conception of ideology that a particular ideology excludes or denies.

CONCLUSION

One important consequence of this approach to the critical assessment of ideologies is that not only is the end of ideology not on the horizon (as McLellan suggested), but it is in principle never possible. As we cannot step out of our ideological shoes we must be aware that ideologies will always be with us. The ideological arena is a constantly shifting battleground, yes, but it is not possible to leave that arena in order to get a bird's-eye view to discover the one true ideology. To put it all too briefly, ideologies generate, in the way they operate, their continuing necessity.

For example, political debate in Britain often refers to the core values of 'ordinary British citizens'. The assumption, however, that core values exist and can be reflected in the political arena, is itself the source of ideological conflict. It is hotly contested by, among others, women's groups and gay rights organisations who disagree with the emphasis such a notion places on 'traditional' family values. Similarly, many educationalists fear that stressing 'core standards', such as speaking 'proper English' to the detriment of local variations, undermines their more liberal approach. In America, similar ideological disputes are generated whenever a politician or pressure group claims to represent the 'moral majority'. Attempting to circumvent ideological dispute by appealing to universal values does, in fact, generate further controversy.

On the global stage, we must be wary of the claim that liberal ideology has been victorious. First, it is highly unlikely that the eastern European revolutions of 1989 that brought about the collapse of the old Soviet bloc will bring an end to ideological conflict. The upsurge in nationalism has proven to be a particularly virulent reminder of this and there is no reason to believe that nationalist ideology will simply disappear. Secondly, even if it was accepted that ideological conflict was no longer a feature of East–West relations (and this is highly problematic), the polarisation of North and South is assuming increasing importance. The disparities of wealth are far greater than they ever were between East and West. Indeed, as long as this is the case, ideological debates about the merits and faults of global capitalism will continue. The ideological battleground is, if anything, growing rather than shrinking. Born in the midst of the French Revolution, in many respects the defining moment of a new Europe, ideologies may mature in a new global arena.

Ideologies do not go away. They will remain a central feature of British politics and of politics in general. The following chapters contribute to these on-going and everlasting debates. That we are aware of the issues that surround the concept of ideology as a whole and the discussions within and between particular ideologies is a necessary part of understanding the political world in which we are engaged every day.

NOTES

1 Malcolm B. Hamilton, 'The Elements of Ideology', *Political Studies*, XXXV, 1987, 18–38.
2 Francis Bacon, *Novum Organon*, Oxford, Oxford University Press, 1855, 3.
3 Karl Mannheim, *Ideology and Utopia: An Introduction to the Sociology of Knowledge*, London, Kegan Paul, Trench Trubner and Co., 1936, 54 (my italics). It is important to note, though, that Mannheim, while discussing the role of Bacon's thought, stresses that it would be wrong to claim a direct line from Bacon to the 'modern conception of ideology' (55).
4 Terry Eagleton, *Ideology: An Introduction*, London, Verso, 1991, 66.
5 Kenneth Minogue, *Alien Powers: The Pure Theory of Ideology*, London, Weidenfeld and Nicolson, 1985. See also his recent article, 'Ideology after the Collapse of Communism', *Political Studies*, Special Issue, 'The End of Isms?', 41, 1993, 4–20.
6 Karl Marx and Friedrich Engels, *The German Ideology* (Students Edition), ed. C.J. Arthur, London, Lawrence and Wishart, 1974, 47.
7 Istvan Meszaros, *The Power of Ideology*, London, Harvester Wheatsheaf, 1989, 10–11.
8 See the further reading for some useful texts on Marx and Engels' theory of ideology.
9 Eagleton, *Ideology: An Introduction*, 72.
10 Meszaros, *The Power of Ideology*, 7–8.
11 Richard Ebeling, 'Liberalism and Collectivism in the 20th Century', *Political Studies*, XLI, 1993, 66–77.

12 R. Boudon, *The Analysis of Ideology*, trans. Malcolm Slater, Cambridge, Polity Press, 1989, 22.

13 Daniel Bell, *The End of Ideology: On the Exhaustion of Political Ideas in the Fifties*, London, Collier-MacMillan, 1962.

14 For an introduction to the work of Aron and Lipset see their contributions to C.L. Waxman, ed., *The End of Ideology Debate*, New York, Funk and Wagnalls, 1968.

15 Francis Fukuyama, *The End of History and the Last Man*, London, Hamish Hamilton, 1992.

16 Bell, *The End of Ideology*, 403.

17 Bell, 'The End of Ideology Revisited – Part One' and 'The End of Ideology Revisited – Part Two', *Government and Opposition*, 23, 1988, 127–50 and 321–31 respectively.

18 Bell, *The End of Ideology*, 13.

19 Bell, 'The End of Ideology Revisited – Part One', 140. Bell is referring to H. Brick, *Daniel Bell and the Decline of Intellectual Radicalism*, University of Wisconsin Press, 1986.

20 Bell, *The End of Ideology*, 404.

21 Bell, 'The End of Ideology Revisited – Part One', 138.

22 Bell, *The End of Ideology*, 400.

23 Francis Fukuyama, 'The End of History?', *The National Interest*, 16, 1989, 3–18.

24 Fukuyama, *The End of History and the Last Man*, 42.

25 Fukuyama, *The End of History and the Last Man*, xiv.

26 Fukuyama, *The End of History and the Last Man*, xv.

27 A sample of the issues at stake can be gleaned from comparing Alan Ryan's critical article 'Professor Hegel Goes to Washington', *The New York Review of Books*, 26 March 1992, with the more sympathetic (though not uncritical) last chapter in Perry Anderson's *A Zone of Engagement*, London, Verso, 1992.

28 Fukuyama, *The End of History and the Last Man*, 48.

29 Fukuyama, *The End of History and the Last Man*, 67.

30 E. Shils, 'The End of Ideology?', in Waxman, ed., *The End of Ideology Debate*, 49–63.

31 C. Wright Mills, 'Letter to the New Left', in Waxman, ed., *The End of Ideology Debate*, 126–40. Originally published in *New Left Review*, 5, 1960.

32 For a useful discussion of the New Left see Michael Kenny, *The First New Left: Britain's Organic Intellectuals?*, London, Lawrence and Wishart, 1994.

33 Ryan, 'Professor Hegel Goes to Washington', 8.
34 Bell, 'The End of Ideology Revisited – Part One', 143–50.
35 Anderson, *A Zone of Engagement*, 350.
36 Minogue, 'Ideology after the Collapse of Communism', 9–10.
37 Christopher Norris, 'The End of Ideology Revisited: The Gulf War, Postmodernism and Realpolitik', *Philosophy and Social Criticism*, 17, 1991, 1–40.
38 Fukuyama, 'Changed Days for Ruritania's Dictator', *The Guardian*, 8 April 1991.
39 Norris, 'The End of Ideology Revisited', 34.
40 Hamilton, 'The Elements of Ideology', 38.
41 Alex Callinicos, 'Premature Obituaries: A Comment on O'Sullivan, Minogue and Marquand', *Political Studies*, XLI, 1993, 57–65, 60.
42 Andrew Vincent, *Modern Political Ideologies*, Oxford, Blackwell, 1992, 20.
43 Boudon, *The Analysis of Ideology*, 18.
44 Louis Althusser, 'Marxism and Humanism', *For Marx*, London, Allen Lane, 1969, 232.
45 David McLellan, *Ideology*, Milton Keynes, Open University Press, 1986, 33.
46 Eagleton, *Ideology: An Introduction*, 145.
47 Stuart Hall, 'The Problem of Ideology – Marxism Without Guarantees', in Betty Matthews, ed., *Marx: A Hundred Years On*, London, Lawrence and Wishart, 1983.
48 McLellan, *Ideology*, 2.
49 McLellan, *Ideology*, 83.
50 Boudon, *The Analysis of Ideology*, 202.

FURTHER READING

General

D. McLellan, *Ideology*, Milton Keynes, Open University Press, 1986, provides a brief yet insightful introduction to many of the issues raised in the Introduction, and can be usefully complemented by T. Eagleton, *Ideology: An Introduction*, London, Verso, 1991, who undertakes a more wide-ranging analysis encompassing current trends in social theory. Similarly, J.B. Thompson, *Studies in the Theory of Ideology*, Cambridge,

Polity Press, 1984, is an excellent guide to traditional debates while also showing how the terms of these debates have shifted in recent years. For a useful survey of the material on ideology see M.B. Hamilton, 'The Elements of the Concept of Ideology', *Political Studies*, XXXV, 1987, 18–38. A very analytical, and at times quite dry, approach to the epistemological problems raised above is given in R. Boudon, *The Analysis of Ideology*, translated by M. Slater, Cambridge, Polity Press, 1989. J. Larrain, *The Concept of Ideology*, London, Hutchison, 1979, also provides a study of ideology that is difficult but rewarding. Interesting, and challenging, accounts of the nature of ideology, at both a theoretical and a practical level, can be found in Centre for Contemporary Cultural Studies, *On Ideology*, London, Hutchison, 1978. N. O'Sullivan, ed., *The Structure of Modern Ideology: Critical Perspectives on Social and Political Theory*, Aldershot, Elgar, 1989, is not afraid to tackle the concept of ideology in terms of an unusual and diverse range of thinkers. Two books that approach the issues surrounding ideology from their own particular (and, it must be said, peculiar) perspectives are L.S. Feuer, *Ideology and the Ideologists*, Oxford, Blackwell, 1975, and W.J. Stankiewicz, *In Search of a Political Philosophy: Ideologies at the Close of the Twentieth Century*, London, Routledge, 1993. Finally, and to return to more traditional approaches, an excellent set of essays in A. Shtromas, ed., 'The End of Isms?', *Political Studies*, XLI, 1993, represents the state of the art in debates regarding ideology. Of particular interest in terms of this Introduction are the chapters by K. Minogue, N. O'Sullivan, D. Marquand and A. Callinicos, some of which I drew upon in the text.

Marxism and ideology

The literature in this area is vast, often very difficult and related to particular debates within Marxism. However, useful starting points are B. Parekh, *Marx's Theory of Ideology*, London, Croom Helm, 1982, and J. Larrain, *Marxism and Ideology*, London, Macmillan, 1983. I would also thoroughly recommend S. Hall, 'The Problem of Ideology – Marxism Without Guarantees' in B. Matthews, ed., *Marx: A Hundred Years On*, London, Lawrence and Wishart, 1983. For the more adventurous in this area I. Meszaros, *The Power of Ideology*, London, Harvester Wheatsheaf, 1989, is a very long (over 500 pages) Marxist discussion of ideology that can be as rewarding as it is frustrating. Another book that can enlighten as much as it confuses, but that is worthy of examination in this area, is F. Rossi-Landi, *Marxism and Ideology*, translated by R. Griffin, foreword by S. Veca, Oxford, Clarendon Press, 1990. Two useful, though different, interpretations can be found in J. McCarney, *The Real World of Ideology*, Sussex, Harvester Wheatsheaf, 1980, and G. Therborn, *The Ideology of Power and the Power of Ideology*, London, Verso, 1980.

The end of ideology

The two classic texts on this issue are D. Bell, *The End of Ideology: On the Exhaustion of Political Ideas in the Fifties*, London, Collier-Macmillan, 1962, and F. Fukuyama, *The End of History and the Last Man*, London, Hamish Hamilton, 1992. To pursue the debates generated by Bell see C.L. Waxman, ed., *The End of Ideology Debate*, New York, Funk and Wagnalls, 1968; D.E. Apter, ed., *Ideology and Discontent*, New York, The Free Press, 1964; M. Rejai, ed., *Decline of Ideology?*, Chicago, Aldine Atherton Inc., 1971. For a clear and up-to-date restatement of his position see D. Bell, 'The End of Ideology Revisited – Part One' and 'The End of Ideology Revisited – Part Two', *Government and Opposition*, 23, 1988.

The literature on Fukuyama is only just beginning to emerge. Probably the most rigorous essay to date is A. Ryan, 'Professor Hegel Goes to Washington', *The New York Review of Books*, 26 March 1992. The last chapter of P. Anderson, *A Zone of Engagement*, London, Verso, 1992, while dealing with a range of thinkers, provides a critical perspective on Fukuyama's work that is ultimately very compelling.

Alternative approaches

Commentaries on Lenin's and Althusser's approaches to ideology can be found in the general reading listed above. To obtain an overall picture of Lenin's political thought see N. Harding, *Lenin's Political Thought*, 2 vols, London, Macmillan, 1977, 1981. On Althusser, a good overall guide can be found in A. Callinicos, *Althusser's Marxism*, London, Pluto Press, 1976. A. Assiter, *Althusser and Feminism*, London, Pluto Press, 1990, is an ambitious attempt to wed Althusserian Marxism with contemporary feminism.

Approaches to ideology that weren't covered in the Introduction, but that prove interesting in terms of a more detailed look at the debates, are: K. Mannheim, *Ideology and Utopia: An Introduction to the Sociology of Knowledge*, London, Kegan Paul, 1936, who provides a useful link between classical accounts of ideology and contemporary discussions; C. Geertz, 'Ideology as a Cultural System', *Ideology and Discontent*, New York, The Free Press, 1964, 25–49, argues for a separation of science and ideology but from a non-Marxist perspective; G. Sartori, 'Politics, Ideology and Belief Systems', *American Political Science Review*, 63, 1969, attempts to define ideology as an analytical tool within the context of empirical social science; E. Shils, 'The Concept and Function of Ideology', *International Encyclopaedia of the Social Sciences*, VII, 1968, argues, to my mind unconvincingly, that scientific knowledge is gradually eroding the need for ideologies.

Chapter 2

Liberalism

Robert Eccleshall

[Liberalism's] aim is to create a nation, not of humble though kindly treated workers dependent upon a small rich class who alone can enjoy the full benefits of a civilized life; and not of proletarians regimented, controlled, and provided with standardised comforts by a group of dictators or bureaucrats acting in the name of the State; but a nation of free, responsible, law-abiding, and self-reliant men and women – free from the grinding servitude of poverty and (so far as is possible for men) from the tyranny of circumstance; with healthy bodies and alert and trained minds; enjoying a real equality of opportunity to make the most and best of their powers for their own advantage and that of the community, and to choose the way of life for which they are best fitted; having a real share of responsibility for regulating the management of their common affairs and the conditions of their own life and work; and secure of sufficient leisure to live a full life and to enjoy the delights of Nature, letters, and the arts.
The Liberal Way: A Survey of Liberal Policy, published by the authority of the National Liberal Federation, with a foreword by Ramsay Muir, London, George Allen and Unwin, 1934, 221–2

PROBLEMS OF DEFINITION

Liberalism has a longer history than the other ideologies considered in this book. Its genesis in the seventeenth century coincided with the dissolution of feudal relations and the emergence of modern, capitalist society. The earliest liberals were radical Protestants who challenged secular and ecclesiastical hierarchies in the name of individual rights, claiming that ordinary people were competent to judge the affairs of government as well as to choose their own path to eternal salvation. Since that time liberals have been at the forefront of movements to emancipate individuals from political, religious, economic and other constraints on their activities, and they have persistently campaigned for a society that is more open, tolerant and diversified, less paternalist and authoritarian, than one which entrenches privilege and illegitimate authority. As such, liberalism provides an ideological map of the principal struggles and developments that have occurred in Britain and elsewhere during the last three hundred years.

Herein lies a principal difficulty in identifying the doctrine's distinctive characteristics. In a sense all but the perverse or temperamentally autocratic are now liberals, for few would wish to discard the individual liberties and democratic rights that have been secured in post-feudal society. Liberalism, in everyday usage, often stands for little more than a collection of values and principles which no decent person would reject: a liberal, the economist J.M. Keynes wrote, 'is anyone who is perfectly sensible'. The effect is to blur the doctrine's peculiar perspective on society as well as the frontiers separating liberals from those who belong to rival ideological camps.

One means, much favoured by academic commentators, of bringing liberalism into sharper focus is to characterise it as a bourgeois creed. 'In its living principle', according to Harold Laski, liberalism 'was the idea by which the new middle class rose to a position of political dominance'.[1] Liberalism has been intimately connected with the evolution of the capitalist world, its adherents have endorsed the right to accumulate private property, and until the end of the nineteenth century their assault upon privilege was directed at the power of the aristocracy. The ideology, as Laski indicates, inevitably took shape from the social interests to which it was attached. In characterising the doctrine as essentially bourgeois, however, some commentators wish to depict it as a narrow, excessively individualistic creed which licenses the members of capitalist society to pursue their private interests unrestrained by any sense of duty to co-operate on behalf of the public good.

According to common understanding, then, liberalism is a nebulous doctrine embracing everyone of goodwill, whereas in academic usage it tends to appear as a coherent but unattractive ideology, unlikely to appeal to anyone with generous impulses. In what follows I suggest that liberalism is neither incoherent nor narrowly individualistic: that what gives the doctrine its distinctive perspective is a strong sense of public duty or citizenship which is linked to the ownership of private property. Liberals, to anticipate the argument, have wished to safeguard individual liberties through a structure of equal rights in the expectation that dutiful citizenship or civic virtue will thereby be enhanced.

AN INCOHERENT DOCTRINE?

The adjective 'liberal' has for centuries denoted an open-minded and tolerant disposition. Only from the early nineteenth century, however, was the noun 'liberalism' used to designate political parties and movements, and eventually historians found the term a convenient concept for classifying ideological strands associated with the evolution of post-feudal society.

Liberals themselves often reinforce the impression that their doctrine is little else than the political expression of those civilised values denoted by the adjective 'liberal'. 'To behave liberally', according to a former leader of the British Liberal Party, 'is to behave generously. It implies lavishness. It evokes ideas of breadth and lightness, reason and beauty.'[2] The story that liberals are inclined to tell of their doctrine's history is of a movement for emancipation from successive forms of arbitrary power and outmoded privilege. It is an heroic venture in which bearers of the torch of freedom emerge as magnanimous individuals intent on creating a fairer, more pluralist society that gives individuals ample space to shape their lives according to their own conscience and preferences. Hence a tendency to characterise liberalism as the mobilisation of decent impulses on behalf of social progress: the spirit of 'liberality', as Lord Selborne put it, 'transferred only to the sphere of politics'.[3] It is also a success story of battles won against such obstacles to individual liberty as absolute monarchy, religious intolerance, economic privilege, an undemocratic franchise, and the poverty flowing from unfettered capitalism. Liberals, on this account, have for three centuries spearheaded the transformation of society from feudal despotism into a structure of liberties equally available to everyone.

This account is not wholly inaccurate. Historically, liberals have indeed been intent on freeing individuals from the clutches of arbitrary power, and as champions of liberty they have advocated a dispersal of authority through society on the assumption that the mass of people can be trusted to act responsibly without interference from the state. The next chapter indicates how Edmund Burke's *Reflections on the Revolution in France* (1790), a classic statement of conservatism, was a reaction to Enlightenment optimism, the belief that in principle all individuals could both make sense of the human world and co-operate to demolish unjust social and political structures. Burke, by contrast, warned of the danger of supposing that society could be dramatically reconstructed in the light of principles that were within the compass of every individual mind. The established order was the product of historical experience, according to Burke, and only arrogant individuals could imagine that their 'private stock' of reason was a more reliable guide in public affairs than the 'general bank and capital of nations, and of ages'. It was naive to suppose that political arrangements should be accountable to reason uninformed by tradition. And the legitimate custodians of tradition were what Burke termed a 'natural aristocracy', those 'chieftains' who knew better than the people themselves how they ought to be governed:

> To enable men to act with the weight and character of a people, and to answer the ends for which they are incorporated into that capacity, we must suppose them (by means immediate or consequential) to be in that state of habitual social discipline, in which the wiser, the more expert, and the more opulent conduct, and by conducting enlighten and protect the weaker, the less knowing, and the less provided with the goods of fortune. When the multitude are not under this discipline, they can scarcely be said to be in civil society.

For Burke, then, a properly organised society consists of a hierarchy or chain of command rather than a structure in which individuals enjoy an equal right to be involved in public affairs, or at least to hold government to account through democratic elections.

One expression of those egalitarian assumptions of the Enlightenment which offended conservatives was the Declaration of Independence, by which in 1776 Americans announced that they were no longer a British colony:

> We hold these truths to be self-evident, that all men are created equal, that they are endowed by their Creator with certain inalienable Rights, that among these are Life, Liberty, and the

pursuit of Happiness. That to secure these rights, Governments are instituted among Men, deriving their just powers from the consent of the governed. – That whenever any Form of Government becomes destructive of these ends, it is the Right of the People to alter or abolish it, and to institute new Government, laying its foundation on such principles and organizing its powers in such form, as to them shall seem most likely to effect their Safety and Happiness.

Contained in this passage are the principles not only of the Enlightenment but of a progressive liberalism. For besides provoking a conservative ideological backlash, the American and French Revolutions stimulated some particularly clear expressions of a liberal perspective: the belief that society is a structure of equal rights in which all are citizens, not a chain of discipline separating a minority of rulers from the mass of subjects; an impatience with those like Burke who shrouded political authority in mystery, instead of judging it by principles that are within the grasp of individual reason; and the conviction not only that government should be democratically accountable, but that in large areas of life individuals are responsible enough to manage their affairs without assistance from a paternalist or busybody state. Whereas Burke feared that the 'private stock' of individual reason undisciplined by law and convention would result in the dissolution of 'civil society', Enlightenment liberals argued that civil society would be vibrant only insofar as the state refrained from trespassing upon individual rights and liberties.

A prominent representative of the kind of Enlightenment thinking detested by Burke was Tom Paine (1737–1809) who left England in 1774 to support the American struggle for independence, later joining the French in their revolution against the *ancien régime*. Paine, whose *Rights of Man* (1791–2) was subtitled *An Answer to Mr Burke's Attack on the French Revolution*, was an exponent of the progressive spirit of the age which we now associate with early liberalism. The Burkean appeal to tradition was an attempt to deflect people from questioning their subordination to illegitimate aristocratic authority, according to Paine, and he repudiated conservative inegalitarianism by claiming that individuals are born with a natural right – by which he meant an innate capacity and equal entitlement – to manage their own affairs. This meant that government had to be based upon the consent of those to whom its authority extended, which for Paine entailed regular democratic elections. If individuals were capable of self-government, moreover, the state had a responsibility not to encroach upon private judgement in, for example, matters of opinion or religion. Paine began *The Age of Reason* (1795–6), in which he ridiculed religious orthodoxies and ecclesiastical establishments, by pronouncing that 'my own mind is my own church'.

Burke, comparing the bodies politic and human, likened the 'natural aristocracy' to the head of the human body whose function was to co-ordinate and direct the other members. But for Paine, displaying Enlightenment impatience with traditional vindications of social hierarchy, Burke's paternalist image of political society as a human body writ large was but an attempt to portray aristocratic exploitation of the majority as natural and just. The proper image of a polity was one in which authority flowed not downwards to subjects from an unaccountable elite, as Burke suggested, but inwards to the centre from the democratic decisions of rational, responsible, essentially self-governing citizens. 'A nation is not a body', Paine argued in response to Burke, 'the figure of which is to be represented by the human body, but is like a body contained within a circle, having a common centre in which every radius meets; and that centre is formed by representation.' This confidence in the capacity of ordinary people to understand and control the human world, coupled with an urge to topple institutions that failed the test of reason, lay at the heart of Enlightenment liberalism.

One means of highlighting the differences between Burke and Paine is to suggest that whereas one endorsed the politics of mistrust, the other celebrated the politics of trust. Burke, in characteristically conservative manner, warned of the dangerous political consequences of unrestrained private judgement. Individuals are frail and fallible, according to this pessimistic account of human nature, and left to their own devices they are likely to engage in behaviour that is morally reprehensible and politically disruptive. Hence the need for a disciplinary state which curbs predatory and anti-social impulses through a firm system of law and order. For Paine, in the spirit of Enlightenment liberalism, individuals can by and large be trusted to exercise their judgement in a manner of benefit to themselves and the wider community. Hence the need for a vigorous civil society, immune from state interference, in which individuals may freely associate, formulate opinions, and follow the dictates of conscience in matters such as religion. So perhaps liberals are not inaccurate in depicting their movement as a continual endeavour to create a structure of liberties available to every citizen.

Individual freedom is clearly a primary liberal value. But a commitment to liberty is insufficient to distinguish liberalism from other doctrines. Freedom is one of those elastic concepts whose meanings can be stretched to convey a range of contrary political messages, and as such is prominent in most ideological perspectives on society. Conservatives, particularly those of the New Right or free-market variety, tend to equate freedom with the unhindered pursuit of economic self-interest. Hence their claim in Britain during the 1980s to be liberating the nation by reducing state regulation of the economy. For socialists, however, conservative freedom is licence for a few entrepreneurs to exploit the mass of people, unrestrained by any government responsibility to ensure social justice by redistributing wealth from rich to poor. A free society, according to socialists, is one in which everyone has access to those material resources without which the human potential is thwarted. And this requires the state to combat the inequalities of the capitalist economy through, for example, the collective provision of health care and social welfare.

The difference between these rival conceptions of freedom is often characterised as a debate as to whether liberty is something negative or positive.[4] Individuals are free, according to free-market conservatives who favour a negative conception of liberty, insofar as they are left alone by government or other external agencies to pursue their private ambitions and shape their lives in light of particular preferences. But individuals cannot be free, socialists retort, unless government assumes active responsibility for the public good in order to ensure that everyone has access to the necessities of a worthwhile existence.

The problem is that during the course of its history liberalism has encompassed the contrary meanings which conservatives and socialists attach to freedom. In challenging arbitrary power and aristocratic privilege, early liberals sought to push back the frontiers of the state. Individual freedom, they argued, depended upon the enjoyment of certain civil liberties immune from government interference, including the right to accumulate property as well as to express opinions and follow conscience in religious matters. In this sense early liberals would seem to have endorsed the conservative conviction that liberty flourishes in a free-enterprise society which imposes few restrictions upon the pursuit of individual ambition. Towards the end of the nineteenth century, however, many liberals abandoned this ideal of a minimal state in which the right to acquire private property was sacrosanct. The gross inequalities of competitive capitalism, they now acknowledged, impaired the freedom of people whose struggle for survival afforded them little opportunity to make the best of their capacities. These progressive or 'new' liberals, as they are sometimes called, advocated political intervention in the economy to eliminate unemployment and low wages, as well as urging public provision of health care and other welfare rights.

In distinguishing themselves from their predecessors, the new liberals sometimes used the terms 'negative' and 'positive' liberty. Earlier liberals were mistaken, they suggested, in viewing society as an arena of self-sufficient and competitive individuals who were free to the extent that they could pursue private interests without coercion. A less individualistic perspective was now required, according to this argument, one which envisaged society as a collectivity of mutually dependent individuals unable to make the best of themselves unless government assumes responsibility for a public good transcending the private interests of a wealthy minority. Only a more active and interventionist state, then, could make a reality of the right to equal citizenship.

New liberals, in rejecting the faith of their predecessors in unbridled capitalism, concur with socialists that freedom is enhanced rather than restricted by the political elimination of poverty and social deprivation. The link between freedom and the collective provision of the material necessities of life was made by Elliott Dodds in a book which, when published in 1957, was announced as the most comprehensive statement in thirty years of the philosophy of British liberalism.

> We argue that Welfare is actually a form of Liberty in as much as it liberates men from social conditions which narrow their choices and thwart their self-development as truly as any governmental or personal coercions. At any rate both, in the Liberal view, have this in common that they should be regarded as means to the full and harmonious development of persons. But the 'new' freedoms differ from the old in that they call for positive measures, whereas the 'old' freedoms require simply the abolition of restraints. Their establishment, though in many ways extending the field for free action, involves restrictions which did not exist before.[5]

But though sharing with socialists a distaste for the gross inequalities of a market economy, new liberals have been reluctant entirely to discard the assumption of their predecessors that a system of economic competition is just in that it distributes rewards on the basis of individual merit. The following passage is taken from Nancy Sear's chapter in the book to which Dodds contributed. If the word 'Liberal' were deleted, her sentiments could be read as a manifesto of free-market conservatism.

> The Liberal society cannot be an egalitarian society, since freedom includes the freedom to make headway or to fall back, and liberals cannot agree to restrict the energetic in the interest of the leisurely. On the contrary we should try to ensure equality of opportunity, accepting the implication that those who seize opportunities will go faster and farther than those who do not.[6]

In some respects, then, modern liberals appear to sit uncomfortably astride the ideological worlds of conservatism and socialism. With conservatives they wish to define freedom as the right of individuals to strive for inequalities of wealth, and yet, like socialists, they want to argue that liberty is diminished unless everyone is given access to the resources necessary for a decent life.

Does the fact that liberalism embraces these conflicting meanings of freedom mean that a firm boundary cannot be drawn between the doctrine and its rivals, and also that the ideology is essentially incoherent? There is a tendency among some academic commentators to depict the transformation of liberalism at the end of the nineteenth century as a seismic shift splitting the ideology into two irreconcilable halves. One argument, favoured by the left, is that liberalism was conceptually robust during its classical phase when the emphasis was upon rolling back the state from civil society in order to eliminate arbitrary power and aristocratic privilege. Liberals had been too energetic pronouncing the desirability of negative liberty to make a plausible case for an economically interventionist state, in this view, and as a consequence their doctrine disintegrated with the passing of the age of *laissez-faire*.[7] Arguments of this sort reinforce the impression that there is now little to liberalism beyond those decent sentiments conveyed by the adjective 'liberal', and that the ideology is so nebulous as to embrace all of a generous disposition who favour an open society which tolerates individual differences. According to this characterisation of the doctrine a liberal is anyone who, for instance, would feel uncomfortable living in a theocratic state such as the Republic of Ireland which in its constitution embraces Roman Catholic teaching on divorce, abortion, and contraception; and who would also be disinclined to join some

Protestant evangelical sects in the North of Ireland because of their antipathy to gay and other minority rights. So a liberal can be expected to dislike authoritarian political regimes, preferring those which give their citizens ample space for self-expression. But does the noun 'liberalism' now signify little else than this disposition to respect individual diversity?

What is clear is that liberty is one of those ambiguous concepts about which there is disagreement both as to its meaning and the social conditions in which it is secured. So to claim that a commitment to freedom is at the core of liberalism is insufficient to identify the doctrine's distinctive characteristics. Of greater analytical value is the recognition that liberalism, in affirming the primacy of freedom, is in a significant sense an egalitarian doctrine. This does not necessarily mean, as one commentator suggests,[8] that the commitment of liberals to equality takes priority over their attachment to liberty. It does mean that they want freedom to be shared equally through society, for in valuing liberty they commit themselves to the proposition that everyone should enjoy as much of it as possible.

Now the claim that individuals are equally entitled to freedom does not in itself resolve the problem of determining the doctrine's identity. It begs the question of which particular liberties should be made available to everyone. Classical liberals believed that authoritarian government was the greatest threat to individual freedom, and so sought to extend the sphere of civil liberties as a safeguard against arbitrary power; whereas later liberals identify minimal or economically inactive government as an impediment to the equal enjoyment of freedom, and in consequence advocate the collective provision of social or welfare rights. There has been little continuity of agreement among liberals about the policies needed to enhance liberty. What nevertheless emerges from the varieties of liberalism is a persistent image of the good society as an association of free persons who are equal in their possession of basic rights. So the manner in which liberals have tended to couple the concepts of liberty and equality does lend to their doctrine a certain coherence and particular social perspective.

A BOURGEOIS CREED?

Historically, then, liberalism can be viewed as having endorsed a succession of strategies for extending the freedoms to which everyone is considered to be equally entitled. But there is a further issue to be tackled in order fully to identify the doctrine's distinctive features. This is the charge of commentators that liberalism is a narrowly individualistic creed which legitimates the maximisation of private satisfactions without regard to the public good. The argument is that, in emphasising the sanctity of individual rights, liberals have an impoverished sense of community as well as of the requirements of citizenship.

Now in a loose sense liberalism is evidently a bourgeois ideology. From its inception the doctrine conveyed ideas associated with the disintegration of feudal society and the eventual triumph of capitalism, and among its exponents were those who stood to gain from an erosion of aristocratic privilege and the wider accumulation of property. In liberal accounts of the struggle to emancipate individuals from the shackles of traditional society, moreover, the middle classes have not infrequently been cast as the heroes of the story. In *Vindicae Gallicae*, which like Paine's *Rights of Man* rebutted Burke's vindication of the *ancien régime*, James Mackintosh depicted the bourgeoisie as the personification of the values of Enlightenment liberalism:

> The commercial, or monied interest, has in all nations of Europe (taken as a body) been less prejudiced, more liberal, and more intelligent, than the landed gentry. Their views are enlarged by a wider intercourse with mankind, and hence the important influence of commerce in liberalizing the modern world. We cannot wonder then that this enlightened class of men ever prove the most ardent in the cause of freedom; the most zealous for political reform. It is not wonderful that philosophy should find in them more docile pupils; and liberty more active friends, than in a haughty and prejudiced aristocracy.[9]

For some commentators, however, liberalism is a bourgeois creed in the stronger sense that its adherents celebrate the acquisitive values associated with the pursuit of self-interest in a competitive economy, and in doing so operate with an atomistic conception of the individual. The 'emphasis on the asocial egoism of the individual', according to Anthony Arblaster, 'plays a permanently important part in liberalism. Without taking it into account it is impossible to understand the importance which liberalism attaches to the principles of personal freedom and privacy.'[10] The basis of this claim is that unlike conservatives such as Burke, who emphasise the inability of people to detach themselves from the traditions and conventions of a particular community, liberals often depict individuals as curiously abstracted from the society they happen to inhabit.

Early liberals challenged arbitrary power by appealing to universal principles. Individuals were said to come into the world with certain natural or inalienable rights, by which was meant an innate capacity and equal entitlement to manage their economic, religious, and other affairs. In the words of the seventeenth-century English philosopher John Locke (1632–1704), whose *Two Treatises of Government* (1690) is a classic exposition of this doctrine of natural rights, human beings are born 'in a state of perfect freedom, to order their actions and dispose of their possessions, and persons, as they see fit'. As residents in political society, runs the argument, individuals are entitled to retain their natural freedom in the form of constitutionally safeguarded civil liberties, and this requires a government that is both bound by the rule of law and limited in scope. Its role is that of an 'umpire', as Locke put it, upholding an impartial framework of law and order within which individuals may safely pursue their private concerns. The thrust of the argument was that legitimate government is rooted in the consent of those to whom its authority extends. To cite the *Two Treatises* again:

> Men being, as has been said, by Nature, all free, equal and independent, no one can be put out of this Estate, and subjected to the Political Power of another, without his own *Consent*. The only way whereby any one divests himself of his Natural Liberty, and *puts on the bonds of Civil Society* is by agreeing with other Men to join and unite into a Community, for their comfortable, safe and peaceable living one among another, in a secure Enjoyment of their Properties, and a greater Security against any that are not of it.

The inference of this consensual theory of political society is that government ought to be accountable to those whose rights it purports to protect, and the principal message of the *Two Treatises* was that arbitrary power might legitimately be resisted by the 'body of the people'.

So the doctrine of natural rights was a conceptual device by which early liberals challenged political authoritarianism. But the doctrine did tend to view individuals as abstract entities, conveying the impression that what is essential to human existence does not depend upon social relations and, further, that membership of political association is of instrumental value in protecting personal freedoms. This is the basis of the suggestion that classical liberalism was grounded in a form of bourgeois or 'possessive' individualism sanctioning the pursuit of private goals, particularly the acquisition of riches, at the expense of wider social obligations.[11] The 'great and chief end of men entering into commonwealths and putting themselves under government', according to the *Two Treatises*, 'is the preservation of their property'. There is a sense, then, in which liberalism can be taken to legitimate a form of government which permits individuals to accumulate property and indulge in other private pursuits without any obligation to co-operate on behalf of the public good.

The tendency to characterise liberalism as a narrowly individualist creed has been reinforced by recent scholarship. Historians of political thought such as J.G.A. Pocock distinguish Lockean liberalism from what they describe as a classical republican or civic humanist tradition of political discourse, articulated by James Harrington and others in the seventeenth century and subsequently refined into a condemnation of government patronage and corruption.[12] Whereas, the argument runs, early liberals licensed the pursuit of private goals, radicals of the civic humanist tradition were inspired by the ancient Greek and Roman ideal of a community whose members set aside self-interest by participating in public affairs for the common good. The emphasis of these radicals was not so much the Lockean one of individual rights against the state, including the right to resist arbitrary power, as the individual and social benefits of active citizenship. Through participation in public affairs citizens supposedly fulfilled their human potential as well as preventing political corruption. So rivalling the early liberal discourse of natural rights and individual self-sufficiency, according to recent historiography, was one which celebrated civic virtue and communal solidarity.

Among political theorists, too, there has been a tendency to depict liberalism as an individualistic doctrine. What has become known as the communitarian critique of liberalism, of which there have been many expressions since the early 1980s,[13] has focused upon John Rawls's *A Theory of Justice*, published in 1971 and regarded as the paradigmatic statement of twentieth-century liberalism. Rawls, an American philosopher, considers what principles of a fair and 'well-ordered' society are most likely to generate widespread assent among its members. His approach is to postulate an hypothetical situation in which free and rational individuals debate the ground rules that would enable them to live together in a polity. Such individuals, according to Rawls, would agree, firstly, that everyone is equally entitled to basic civil liberties and, secondly, on the desirability of redistributive welfare policies to ensure equality of opportunity. Of relevance is less the consensus about principles of justice which Rawls attributes to the 'original position' – as he describes the natural condition in which individuals discuss the terms of their political co-operation – as the fact that his hypothetical account of the origins of government is in the tradition of Lockean contractualism. This is why the Rawlsian theory of justice is taken by communitarians to confirm that liberalism is a form of asocial individualism. For both Locke and Rawls consider the foundations of a sound political society by abstracting individuals from it. And in making the self independent of and logically prior to the community in which it resides, communitarians contend, liberals conceive of political association as an instrumental arrangement for people pursuing essentially private interests.

This accusation of asocial individualism can be legitimately levelled against libertarian or free-market conservatives who do tend to view society as a collection of competitive individuals joined by a common desire for security rather than an awareness of citizenship. 'There is no such thing as society', Margaret Thatcher pronounced, 'there are only individuals.' But there is little evidence, in spite of the communitarian critique, that liberalism is a form of possessive individualism sanctioning the pursuit of private goals to the neglect of the public sphere. There is a sense of the common good even among those liberals, from Locke to Rawls, who have grounded government in the hypothetical consent of naturally independent individuals. Fair political arrangements are not only the shared achievement of free and equal individuals, according to this theory, they are maintained by vigilant citizenship alert to the danger of arbitrary power. Locke argued that the 'body of the people' had a right to resist unjust government, and later liberals have advocated democratic elections and other forms of public participation. For Rawls the preservation of fair democratic institutions is itself a common good achieved, as he writes in A Theory of Justice, 'through citizens' joint activity in mutual dependence on the appropriate action being taken by others'. Among early liberals, too, there was a conviction that a healthy polity presupposes a moral community of public-spirited individuals co-operating on behalf of common objectives. Historians such as J.G.A. Pocock, we have seen, highlight the existence of two competing political discourses in the seventeenth and eighteenth centuries: the liberal one of individual rights as against the classical republican language of civic virtue. The differences between these discourses have been exaggerated, in my view, because the classical republican ideal of citizen self-government was a hallmark of liberalism itself.

For early liberals this ideal of citizen self-rule was to be achieved through a dispersal of power and authority from existing elites to a much larger body of people. Central to their strategy was a belief in the benefits of a widespread ownership of property. Private property, they argued, engenders in its owners the moral discipline and mutual tolerance by which a just society is sustained. In this loose sense liberals did indeed construct a bourgeois ideology, arguing as they did that a well-ordered society depends upon virtues associated with the acquisition of private property. In endorsing the spread of bourgeois attitudes through society, however, their wish was to promote, not the asocial egoism of a self unencumbered by public responsibilities, but the virtues of citizens conscious of their obligations within the body politic.

To facilitate this process of *embourgeoisement*, early liberals advocated a twofold strategy that has remained a characteristic of the doctrine. They sought, on one hand, to undermine the power of inherited wealth derived from the ownership of land. The aristocracy was depicted as an idle and parasitic class which reaped an unearned income from rent, and whose privilege and monopolies prevented others from achieving independence. Its ethos of paternalism, moreover, was said to foster among the mass of the population an attitude of deference that was incompatible with a life of autonomy and citizenship. And so, on the other side, liberals wished to make the labouring classes virtuous. In becoming prudent and self-reliant, it was said, the poor would free themselves from dependence on the aristocracy, as well as acquiring those civic virtues which ensured political stability. Historically, then, liberals have been hostile to the undeserved benefits of aristocratic privilege, and also intent on the moral elevation of the poor. This persistent impulse to universalise bourgeois virtues provides a significant clue in the search for the ideology's identity.

The image that emerges from the concern of liberals to make everyone virtuous through the implementation of equal rights is of a one-class society in which, despite inequalities of wealth, there are common habits of self-discipline and responsible citizenship. It differs from the conservative picture of a class or command structure in which the rich and powerful exercise leadership and discipline over the majority; and also from the socialist ideal of a classless society which eliminates the inequalities of economic competition.

A BRIEF HISTORY

This persistent ideal of a community of free, independent, propertied and virtuous citizens can be illustrated by glancing at the ideology's evolution in a British context.

In its classical phase, we have seen, liberalism took shape around the idea of natural rights, a concept which was given clear expression during the Civil War period of the 1640s. The conflict between royalists and parliamentarians unleashed a torrent of radical thinking in which the traditional perception of society as a rigid hierarchy was displaced by that of a structure of equal rights where individuals exercise autonomy in crucial areas of their lives. Among these radicals were the Levellers, a group formed in 1646, whose extensive programme of political reform took its bearings from the assumption of natural freedom and equality. In *The Freeman's Freedom Vindicated* (1646) a Leveller leader, John Lilburne, articulated the view pivotal to natural rights doctrine, that no form of authority is legitimate unless grounded in the consent of those affected by it.

> Unnatural, irrational, sinful, wicked, unjust, devilish, and tyrannical it is, for any man whatsoever, spiritual or temporal, clergyman or layman, to appropriate and assume unto himself a power, authority and jurisdiction, to rule, govern, or reign over any sort of men in the world, without their free consent.

The 'freeborn' English had been deprived of their fundamental liberties with the introduction during the Norman Conquest of a system of hereditary privilege, according to the Levellers, but the time had come to reclaim those freedoms through a dispersal of power and wealth from elites to the people at large.

Leveller proposals for redistributing authority to ordinary people included a written constitution to protect civil liberties by ensuring that government was bound by the rule of law and limited in scope. Prominent among these liberties was the right to follow conscience in spiritual matters. Leveller antipathy to religious orthodoxy and ecclesiastical hierarchy derived from the radical Protestant commitment to the priesthood of all believers, which meant that everyone was entitled to choose their own way to truth in a society practising toleration and permitting heterodoxy.

The Leveller programme also advocated the abolition of monarchy and the lords, perceived to be bastions of arbitrary power and economic privilege, and the establishment of a representative commons elected annually by a larger electorate than before. How large has been a matter of dispute among commentators, deriving from their disagreement as to whether liberalism is a narrowly bourgeois creed. The Levellers appear to have been reluctant to endorse universal suffrage, excluding from their proposals for an extended franchise servants and alms-takers as well as women. One explanation is that Levellers were early exponents of a possessive individualism that licensed the pursuit of economic self-interest.[14] In linking political rights to property owner-ship, runs the argument, they revealed their conviction that individuals who failed successfully to compete in a market economy thereby forfeited the right to be a citizen. But though Leveller radicalism was certainly moderated by patriarchal and other prevailing assumptions, their caution about the extent of the suffrage did not necessarily stem from an impulse to endorse the inequalities of an embryonic capitalism. A more plausible explanation of their readiness to exclude servants and alms-takers from the suffrage was the view that, as Maximilian Petty suggested at the time, such 'persons depend upon the will of other men and should be afraid to displease them'. The Leveller objection to aristocratic privilege was that it sustained a hierarchy of social relation-ships – ruler and subject, master and servant – contrary to the natural human condition of freedom and equality. Those at the bottom of the hierarchy, Levellers believed, were unable to make autonomous polit-ical choices because of the mechanisms of social control ensuring their subordination to landlords.

The Leveller strategy for restoring the natural condition of freedom and equality was to construct a society in which no one depended upon the will of another. Without intending to 'level mens Estates, destroy Propriety, or make all things Common', as their manifesto, *An Agree-ment of the Free People of England*, put it, the Levellers nevertheless proposed to disperse property ownership as widely as possible by eliminating economic monopolies, the practice of primogeniture and other bulwarks of landed privilege. In this way those groups dependent on aristocratic paternalism, including servants and alms-takers, would eventually disappear, enabling every adult male to enjoy full political rights in a property-owning democracy. Allied to Leveller measures for ensuring the economic self-sufficiency of the poor was an educational plan to make them literate and knowledgeable. A community of educated and masterless individuals would consist of virtuous citizens, according to the Levellers, exercising their birthright as freeborn Englishmen in a civilised manner.

So the Levellers were not narrowly bourgeois ideologues who anticipated a new age of capital accumulation and wage labour. Their ideal was a society of independent proprietors, enjoying ample space within civil society to shape their lives in a responsible manner, respecting the liberties of others, and using their rights as citizens to co-operate in ensuring the preservation of a fair and just polity. Here was the image that recurred in later liberal writings: a one-class community of autonomous citizens, each responsible for their own affairs and making a particular contribution to the common good.

The Leveller conception of democracy was gendered. Women did not need to be enfranchised, even radicals assumed, because their welfare and interests were included in those of their husbands as household heads. This inclination to exclude women from citizenship persisted until the nineteenth century. Not all liberals, moreover, were as eager as the Levellers to redistribute wealth more evenly through the community as a prelude to full citizenship.

In the eighteenth century those claiming to be heirs of the struggles of the previous century against absolute monarchy and religious conformity were the Whigs, who favoured a system of parliamentary government and a degree of religious toleration. But as men of wealth and rank, many of them beneficiaries of government patronage, the Whigs were disinclined either to oppose the established order or to advocate democracy, which they equated with rule by the rabble. Government was best left to a propertied minority, they believed, with enough of an economic 'stake' in the community to know better than the masses themselves what was in their political interests. Hence the Whig preference for the English system of mixed government where king, lords and commons checked one another against arbitrary power because of their overlapping powers, and in which the 'popular' branch of the legislature was elected by men of substantial property.

Most Whigs, embarrassed by that aspect of their ideological legacy which gave credence to demands for political and economic equality, side-stepped the concept of natural rights. But from the middle of the century, responding to an increasing demand of radicals for an extension of civil and political liberties, they condemned John Locke as the principal proponent of natural rights. Having characterised Locke as 'the Idol of the Levellers of England', Josiah Tucker proceeded in *Four Letters on Important National Subjects* (1783) to explain why the mass of people were politically incompetent:

> When a Multitude are invested with the Power of governing, they prove the very worst of Governors. They are rash and precipitate, giddy and inconstant, and ever the Dupes of designing Men, who lead them to commit the most atrocious Crimes, in order to make them subservient to their own Purposes. Besides, a democratic Government is despotic in its very Nature; because it supposes itself to be the only Fountain of Power, from which there can be no Appeal. Hence, therefore, it comes to pass, that this many headed Monster, an absolute Democracy, has all the Vices and Imperfections of its Brother-Tyrant, an absolute Monarchy, without any of the shining Qualities of the latter to hide its Deformity.

Tucker then extolled the virtues of mixed government in which the 'hereditary Nobility' were pivotal in preserving the balance of the constitution.

This vindication of inherited wealth was a world removed from the Leveller assault upon every form of customary privilege. Whig support for limited government and religious toleration provided a tenuous link with the radicalism of the previous century. Yet the liberal kernel – if liberal it really was – of aristocratic Whiggism was contained within a conservative shell. There was a point, probably reached with the denunciation of natural rights thinking, when establishment liberalism – if we can so describe Whiggism – lost touch with its doctrinal roots and shaded into conservatism. Edmund Burke made conformity to tradition rather than natural rights the measure of a fair and just polity, and his eloquent defence of social hierarchy earned him a reputation as a scourge of Enlightenment liberalism and the progenitor of English conservatism. Burke was a Whig.

Although most eighteenth-century Whigs retreated from the radicalism of the previous century, others continued to resort to the idea of natural rights to urge an extension of civil liberties and political rights. In the early decades of the century some of them, disturbed by what they perceived as a tendency towards financial corruption and executive tyranny by the Whig establishment, followed the Levellers in advocating a more even spread of private property as a bulwark against arbitrary power. In *Cato's Letters*, popular expressions of radical Whiggism that appeared as newspaper articles in the 1720s, John Trenchard proposed the implementation of an agrarian law to ensure a more equitable distribution of wealth, as well as other measures to extend individual liberties. Economically self-sufficient individuals with a firm sense of their own autonomy within a structure of equal rights, argued Trenchard, would be model citizens alert to the dangers of arbitrary power.

> Every Man's honest Industry and useful Talents, while they are employed for the Publick, will be employed for himself; and while he serves himself, he will serve the Publick: Publick and private Interest will secure each other; all will cheerfully give a Part to secure the Whole, and be brave to defend it.

Here again was the ideal of a community of self-reliant and politically responsible individuals.

The concept of natural rights was also used by dissenters in their bid for greater religious freedom. Their principal target was the Test and Corporations Acts which entrenched the privileges of the established Church by reserving many public offices for Anglicans. A state religion, according to dissenters, violated the natural condition of freedom and equality by infringing upon the sovereignty of private judgement in spiritual matters. It was the business of government, wrote Richard Price in *The Evidence for a Future Period of Improvement in the State of Mankind* (1787), 'to defend the *properties* of men, not to take care of their *souls* – And to protect *equally* all honest citizens of all persuasions, not to set up one religious sect above another'. A society enshrining natural freedom in its arrangements would consist of religious denominations that were voluntary and equal.

By the time Price was writing, radicals such as Paine, we have seen, were demanding an equality not only of civil liberties but of political rights by means of manhood suffrage. The failure of Britain to become a democratic republic at the time of the French Revolution spurred radicals to use the idea of universal rights well into the next century. The *Nonconformist* weekly, established by the Reverend Edward Miall, campaigned for the disestablishment of the Church of England and the admission of all adult males to the suffrage, depicting the latter as a means of nurturing a virtuous citizenry no longer inhibited by attitudes of deference and subordination. Not only were labouring men entitled to the vote as a natural right, according to the *Nonconformist*, their enfranchisement would be an incentive to acquire those virtues of self-discipline and mutual respect by which a sound polity is sustained. *Reconciliation Between the Middle and Labouring Classes* (1842), which consisted of articles printed in the *Nonconformist*, depicted democracy as an educative process of benefit to individuals and the community:

Only let the poor be taken politically by the hand – placed on a level with other classes – brought forward into association with these whose social position is above them – and the spirit within them will naturally awake to new life, and become sensible to wants before unknown. Education will not need then to be forced upon the poor. They will pant for education. Man soon accommodates himself to a new sphere, when once he is allowed to move in it – seldom qualifies himself for that sphere before he is called to occupy it. Raise the tone of his self-respect by raising his position, and you awaken in his bosom an honourable ambition to act his part with becoming dignity. The extension to the people of complete suffrage, so far from exciting insubordination, would, calculating upon the ordinary laws of human nature, give a mighty impulse to popular intelligence and morality; and in the course of a short time would secure an amount of education, order, and even religion, which no other means could possibly effect.

The great *consideratum* of society is that all classes should be guided in their conduct by systematic self-government, rather than by the external restraints of law. But men never care to obey, themselves, until they receive from others the respect to which they are entitled. Until then, apart from religion, with which human governments have nothing to do, the grand motive is wanting – the inner spring is sealed up – and men are what they are forced to be, rather than what they wish to be. The way to make them aspire is not to treat them as things of nought – to make them love order and revere law is not to refuse them the benefits of order, and turn law into an engine for their oppression. Place them where they are entitled to be, give them what they are entitled to have, and while you take away the main inducement to insubordination, you supply at the same time the main motive to industrious, sober, and peaceable behaviour . . .

So manhood suffrage would provide the poor with that sense of autonomy from which civic virtue flowed.

By this time the case for an extension of individual liberties tended to be made without recourse to the idea of natural rights. The concept did not feature in Adam Smith's *Wealth of Nations* (1776), the classic statement on behalf of a free-market economy. Arguments for a 'system of natural liberty', as Smith described an economy in which individuals can pursue their interests unencumbered by government intervention, are often cited as evidence that liberalism is the narrowly individualistic creed depicted by some commentators, and also that the mantle of the doctrine in its classical phase has been inherited by free-market conservatives. In using the discourse of a competitive economy, however, eighteenth- and nineteenth-century liberals were neither licensing the maximisation of private interests without regard to the common good nor – as libertarian conservatives do – defending the inequalities and privileges of capitalist enterprise. The idea of an unbridled economy was a means by which they continued to condemn the privileges of inherited wealth and advocate greater scope for individual autonomy on the part of ordinary people.

The New Right of the 1980s is sometimes said to have been in the tradition of the nineteenth-century Manchester School of liberalism. But members of the Manchester School, unlike modern conservatives, were intent on eliminating prevailing inequalities. Some of them were involved in a free-trade movement which culminated in 1846 with the abolition of tariffs on imported grain. The Corn Laws, they believed, inflated the price of domestic bread, and were therefore a form of taxation on the poor for the benefit of landowners. The leaders of the Anti-Corn Law League, Richard Cobden and John Bright, attributed current injustices to the system of hereditary privilege introduced with the Norman Conquest – as the Levellers had done – and they argued that the balanced constitution extolled by mainstream Whigs was designed to preserve the undeserved wealth of the 'great territorial families of England'. Cobden and Bright linked their arguments against economic protectionism with proposals, including household suffrage and an educational scheme, to enable the mass of people to attain that independence on which virtuous citizenship was said to depend. Instead of being used to endorse the acquisitive impulses of competitive individuals, then, the concept of a free economy underpinned the liberal vision of a society of autonomous citizens equal in their possession of basic rights.

The concept of natural rights was absent too from the writings of John Stuart Mill (1806–73), one of the most influential of British liberal thinkers. Mill argued that individuals secure in their independence and intent on fulfilling themselves would contribute to the welfare and progress of society, and in this sense his work was a sophisticated expression of the now familiar assumption that a sound polity emanates from a virtuous citizenry. Of interest are the novelty of Mill's arguments and his proposals for constructing a community in which autonomous individuals co-operate in the pursuit of shared objectives. *On Liberty* (1859) was in some respects an orthodox, though elegant, argument for limited government that did not encroach upon civil liberties. But whereas earlier liberals had condemned arbitrary government, Mill used the concept of liberty to warn of the danger of the tyranny of public opinion. In modern society, according to Mill, there were growing pressures to conform which inhibited individual spontaneity and cultural diversity. Without the space for individual experimentation with life, however, the human potential would be thwarted and society would stagnate.

Mill's desire for a more open, pluralist society shaped his attitude to democracy. He favoured adult male and, unlike earlier liberals, female suffrage, linking the latter in *The Subjection of Women* (1869) with proposals to secure for women equal legal as well as political rights with men. Mill advocated universal suffrage partly on the ground that the disenfranchised were invariably exploited by those with political power, but also because the virtues of citizenship were cultivated by the exercise of democratic rights. The case that Mill made for democracy in *Thoughts on Parliamentary Reform* (1859) is not dissimilar from that put in the *Nonconformist*:

It is important that every one of the governed should have a voice in the government, because it can hardly be expected that those who have no voice will be unjustly postponed to those who have. It is still more important as one of the means of national education. A person who is excluded from all participation in political business is not a citizen. He has not the feelings of a citizen. To take an active interest in politics is, in modern times, the first thing which elevates the mind to large interests and contemplations; the first step out of the narrow bounds of individual and family selfishness, the first opening in the contracted round of daily occupations . . . The possession and the exercise of political, and among others of electoral, rights, is one of the chief instruments both of moral and of intellectual training for the popular mind; and all governments must be regarded as extremely imperfect, until every one who is required to obey the laws, has a voice, or the prospect of a voice, in their enactment and administration.

Although in favour of admitting everyone to the franchise, Mill advocated a graduated suffrage in which additional votes were rewarded to those who by their occupation and professional qualifications 'could afford a reasonable presumption of superior knowledge and cultivation'. His intention in wishing to weight democracy in favour of an enlightened opinion was to counteract what he described in *On Liberty* as the tyranny of 'collective mediocrity'. A system of plural voting, he hoped, would ensure that legislation reflected informed opinion.

Mill's preoccupation with the stifling of individuality by mass conformity may appear to run contrary to the liberal conviction that ordinary people can be trusted to act in a civilised manner. Like the Levellers, however, he believed that the labouring classes had been inhibited from practising the art of self-government because of their subordination to a propertied minority. His strategy, also like that of the Levellers, was for a society in which everyone had both the incentive and opportunity to be autonomous in a socially responsible manner. He believed that making the number of votes dependent on educational and other achievements would spur the poor to improve themselves. Another proposal, outlined in *Principles of Political Economy* (1848), was for a network of economic co-operatives in which workers themselves would own capital and take managerial decisions. The effect would be a 'moral revolution' providing the labouring classes with a sense of autonomy and of being engaged in the pursuit, not of competing private and sectional interests, but of a common good. Society had advanced to a stage where the poor had to be treated as citizens rather than subjects, Mill wrote in the same book, so that the 'prospect of the future depends on the degree in which they can be made rational beings'. The problem of how to universalise a disposition to intelligent self-government was one to which Mill persistently returned in his writings.

The liberal concern with virtuous citizenship prompted some writers in the decades after Mill's death to provide a sharper, more robust conceptualisation of the common good. In doing so they suggested that the state, as custodian of the public interest, had a responsibility to eliminate social and economic obstacles preventing individuals from making their particular contribution to the well-being of the community. Many of these new or progressive liberals, as they are known, were influenced by the claim of the Oxford philosopher and Liberal city councillor T.H. Green (1836–82), that liberty ought to be understood not merely in a negative sense as the absence of external constraints upon individual conduct. Individual freedom was not necessarily secured through competition for scarce resources within the framework of a minimal state confined to preserving law and order. Individuals were free insofar as they fulfilled their potential for rational and moral conduct, according to Green, and for him this meant transcending the narrow concerns of self-interest to participate in a shared way of life. Freedom was to be understood, then, as a positive capacity for citizenship. In a famous lecture, 'Liberal Legislation and Freedom of Contract' (1881), Green said that government should 'maintain the conditions without which a free exercise of the human faculties is impossible' by emancipating the poor from ignorance, disease, squalid housing and exploitation at work. Advocates of a free-market economy believed that regulations of this kind infringed the property rights of landlords and employers. Freedom, Green retorted, was not a licence for a minority to frustrate the potential of others to contribute to the common good by making the best of themselves.

Green did not think that the state had much to do in removing social and economic impediments to virtuous citizenship. He believed, like earlier liberals, that most of the ills of British society derived from the system of hereditary privilege established at the Norman Conquest. The persistent influence of aristocratic power explained lingering attitudes of deference and subordination among the labouring classes, according to Green, as well as political reluctance to tackle the evils of landlordism. Once the feudal debris had been cleared by measures such as the taxation of inherited wealth, the poor would acquire the virtues of citizenship within a predominantly competitive economy.

Other liberals, influenced by Green's characterisation of freedom as a positive capacity of individuals to make the best of themselves, were less convinced of the efficacy of unregulated capitalism. What prompted them to formulate the philosophy of an enlarged state was the use made by advocates of a free economy, considered in the next chapter, of the Darwinian discourse of natural selection to contend that society progresses through a competitive struggle in which 'fit' entrepreneurs accumulate riches and the 'unfit' poor suffer the consequences of their incompetence. New liberals responded by formulating their own evolutionary theory to demonstrate that the 'unfitness' of the masses was perpetuated by government inactivity. L.T. Hobhouse (1864–1929), a prolific publicist of the new liberalism, detected in modern society the emergence of a higher form of morality because citizens were increasingly willing to set aside private interests for the sake of the common good. Among the manifestations of social progress was the spread of democratic values, a dimunition of class conflicts, and a readiness to embody altruism in public policy through, for example, factory and sanitary legislation.

Hobhouse used his theory of evolutionary collectivism to justify a more extensive programme of social reform than Green had envisaged. In *Liberalism* (1911) he argued that the state ought to establish a 'living equality of rights' through welfare policies financed by taxation. Hobhouse's intention was to vindicate the measures implemented by the reforming Liberal government between 1906 and 1911, including the provision of old-age pensions and an insurance scheme for sickness and unemployment. In arguing for a minimum wage and other social rights, moreover, he discarded the assumption of earlier liberals that a market economy could provide everyone with the material basis of individual autonomy. Poverty and unemployment signified not a moral failure or character defect on the part of individuals, as Social Darwinists claimed, but the structural imperfections of an economy which invariably deprived some people of the necessities of a worthwhile existence. It was the business of government to deal with the flaws of market capitalism by mobilising the 'collective resources and organised power of the community for public needs'. Hobhouse challenged the idea that the rights of private property are sacrosanct by arguing that wealth is neither accumulated nor secured by individuals in isolation from one another. The social dimension of wealth creation entitled government to treat a proportion of individual income as surplus that could be taxed to provide the poor with a basic wage and other benefits.

Hobhouse derived the idea of a surplus from his friend, J.A. Hobson (1858–1940), who argued that the redistribution of wealth into a living wage for the poor would secure economic efficiency by providing them with new purchasing power. In the *Crisis of Liberalism* (1909), Hobson urged a measure of political regulation of the economy as well as welfare policies:

> Liberalism is now formally committed to a task which certainly involves a new conception of the State in its relation to the individual life and to private enterprise. That conception is not Socialism, in any accredited meaning of that term, though implying a considerable amount of increased public ownership and control of industry. From the standpoint which best presents its continuity with earlier Liberalism, it appears as a fuller appreciation and realisation of individual liberty contained in the provision of equal opportunities for self-development. But to this individual standpoint must be joined a just apprehension of the social, viz., the insistence that these claims or rights of self-development be adjusted to the sovereignty of social welfare.

A positive understanding of liberty as a capacity for human fulfilment entailed the public provision of welfare and other social rights, in this view, to achieve the conventional liberal ideal of equal freedom for everyone.

Two men, both members of the Liberal Party, are regarded as the principal architects of the welfare or humanised capitalism which prevailed in Britain from 1945 until the ascendancy of the New Right in the 1980s. In *The General Theory of Employment, Interest and Money* (1936), J.M. Keynes (1883–1948) provided the classic vindication of a mixed economy in which the state assumes overall management of investment and consumption, while leaving production in the hands of private enterprise. This kind of hybrid economy preserved personal liberties and cultural diversity, according to Keynes, while eradicating mass unemployment and other social ills which nurtured authoritarian political regimes.

The other man, William Beveridge (1879–1963), an unsuccessful Liberal Party candidate, wrote several reports in the 1940s which became the ideological foundation of the post-war welfare state. The business of government was to eliminate deprivation and unemployment, according to Beveridge, through such measures as comprehensive social insurance, free health care, provision of a minimum wage, and Keynesian management of the economy. Liberty, he told the Liberal Assembly,

> means more than freedom from the arbitrary power of Governments. It means freedom from economic servitude to Want and Squalor and other social evils; it means freedom from arbitrary

power in any form. A starving man is not free, because till he is fed, he cannot have a thought for anything but how to meet his urgent physical needs; he is reduced from a man to an animal. A man who dare not resent what he feels to be an injustice from an employer or a foreman, lest this condemn him to chronic un-employment, is not free.

So the provision of full employment in a welfare state was another tactic in the liberal strategy to achieve an equality of rights.

CONCLUSION

The principal argument of this chapter is that the coherence of liberal-ism is to be detected in the way in which a persistent commitment to an equal right to liberty has been given substance in different historical contexts. A related, less explicit, argument is that liberalism is essen-tially an ideology of the left. Its adherents have endorsed not the unrestrained egoism of enterprising individuals intent on capital accumulation, as commentators frequently suggest, but the rights of citizens engaged in a mutual endeavour to sustain a just polity. The final issue to be addressed is the location of liberalism in modern society. In Britain the doctrine has been attached to a political party for a com-paratively short period of its history. The Liberal Party was formed in the 1850s, began to lose electoral support during the First World War, and merged with the Social Democratic Party in the 1980s. The dis-appearance of the Liberal Party does not necessarily signify the dis-integration of liberalism as a set of principles embraced by people who believe in an equal right to freedom. Now, as in earlier centuries, those whom we identify as liberals may not describe themselves as such. Liberal values can be discerned, for example, in arguments against sexual and racial discrimination, on behalf of minority rights, and in a renewed campaign in Britain since the 1980s to safeguard citizens against arbitrary government through, for example, the establishment of a Bill of Rights or the introduction of a written constitution. Liberalism in a broad sense is diffused throughout society.

There are limits, however, to this diffusion. In the 1980s some libertarian conservatives were eager to unfurl the banner of liberalism in their crusade to roll back the state from the economy. But, not-withstanding endorsement from those commentators who depict the doctrine as a form of asocial individualism, the New Right was incorrect in perceiving itself as a reincarnation of classical liberalism. The free market, like the idea of liberty itself, is one of those slippery concepts that has been put to various political uses. Whereas classical liberals honed it into an assault upon every form of privilege and patronage, conservative individualists from Robert Peel to Margaret Thatcher have used it to defend the wealth and authority of a minority. The authoritarian individualism of the right has little in common with any form of liberalism.

Socialists can with greater legitimacy claim to have inherited the mantle of liberalism. With liberals, and unlike conservatives, they believe that a more even distribution of wealth is necessary to secure an equal right to freedom. The difference is that socialists have tended to assume that their objectives are incompatible with the continuation of a system of private property. 'We are not among those communists who are out to destroy personal liberty', wrote Marx and Engels in the first issue of the *Communist Journal* (1847),

> who wish to turn the world into one huge barrack or into a gigantic workhouse. There are certainly some communists who, with an easy conscience, refuse to countenance personal liberty and would like to shuffle it out of the world because they consider that it is a hindrance to complete harmony. But we have no desire to exchange freedom for equality. We are convinced . . . that in no social order will personal freedom be so assured as in a society based upon communal ownership.

The problem for socialists, of course, is that public ownership has been discredited by the failure of certain forms of state planning in Western societies and more spectacularly by the collapse from the late 1980s of communist regimes elsewhere. Hence the attraction now of 'market' and other forms of socialism whose adherents advocate a more even dispersal of wealth within a structure of private property and economic competition. But market socialism, though not described as such, has been a feature of liberal thinking since the Levellers.

One criticism of the new liberalism, made at the time by individualists, was that it was socialist in endorsing collectivist policies. The same charge is sometimes made by those commentators who suggest that the doctrine in its post-classical phase became indistinct and incoherent. The accusation rests on the false assumption that early liberalism was an individualistic creed. A more plausible view is that modern socialists, with their attachment to economic competition, are liberals in disguise and that the on-going struggle to give substance to the idea of equal rights will ensure the survival of the doctrine as an intellectually rigorous and persuasive set of values and principles – even though those engaged in the struggle may not be labelled liberal.

NOTES

1 Harold Laski, *The Rise of European Liberalism*, London, Allen and Unwin, 1936, 17.
2 Joseph Grimond, *The Liberal Challenge*, London, Hollis and Carter, 1963, 33.
3 In Andrew Reid, ed., *Why I am a Liberal: Being Definitions and Confessions of Faith by the Best Minds of the Liberal Party*, London, Cassell, 1885, 82.
4 See Isaiah Berlin, 'Two Concepts of Liberty', in his *Four Essays on Liberty*, Oxford, Oxford University Press, 1969, 118–72.
5 In George Watson, ed., *The Unservile State: Essays in Liberty and Welfare*, London, Allen and Unwin, 1957, 17.
6 *Ibid.*, 192.
7 Harold Laski, *The Decline of Liberalism*, L.T. Hobhouse Memorial Lecture No. 10, Oxford, Oxford University Press, 1940.
8 Ronald Dworkin, 'Liberalism', in Stuart Hampshire, ed., *Public and Private Morality*, Cambridge, Cambridge University Press, 1978, 113–43.
9 James Mackintosh, *Vindicae Gallicae: Defence of the French Revolution and its English Admirers, Against the Accusations of the Right Hon. Edmund Burke*, London, G.G.J. and J. Robinson, 1792.
10 Anthony Arblaster, *The Rise and Decline of Western Liberalism*, Oxford, Blackwell, 1984, 43.
11 C.B. MacPherson, *The Political Theory of Possessive Individualism: Hobbes to Locke*, Oxford, Oxford University Press, 1968.
12 J.G.A. Pocock, *The Machiavellian Moment: Florentine Political Thought and the Atlantic Republican Tradition*, Princeton, Princeton University Press, 1975.
13 E.g. Alasdair MacIntyre, *After Virtue: A Study in Moral Theory*,

London, Duckworth, 1981; Michael Sandel, *Liberalism and the Limits of Justice*, Cambridge, Cambridge University Press, 1982.
14 MacPherson, *The Political Theory of Possessive Individualism*.

FURTHER READING

Anthony Arblaster, *The Rise and Decline of Western Liberalism*, Oxford, Blackwell, 1984, is a wide-ranging and enjoyable history of the doctrine, even though as a critic of liberalism from the left he depicts it as an individualistic creed which became incoherent at the end of the nineteenth century. A brief but sharp history from Locke to modern liberals such as Rawls is John Gray, *Liberalism*, Milton Keynes, Open University Press, 1986, though like Arblaster – but from an alternative ideological perspective – he too portrays liberalism as a 'project of theorising political institutions for the government of an individualist society' which foundered in its post-classical phase. A sympathetic and more balanced account is John A. Hall, *Liberalism: Politics, Ideology and the Market*, London, Paladin, 1987. E.K. Bramsted and K.J. Melhuish, eds, *Western Liberalism: A History in Documents from Locke to Crowe*, London, Longman, 1978, provides 800 pages of texts and sound commentaries. Some of the arguments of the chapter can also be found in Robert Eccleshall, *British Liberalism: Liberal Thought from the 1640s to 1980*, London, Longman, 1986, which is an anthology of liberal writings prefaced by an introductory essay. Richard Bellamy, *Liberalism and Modern Society: An Historical Argument*, London, Polity Press, 1992, is a wide-ranging analysis of the development of liberalism in Britain, France, Germany and Italy from the nineteenth century to the present. Carole Pateman, *The Problem of Political Obligation: A Critical Analysis of Liberal Theory*, New York, Wiley, 1979, is a penetrating critique of social contract theorists with chapters on Locke and Rawls. Amy Gutman, *Liberal Equality*, Cambridge, Cambridge University Press, 1980, is interesting on liberal theories of equality from Locke to Rawls. Susan Mendus, *Toleration and the Limits of Liberalism*, Houndmills, Macmillan, 1989, focuses on the arguments of Locke and Mill for toleration. Gerald F. Gaus, *The Modern Liberal Theory of Man*, London, Croom Helm, 1983, focuses on Mill, Green, Hobhouse, Rawls, and others, arguing that the theme of modern liberalism is that of 'combining and reconciling individuality and sociability'. Stephen Mulhall and Adam Swift, *Liberals and Communitarians*, Oxford, Blackwell, 1992, provides a clear account not only of communitarian objections to liberalism but also of Rawls's theory.

With regard to thinkers mentioned in the chapter, John Sanderson, *'But the People's Creatures': The Philosophical Basis of the English Civil War*, Manchester, Manchester University Press, 1989, is a crisp account of the thinking of the Levellers and other radicals in the 1640s. Richard Aschraft, *Revolutionary Politics and Locke's Two Treatises of Government*, Princeton, New York, Princeton University Press, 1986, persuasively argues that Locke was far from being the bourgeois ideologue of many accounts. Among the better books on Paine are Mark Philp, *Paine*, Oxford, Oxford University Press, 1989, and Gregory Claeys, *Thomas Paine: Social and Political Thought*, London, Unwin Hyman, 1989. Richard Bellamy, ed., *Victorian Liberalism: Nineteenth-Century Political Thought and Practice*, London, Routledge, 1990, includes chapters on Adam Smith, Mill, Green, and the new liberalism. An authoritative introduction to Mill's thinking is William Thomas, *Mill*, Oxford, Oxford University Press, 1985. A book rich with insight into Green's intellectual milieu is Melvin Richter, *The Politics of Conscience: T.H. Green and His Age*, London, Weidenfeld and Nicolson, 1964. Good accounts of the new liberalism include Stefan Collini, *Liberalism and Sociology: L.T. Hobhouse and Political Argument in England 1880–1914*, Cambridge, Cambridge University Press, 1979; Michael Freeden, *The New Liberalism: An Ideology of Social Reform*, Oxford, Clarendon Press, 1978; Peter Clarke, *Liberals and Social Democrats*, Cambridge, Cambridge University Press, 1978; Peter Weiler, *Liberal Social Theory in Great Britain 1889–1914*, New York, Garland, 1982; and John Allett, *New Liberalism: The Political Economy of J.A. Hobson*, Toronto, Toronto University Press, 1982. Beveridge is well served by Jose Harris, *William Beveridge*, Oxford, Oxford University Press, 1977. On Rawls see Chandran Kukathas and Philip Pettit, *Rawls' 'A Theory of Justice' and Its Critics*, Cambridge, Polity, 1990, as well as his own revision of the ideas of *A Theory of Justice* in John Rawls, *Political Liberalism*, New York, Columbia University Press, 1993.

Chapter 3

Conservatism

Robert Eccleshall

The common antithesis between a society organised for the good of all and a society run in the interest of a governing class is a false one. Everyone must agree that society should be organised for the general good, but the whole question is whether it is for the general good that there should be a governing class or not.

Christopher Hollis, *Death of a Gentleman: The Letters of Robert Fossett*, Glasgow, William Collins, 1957, 35

Conservatives, if they talk about freedom long enough, begin to believe that that is what they want. But it is not freedom that Conservatives want; what they want is the sort of freedom that will maintain existing inequalities or restore lost ones, so far as political action can do this.

Maurice Cowling, 'The Present Condition', in M. Cowling, ed., *Conservative Essays*, London, Cassell, 1978, 9

PROBLEMS OF DEFINITION

One problem in defining conservatism is the reluctance of some, conservatives themselves as well as academic commentators, to acknowledge that the ideology poses serious conceptual difficulties. In the common-sense approach the meaning of the doctrine is literally given in the verb 'conserve', and conservatism is taken to be a set of preferences or beliefs regarding social change. Conservatives are said to be sceptical about ambitious schemes for improving the human condition. Instead of speculating about a future earthly paradise, they settle for the benefits of a customary way of life; and rejecting the nostrums of the social engineer, they favour the piecemeal reforms that are needed to keep the ship of state on an even keel.

This approach is unsatisfactory for several reasons, not least because self-styled conservatives do sometimes advocate radical change. In the 1980s, for example, the so-called New Right assailed institutions that impeded market forces, justifying their programme of social reconstruction with the sort of abstract ideas which conservatives reputedly abhor. It is of course possible to argue that those who wish to unsettle established institutions are not genuine conservatives, no matter how they designate themselves. Old-style British Tories were inclined to depict Thatcherites as a throwback to the nineteenth-century Manchester School of liberalism, economic dogmatists who had ideologically misled the Conservative Party; and some academics also prefer to describe New Right radicals as neo- or classical liberals rather than conservatives. But this excommunication of avowed conservatives whose views fail to conform to some stereotype is rather arbitrary, as well as being insensitive to the historically varied forms of the doctrine. It seems preferable to recognise that conservatives can be radical or traditional in their attitude to social change, and to characterise the ideology in a manner that accommodates both types.

Sensitivity to historical diversity, however, can create its own kind of conceptual hazard. Some commentators, alert to differences within conservatism, write as if the representatives of its various strands are distant cousins, members of an extended family with nothing in common besides a surname. The effect is to lose sight of the ideology's peculiar characteristics, leaving little sense of the frontiers that separate conservatives from liberals, socialists and others.

In what follows I suggest that there are enough resemblances among members of the conservative family to identify some common ideological traits, and that what distinguishes the doctrine from its rivals is a vindication of inequality. The argument will unfold through a closer inspection of the two alternative approaches just outlined.

CONSERVATISM AND TRADITION

Those who define conservatism as an attitude to change often portray it as superior to rival ideologies. Their argument is that other ideologies encourage impractical schemes of social improvement. But conservatism affirms the value of what has been tried and tested by historical experience, and in doing so dispels any illusion that the imperfections of human arrangements can be eliminated in some future golden age. In making a virtue of what has been called the 'politics of imperfection',[1] conservatism purportedly corresponds to timeless instincts. In his spirited *Conservatism in England* (1933), F.J.C. Hearnshaw traced the origins of the doctrine to Adam's caution in the Garden of Eden. Eve, according to Hearnshaw, was the first radical: reckless, starry-eyed, easily tempted by the false promises made by the serpent – the latter perceived as a forebear of Karl Marx. Other writers also take the view that conservatism stems from a temperamental preference for the familiar, coupled with a distaste for theoretical speculation. 'Conservatism is less a political doctrine than a habit of mind', wrote R.J. White at the beginning of a book published in 1950, 'a mode of feeling, a way of living.'[2] Phrases such as these still appear in the opening sentences of some books about conservatism.[3]

The proposition that conservatism is rooted in a natural dislike of change is of negligible analytical value, conflating as it does ahistorical patterns of individual behaviour with the emergence – at a specific moment in Western culture and among particular social groups – of a cluster of ideas about the purposes of government and the organisation of society. Conservatism is to be understood not as the expression of recurring habits and instincts, but as a distinctive perspective on society shaped by the political struggles and class divisions of the post-medieval state.

Nor should much credence be given to the suggestion that conservatism is qualitatively different from other political doctrines because it belongs outside the realm of ideology. Those who characterise conservatism as a frame of mind often denigrate ideology as a perverted or 'alien' form of knowledge,[4] consisting of speculative notions which foster the illusion that the political order can be dramatically improved. Conservatives, in contrast, allegedly attain genuine understanding of human affairs because of their pragmatic attachment to existing institutions. This insistence that conservatism is not an ideology is itself an ideological ploy by those sympathetic to the doctrine, part of the rough-and-tumble of political argument rather than an analytical exercise.

Not everyone who equates conservatism with opposition to fundamental change is so unsophisticated. S.P. Huntington has made an interesting case for understanding conservatism as a 'positional' ideology, differing from its rivals in not providing an ideal of how society

ought to be organised.[5] Whereas other ideologies stand *for* something –
a more even distribution of resources, for example, or an extension of
civil liberties – conservatism warns *against* dismantling established
institutions. If other ideologies are concerned with what should be
done, conservatism is about the hazards of doing anything too different
from what already has been done.

In a sparkling book, A.O. Hirschman, not himself a conservative, has
identified a triad of arguments or theses by which conservatives
typically vindicate the *status quo*: the perversity thesis, according to
which goal-directed or purposive politics produce consequences contrary to those intended, an example of this kind of argument being the
contention of opponents of the French Revolution that the bid for liberty
would backfire into tyranny; the futility thesis, by which society cannot
possibly be turned upside down, as in the claim that no amount of social
engineering will succeed in eliminating inequalities of wealth and
power; and the jeopardy thesis, which holds that the benefits of radical
reform are always outweighed by the costs, an example being the
argument of nineteenth-century conservatives that an extended franchise would disturb the balance of the constitution.[6] In these ways
conservatism is a kind of counterblast to conviction ideologies, its
adherents persistently rehearsing the same catechism of objections to
promises of a brighter tomorrow.

As a warning against conviction politics conservatism is a reaction
to modernity, the belief that communities can be liberated from the
superstition and tyranny of the past through social engineering on a
grand scale. The optimism of the modern world was expressed in
Enlightenment liberalism with its assumption that each individual
could in principle make sense of the world, apprehending the rules of
a just social order and co-operating with others to make institutions
accountable to the tribunal of reason. It was during the Enlightenment,
particularly at the time of the American and French Revolutions, that
many of what are now taken to be classic statements of conservatism
were formulated. In America John Adams and Alexander Hamilton
advocated a 'natural aristocracy' of wealth and moral leadership as a
means of giving to a new society the stability of a semi-feudal state
such as Britain. In France Joseph de Maistre and others countered the
call for liberty, equality and fraternity with a counter-revolutionary
demand to restore the absolute power of a theocratic state. England's
most notable champion of the *ancien régime* was Edmund Burke, Irish

by birth, who vindicated the legacy of the past by challenging the Enlightenment belief in human perfectibility.

Central to Burke's repudiation, in *Reflections on the Revolution in France* (1790), of French Jacobins and their English allies was his claim that historical experience is more reliable than abstract speculation in the conduct of public affairs. Society is the product of organic growth, according to Burke, accumulating the wisdom of generations who had learned what was prudent through trial and error rather than by attending philosophy seminars to discuss the rights of man. The political order exists not to implement universal rights but to secure certain needs such as food, shelter and education, and each community satisfies these needs in a manner appropriate to itself. Burke warned of the dangers of discarding the 'prescriptive' authority of a customary way of life in the illusion that social progress can be deliberately planned, and he predicted that the quest of revolutionaries for liberty and equality would result in forms of despotism and oligarchy more oppressive than any of the inconveniences and imperfections of the *ancien régime*.

Burke also repudiated the assumption of the 'age of reason' that the principles of a just political order are within the compass of every individual mind. Individuals are weak and fallible because of sinful human nature, he argued, often passionate instead of rational, prone to selfishness and mistaken judgement, and therefore each in isolation cannot apprehend the complexities of the public interest. Burke contrasted the small 'private stock' of individual reason with the inexhaustible 'general bank and capital of nations, and of ages'. Political practices are the outcome of a traditional and corporate wisdom, the consensus of generations forming a bulwark against the fanciful schemes which emanate from the vanity of individual minds. 'The individual is foolish', said Burke in his *Speech on the Reform of the Representation in the House of Commons* (1782), 'the multitude, for the moment, is foolish when they act without deliberation, but the species is wise, and when time is given to it, as a species, it always acts right.' If liberalism can be said to endorse the politics of trust – the argument being that society benefits, morally and politically, from the relatively unrestricted exercise of individual judgement – Burkean conservatism emphasises the socially undesirable consequences of private reason undisciplined by custom and convention. And the doctrine of natural rights, in Burke's view, was the product of faulty judgement, formulated by individuals intoxicated with their capacity for abstract thinking disconnected from historical realities.

Burke's distaste for doctrinal simplicity in politics has found frequent echoes in British conservatism. John Reeves (1752?-1829), Burke's contemporary and the founder in 1792 of the Loyalist Association for the Preservation of Liberty and Property against Republicans and Levellers, attributed the spread of Jacobinism at home to the 'loose metaphysical' idea of inalienable rights, a superficially attractive concept temporarily obscuring in the popular mind the significance of political practices that had evolved to suit the particular circumstances of the nation. His *Thoughts on the English Government* (1795) was *Addressed to the Quiet Good Sense of the People of England*, by which Reeves meant a disposition to regard 'high pretensions founded on visionary and refined theories, as the air in which they were built . . . because they were positions that had no warrant from the known express Laws of the Land, but rested on general reasoning, from topics not known to the usage and laws of the country'. In 1872 Benjamin Disraeli (1804–81), then leader of the Conservative opposition, castigated Whigs for persistently seeking to govern Britain according to intellectual abstractions fashionable in continental Europe – substituting, as he put it, 'cosmopolitan for national principles' – and as a consequence waging 'war on the manners and customs of the people of this country under the pretext of Progress'. And in this century the case against viewing politics as the pursuit of dogmatic certainty has been eloquently made by Michael Oakeshott (1901–90), regarded by many as the finest British conservative philosopher since Burke.

Politics, for Oakeshott, 'is not the science of setting up a permanently impregnable society, it is the art of knowing where to go next in the exploration of an already existing traditional kind of society'.[7] Wise politicians neither equip themselves with universal, supposedly infallible guidelines such as the 'rights of man', nor set their sights on some ultimate destination – the classless society or whatever. Instead, they become familiar with the conventions of a settled way of life, using their experience to pick up 'intimations' of what to do next amidst its shifting complexities. An example he gives of how politicians find their way around was the enfranchisement of women in Britain at the beginning of the twentieth century. Women were granted the vote not because of the compelling logic of some abstract idea such as natural justice or universal rights, but because of their gradually improving legal and social status. In these circumstances the lack of female suffrage was correctly perceived to be an incongruity in the English way of life that ought to be rectified, a mischief that had become apparent through the passage of time rather than by the application of deductive logic.

Oakeshott underlined the folly of misunderstanding politics as the pursuit of doctrinal simplicities by distinguishing two types of knowledge, technical and practical. The former can be precisely formulated into rules – as in the Highway Code, for instance – and learned in advance of an activity. Practical knowledge, on the other hand, is imprecise because acquired by experience rather than learned in a mechanical fashion. The technique of cooking can be read in a book, but we become accomplished cooks only by practising the art. Good politicians, like proficient cooks, do not acquire their skills by poring over manuals that contain the science of governing, but from immersion in those habitual patterns of conduct which signal 'where to go next' among the uncertainties of the practical world to which politics belongs. In political activity, as Oakeshott put it in an often-quoted metaphor of the ship of state:

> Men sail a boundless and bottomless sea; there is neither harbour for shelter nor floor for anchorage, neither starting-place nor appointed destination. The enterprise is to keep afloat on an even keel; the sea is both friend and enemy; and the seamanship consists in using the resources of a traditional manner of behaviour in order to make a friend of every hostile occasion.

Oakeshott's critique of the deficiencies of technical knowledge as a basis for public affairs is another example of the conservative condemnation, persistent since the age of Burke and Reeves, of those who naively imagine politics to be the pursuit of some 'loose metaphysical' enterprise.

Oakeshott labelled the disposition to retreat into theoretical abstractions as rationalism in politics. Rationalists are social engineers eager to set in place a deliberately planned society, tidily managed according to the axioms of technical knowledge. Unaware that there can be no ultimate purpose in politics beyond ensuring the continuity of a particular way of life, they dream of finally eradicating poverty and unemployment, of putting an end to war, and so on. But the conduct of human arrangements according to such simple formulae is bound to fail, and like the biblical Tower of Babel every project to build an earthly paradise will eventually collapse.

The Tower of Babel can serve as a metaphor for conservative objections to socialist or liberal programmes of social transformation. Clearly, conservatives have frequently vindicated the latent wisdom of existing institutions, accusing their ideological adversaries of succumbing to the illusion that politics is the science of human perfection. Does this mean that traditionalism is the key to the conservative sanctum, providing a sort of creed which all who subscribe to the doctrine readily profess? There are four related reasons for supposing that the heart of conservatism lies elsewhere.

The first is that conservatives do not invariably shun abstract thinking in favour of a pragmatic style of politics. There are numerous examples of the conservative predilection for 'loose metaphysical' speculation. Benjamin Disraeli, though scornful of Whigs for succumbing to continental rationalism, was himself prone to ideological flights of fancy. In the 1840s, he opposed advocates of a capitalist market economy, among them members of his own party as well as Whigs, by fabricating from 'the principle of the feudal system' an image of an idyllic past: a mythical Merrie England in which the propertied classes had benevolently discharged their custodial responsibilities to the poor, who had reciprocated with affectionate deference.

Among the kind of free-market conservatives whom Disraeli lambasted there is ample evidence of a fondness for dogmatic certainties. Tory opponents of Thatcherism used to complain that the party had been captured by alien ideologues, as though all former conservatives had quietly practised the art of prudent statecraft without recourse to the certainties of political economy. Yet there have always been conservatives who believed that politics ought to consist in the application of the infallible laws of supply and demand. The Liberty and Property Defence League was founded in 1882, largely by conservatives, with the intention of preventing government from providing welfare or meddling in economic matters. Its principal publicist, Lord Elcho, believed that political economy was 'simply the law of gravitation applied to social matters'. And W.H. Mallock (1849–1923), a member of the League, spent four decades attempting to formulate a 'scientific conservatism' of sufficient theoretical sophistication to combat the superficially persuasive logic of socialism. Mallock's systematic conservatism was intended to demonstrate, by a combination of deduction and empirical evidence, that the mildest deviation from unfettered capitalism would result in economic decline and cultural stagnation. Even Burke, whose writings are supposed to be a clear expression of the conservative aversion to intellectual abstractions, was a dogmatic free-marketeer. Politicians who fancied they could alleviate poverty by ignoring economic imperatives were, according to him, impious. Government was not competent

> to supply to the poor, those necessaries which it has pleased the Divine Providence for a while to withhold from them. We, the people, ought to be made sensible that it is not in breaking the laws of commerce, which are the laws of nature, and consequently the laws of God, that we are to place our hope of softening the divine displeasure to remove any calamity under which we suffer.

Conservatives, then, are no less capable than their ideological adversaries of supposing that sound political conduct consists in the application of the correct intellectual formulae.

This inclination to build theoretical castles in the air means, secondly, that conservatives sometimes indulge in their own form of rationalism. Their attraction to purposive politics is obscured by the right's caricature of the rationalist as a starry-eyed optimist on the ideological left, someone naive enough to suppose that a classless society can be delivered by application of the appropriate axioms. But some conservatives also imagine that the ship of state can be guided, contrary to the message of Oakeshott's metaphor, towards an 'appropriate destination'. Thatcherism was one manifestation of this sort of perfectionism of the right. There was little evidence of distaste for doctrinal certainties in the New Right's flirtation with monetarism and other refinements of the science of political economy, of preference for gradual reform in its crusade to push back the state from the economy, of respect for a customary way of life in its assault upon the post-war settlement, or of an aversion to simplistic solutions in its portrayal of a brave new world of competitive individualism. The ideological right is no less capable than the left of utopian speculation.

The third reason why conservatism cannot be equated with traditionalism is that the right is not invariably against radical change. Conservatives certainly possess a stock of arguments, inherited from the counter-revolutionary response of Burke and others to the attack upon the *ancien régime*, by which they have frequently defended the established political order. The point is that these arguments have been used to oppose political programmes of which the right disapproves.

On other occasions, as in the 1980s, conservatives can be as fervent as their adversaries in advocating schemes of political reconstruction.

This is so because, fourthly, conservativism is not – contrary to S.P. Huntington – a negative or 'positional' ideology which warns against tampering with the *status quo*, whatever that happens to be at a particular historical moment. Conservatism, like other ideologies, does stand *for* something in that its adherents have a clear conception of how society ought to be organised. Not every conservative would claim that there is a divine blueprint for social arrangements – as Burke suggested when vindicating the brutalities of an unshackled market economy. Yet all favour a society in which certain inequalities are preserved, and in condemning purposive politics their intention is to ridicule the egalitarian ideals of their opponents. When John Reeves, for example, lamented the inclination of some to conduct politics according to 'visionary' theories, his target was those democratic republicans who 'tell men that they are by nature equal to their superiors, and that the present inequality between them is brought about by oppression and tyranny'. What prompted Michael Oakeshott to identify conservatism with an antipathy to social engineering was his hostility to post-war planning for full employment in a welfare state. When conservatives themselves assume the mantle of rationalism their intention is to reverse the damage done by rival political projects. A principal objection of the New Right to welfare capitalism was that redistributive taxation had deprived the rich of the incentive to create wealth and discouraged the poor from improving themselves. Hence Thatcherites set sail towards the beguiling horizon of a market economy in order to escape those features of the post-war settlement that had also offended Oakeshott.

Conservatives, then, can vary in their attitude to political change because at the heart of their doctrine is a distinctive image of the sound political order. Whether their political programme is radical or conservative depends upon their intention at any particular moment either, in the words of Maurice Cowling cited at the beginning of this chapter, to 'maintain existing equalities or restore lost ones'.

A PLURALITY OF CONSERVATISMS?

There is one further conceptual obstacle to be overcome in defining conservatism. To claim that central to the doctrine is a commitment to inequality may appear insensitive to marked differences within conservatism. In his contribution to this book Michael Kenny has depicted the varieties of ecologism in shades of green. It has become fashionable since about 1980 to characterise the antinomies of conservatism using aquatic imagery, 'dry' free-marketeers being contrasted with those 'wet' members of the British Conservative Party who are not convinced of the benefits of an unfettered economy. The wet–dry dichotomy highlights a disagreement about the proper scope of government that has been present within conservatism since the early decades of the nineteenth century. There have always been squabbles between those representing the libertarian as against the collectivist strands of the ideology – the former arguing that the state should do little more than safeguard property rights, and collectivists believing that government has responsibility to pursue a common purpose that transcends the sum of particular interests. Does this mean that conservatism lacks a core identity, so that instead of searching for a nucleus of beliefs we should convey the ideology's diversity and contrariety?

According to W.H. Greenleaf, a distinguished historian of the British political tradition, we should be wary not only of searching for a cluster of concepts which conservatives share, but of supposing that there are clear boundaries between the ideology and its rivals. This is because the debate within conservatism between libertarians and collectivists has been reflected in both liberalism and socialism. Ideological divergences are sometimes as acute within as they are between political creeds. Instead, then, of fruitlessly probing for the kernel of a political doctrine, we should seek to convey its ambivalence. And this is done by identifying the interplay of antithetical ideas at work within each ideology.[8]

An even stronger case can be made for the doctrine's essential disunity. The collectivist and libertarian strands of conservatism tend to be associated with apparently incompatible conceptions of society. One derives from the aristocratic ethos of the eighteenth-century when rank was determined primarily by birth rather than individual achievement. In this conception the community is an organic whole bound by a hierarchy of privileges and obligations in which wealth is held in trust for the common benefit, and where in consequence those with power have a responsibility to attend to the welfare of the mass of people. In the other conception, which is rooted in the bourgeois rhetoric of nineteenth-century capitalism, society is a collection of self-interested individuals united by little beyond a common desire for security, and where wealth and prestige are the outcome of individual success rather than the accident of birth. Here the function of the state is not to promote the public welfare at the expense of private interests, but to secure property rights by maintaining law and order. According to Keith Joseph, one of the architects of Thatcherism, human beings

> are so constituted that it is natural to them to pursue private rather than public ends. This is a simple matter of observation. The duty of government is to accommodate themselves to this immutable fact about human nature. Their object (and one must assume the original purpose for which they were created) is merely to avoid the inconveniences which attend the uncontrolled pursuits by private individuals of private ends . . . Men have a natural right to their ambitions because it was not for the purpose of abolishing competitiveness that they submitted to government; it was for the purpose of regulating competitiveness and preventing it from taking violent, fraudulent or anti-social forms.[9]

This is a particularly clear argument for minimal government, and most conservatives lack Joseph's analytical precision when identifying the features of a sound political order. Yet the contrasting conceptions of society are implicit in the disagreements among British conservatives since the beginning of the nineteenth century. Is there, then, no common ground where libertarians and collectivists meet?

There is certainly little common ground on the issue of how the powerful should discharge their responsibilities. In the patrician image of society the privileged classes are obligated to attend to what Disraeli called 'the condition of the people' by, for example, the provision of decent housing and adequate welfare. Conservatives often cite Disraeli when urging the aristocratic ethos of *noblesse oblige* to be adapted to modern conditions through state planning for full employment. And they have often used the ideal of beneficent social hierarchy as a stick with which to beat libertarian conservatives for their cruel indifference to the poor. In the early decades of the nineteenth century, for example, Tories opposed to the growth of market capitalism accused free-traders in their party of succumbing to a spirit of acquisitive individualism; Edwardian conservatives lamented the corruption of their party by a new breed of plutocrats who were creating what Lord Henry Bentinck called a 'bagman's Paradise' for the exploiters of the people; while a frequent complaint of Tory 'wets' was that Thatcherites had abdicated their responsibilities for the casualties of a market economy.

Collectivist conservatives, then, have denounced attempts to emancipate the economy from political regulation as a pretext for the rich to exploit the poor. But libertarians are no less anxious to occupy the high ground of morality, which they do by accusing patrician Tories of obscuring economic realities in a fog of sentimentality. Their argument for minimal government is threefold. There is, firstly, the claim that a free market is just because rewards of wealth and esteem reflect the diversity of human talent. Unrestricted economic competition results in 'an infinitely mobile society' with 'an infinite number of snakes and ladders', argues Keith Joseph, because individuals are permitted to rise and fall according to merit. An unshackled market, secondly, is said to nurture habits of prudence and self-reliance. If poverty reflects a lack of individual skill and effort, then the indigent will not be prompted to improve themselves unless made to bear some of the consequences of their own failure. The welfare state, in this view, creates a permanent underclass of what Margaret Thatcher called 'moral cripples', people who are induced by a dependency culture to delegate personal responsibility to officialdom.

The third argument against state intervention in the market is that rich and poor alike benefit from the unrestricted pursuit of self-interest. Ultimately there are no losers from competitive individualism because in leaping ahead themselves, wealth-creators drag the poor some way after them. Without the expectation of large rewards, however, entrepreneurial individuals will be disinclined to generate the prosperity which raises the living standards of everyone. At the beginning of this century John St Loe Strachey was among libertarian conservatives who opposed a policy of redistributive taxation as a means of financing the public provision of, for example, old-age pensions and free school meals for the poor. 'You will never be able to give every man on a hot day a bigger drink of water', he wrote, 'if you begin by stopping up the pipe that feeds the cistern.' A crude paraphrase of this style of thinking might be

'I'm a successful entrepreneur because of my flair and energy. You're unemployed and in receipt of social benefits because, being lazy, you refuse to 'get on your bike' in search of a job. And if I'm heavily taxed to enable you to remain a 'lounger and scrounger', then I'll no longer bother to create the wealth that eventually trickles down to you.'

The rich, then, are creators of prosperity rather than plunderers of the poor, and any attempt by government to curtail their activities will result in economic stagnation.

In the bourgeois rhetoric of libertarian conservatism society appears as a collection of independent individuals, and government has few functions beyond policing the pursuit of self-interest; whereas in the patrician imagery of an organic nation the state can override particular interests to secure the common welfare. Is conservatism, then, marked by an absent centre? Are we dealing with different types of conservatism, perhaps even two conservatisms, with little or nothing in common? Notwithstanding their differences conservatives do share a perspective on society that distinguishes them from adherents to rival ideologies. Running through the varieties of conservatism is the theme of inequality. Conservatives do not object to rationalism in politics *per se* – otherwise we should not be able to explain right-wing forms of radicalism such as Thatcherism – but to the kind of social engineering intended to level distinctions of wealth and power.

The conservative vindication of inequality is threefold. Human beings are said to be naturally diverse in energy and talents, so that any project to construct a classless society will be futile. Misconceived schemes of social levelling may appear successful for a while, wrote Bernard Braine in *Tory Democracy* (1948), but 'within a very short space of time this new equality will have vanished into the mist. Some men will be rich, some will be poor. Some will be masters, some will be servants. A few will lead, the rest will follow.' Egalitarian programmes, secondly, are dangerous because they entail authoritarian measures which crush individual liberty. And, thirdly, social hierarchy is desirable because the majority benefit from the leadership of a few. The conservative case for inequality was clearly made by Harold Macmillan (1894–1986), Prime Minister from 1957 to 1963:

Human beings, widely various in their capacity, character, talent and ambition, tend to differentiate at all times and in all places. To deny them the right to differ, to enforce economic and social uniformity upon them, is to throttle one of the most powerful and creative of human appetites. It is wrong, and it is three times wrong. It is morally wrong; because to deny the bold, the strong, the prudent and the clever the rewards and privileges of exercising their qualities is to enthrone in society the worst and basest of human attributes: envy, jealousy and spite. It is wrong practically

. . . because it is only by giving their heads to the strong and to the able that we shall ever have the means to provide real protection for the weak and for the old. Finally it is wrong politically; because I do not see how Britain, with all its rich diversity and vitality, could be turned into an egalitarian society without, as we have seen in Eastern Europe, a gigantic exercise in despotism.

Within this general vindication of social inequality there is scope for particular emphasis, and a major point of difference has been the justification of wealth and power.

In patrician language the emphasis is upon the social breeding of those who constitute a ruling elite. The argument is that those who belong to what Burke called a 'natural aristocracy' can acquire knowledge and wisdom and cultivate taste and virtue, and are also inculcated with an ethos of public service. And owning substantial property – having a 'stake' in the community, as it used to be put – they are unlikely to be excited by the false expectations which prompt others to engage in reckless schemes of political reconstruction. In bourgeois rhetoric, on the other hand, the emphasis is on the contribution of exceptional individuals who ascend the social scale through their own merit. These 'wonderful people' – Margaret Thatcher's description of entrepreneurs and other wealth-creators – supposedly possess rare qualities of ambition and vision, so that from their dynamic leadership flows the prosperity which benefit the less energetic majority.

Common to these two strands of conservatism is the image of a chain of social discipline linked by habits of obedience and submission among the majority, as well as by qualities of wise and firm leadership on the part of an elite. As Burke wrote in *An Appeal from the New to the Old Whigs* (1791):

> To enable men to act with the weight and character of a people, and to answer the ends for which they are incorporated with that capacity, we must suppose them . . . to be in that state of habitual social discipline, in which the wiser, the more expert, and the more opulent conduct, and by conducting enlighten and protect the weaker, the less knowing, and the less provided with the goods of fortune. When the multitude are not under this discipline, they can scarcely be said to be in civil society.

The depiction of society as a command structure distinguishes conservatism from the varieties of socialism which advocate at least the erosion of inequalities, and possibly their elimination.

But what of liberalism, particularly as libertarian conservatives are often assumed to be the heirs of classical liberals in endorsing the inequalities attendant upon a market economy? Commentators who suggest that conservative advocates of a minimal state are liberals in disguise tend to forget that the free market is an ambivalent concept susceptible to different ideological meanings. The ideal of a market economy featured in the campaign of nineteenth-century liberals to eradicate aristocratic privilege and extend individual rights, and as such its use was consistent with the enduring liberal ideal of a community of self-governing citizens free of the tutelage of either an elite or an overbearing state.

In conservative usage, however, the concept of unregulated capitalism has been used to justify rather than undermine the authority of both an elite and a strong state. Conservatives are more pessimistic than liberals about the potential of the mass of people for rational and orderly conduct. The diversity of the human condition, coupled with its frailties and 'inherent wickedness', means that not everyone can respond to the imperatives of a self-help society of competitive individualism. Poverty is said to reflect a moral as well as an economic failure, and morally feeble individuals lacking bourgeois habits of self-discipline pose a threat to the stability of the political order. Hence the argument of libertarian conservatives for government that is limited in scope yet firm in maintaining law and order. In campaigning at the end of the nineteenth century for economic individualism, the intention of the Liberty and Property Defence League was neither to diminish the authority of the state nor to subvert ordered hierarchy. Their fear was that government would become incapable of preserving the inequalities of private property because of irrepressible demands from a recently enfranchised working class for collectivist programmes of social welfare. Similarly, the intention of the New Right in rolling back government from the economy was to restore social discipline rather than erode the state's authority. A frequent complaint of Thatcherites was that the egalitarian policies of the post-war welfare state had created a dependency culture which had sapped the moral energy and self-discipline of many individuals. In pruning the state they sought not only to remove fetters from wealth-creators, but also to make it more efficient in curbing socially unruly behaviour. In this sense, Thatcherism was a variant on the enduring conservative theme that society, properly organised, is a chain of command in which leadership is exercised within the framework of firm government.

A BRIEF HISTORY

Some of these conceptual issues can be clarified by glancing at the evolution of British conservatism. The sobriquet 'Tory' was first used to designate a political group in the 1680s, when it became attached to royalists who were opposed to the Whig doctrine that parliament could correct or depose a tyrannical monarch. In the modern sense, however, the ideology derives from the early decades of the nineteenth century, when the adjective 'Conservative' was attached to a political party and the noun 'conservatism' came to denote the principles of its members. It was during this period, too, that doctrinal fissures between patrician and free-market conservatives began to appear.

The social ideal of Tory paternalists was of a beneficent hierarchy in which a generous exercise of their custodial responsibilities on the part of the privileged was reciprocated with grateful deference by those in their charge. 'As Tories', William Johnstone wrote in *Blackwood's Magazine* in 1829.

> we maintain that it is the duty of the people to pay obedience to those set in authority over them: but it is also the duty of those in authority to protect the people who are placed below them. They are not to sit in stately grandeur, and see the people perish, nor, indeed, are they ever to forget that they hold their power and their possessions upon the understanding that they administer both more for the good of the people at large, than the people would do, if they had the administration of both themselves.

The objection of Tory paternalists to the modern age was that the people were being severed from traditional sources of protection and discipline. Their argument was that some landlords, as well as the captains of a rapidly developing manufacturing industry, had been misled by the 'theoretic folly' of the new science of political economy into supposing that, for the sake of material advance, the emotional ties of benevolent hierarchy had to be displaced by the harsh, impersonal relations of the capitalist market. This abdication of their responsibilities for the people was said to be politically dangerous as well as morally reprehensible. 'I wish for reform', said the poet Robert Southey, 'because I cannot but see that all things are tending towards revolution, and nothing but reform can by any possibility prevent it.' Unless extensive measures were taken to deal with poverty and squalor, warned the great Tory philanthropist Lord Ashley (1801–85), many would fall prey to the

> two great demons in morals and politics, Socialism and Chartism [which] are but symptoms of a universal disease, spread through-out the vast mass of the people, who, so far from concurring in the *status quo*, suppose that anything must be better than the present condition.

Various remedies were proposed. Southey favoured greater public expenditure on poor relief together with a national system of education; and Ashley campaigned to improve conditions of work in factories and mines, as well as to provide the poor with decent education, housing, and public health care. Central to this strategy for countering the socially disruptive effects of the capitalist market was a bid to renew the bonds between responsible proprietors and the bulk of people.

Patrician Tories hoped that traditional social relations would stem the growth of mercenary capitalism. For other conservatives, however, the future lay not in a revived partnership between some of the propertied classes and the masses, but rather in a new alliance of aristocracy and emerging bourgeoisie strong enough to withstand democratic and egalitarian demands from below. Foremost among them was Sir Robert Peel (1788–1850), Prime Minister in 1835 and from 1841 to 1846, whom paternalists detested for succumbing to the nostrums of political economy. Peel's recipe for political stability was a free market allied to firm government. He derided Ashley's campaign for factory reform, for example, on the ground that regulation of the hours and conditions of work would reduce productivity. Manufacturers would respond to this breaking of the 'strict rules of political economy' by cutting wages to remain competitive in the world market, and as a consequence labourers rather than capitalists would suffer from the meddling of philanthropists whose grasp of economic realities was obscured by sentimentality. Peel wanted the free market to operate within a strong state, and in a speech of 1835 he urged landed and middle classes to 'protect the interests of order and property' by forming a 'cordial union' against popular pressures to disperse power and wealth. Peel's bid to emancipate the economy from political constraints culminated in his policy of the 1840s to reduce tariffs on imported grain, eventually eliminating them in 1846. His argument against the Corn Laws was partly that protectionism curtailed economic prosperity, but also that a 'continued relaxation of commercial restrictions' would secure law and order by strengthening the alliance of landed and manufacturing interests.

For Tory paternalists, however, the Corn Laws symbolised not the vested interests of land, but the intimate social hierarchy now threatened by the brutalising spirit of commerce. Among opponents of Peel in the 1840s was a group of Tories known as Young England who rhapsodised about an idyllic past of feudal social relations in which, according to Lord John Manners:

> Each knew his place – king, peasant, peer or priest,
> The greatest owned connexion with the least;
> From rank to rank the generous feeling ran,
> And linked society as man to man.

Manners' proposals for retrieving this golden age included the revival of holy days, during which the poor would be spiritually edified as well as physically restored through pastimes such as maypole dancing. From 1842 Young England was led by Benjamin Disraeli who used the feudal ideal – the principle, in his words, that 'the tenure of all property should be the performance of its duties' – to condemn Peelites for reducing the Conservative Party to a selfish faction with no regard for the condition of the people. In *Sybil*, one of a trilogy of novels written at this time, he depicted an England divided into two nations of rich and poor, 'with an innate inability of mutual comprehension', because those with power no longer viewed their wealth as a trust for the benefit of all.

The Conservative Party was split in two by the repeal of the Corn Laws, regaining a sense of direction only after the Second Reform Act. Disraeli, who now led the party, used the 'one nation' ideal to appeal to an expanding electorate. Conservatives, he said in 1872, would not be deterred by free-market dogma from improving the 'condition of the people' through, for example, slum clearance and public health regulations. Only by means of a programme of social improvement, according to Disraeli, might the privileged classes persuade a mass electorate to endorse institutions of ordered hierarchy. Soon after Disraeli's death his brand of patrician conservatism became known as Tory Democracy, though some who used the phrase were less concerned to advocate social reform than to convince 'the people' of the natural affinity between themselves and men of property.

But even the mildest proposal for social improvement annoyed those libertarian conservatives who in the last decades of the century joined organisations such as the Liberty and Property Defence League. Fearing that power and property would be submerged in a democratic deluge, they denounced Tory Democrats and other proponents of an enlarged state for heading 'straight to State-Socialism'. Many 'individualists', as those who favoured minimal government became known at this time, found inspiration in Herbert Spencer's *The Man versus the State* (1885), which appeared to find in Charles Darwin's theory of natural selection the key to human evolution. Although some commentators doubt that Spencer was a Social Darwinist, he certainly condemned modern government for promoting the 'survival of the unfittest' through misconceived schemes for eliminating poverty. His argument was that society progresses by means of a harsh struggle for survival in which the weak and indolent bear the consequences of their imprudence, whereas efficient and talented individuals are permitted to reap economic rewards and social prestige in abundance. Public provision of welfare encourages undesirable moral habits by rewarding inefficient members of society, Spencer believed, and also deters 'fit' individuals by taxing them to subsidise the 'undeserving' poor:

> Men who are so sympathetic that they cannot let the struggle for existence bring on the unworthy the suffering consequent on their incapacity or misconduct are so unsympathetic that they can, deliberately, make the struggle for existence harder for the worthy, and inflict on them and on their children artificial evils in addition to the natural evil they have to bear.

The poor themselves would suffer from misguided philanthropic efforts to mitigate their condition, according to Spencer, because taxation would deprive efficient members of society of incentive to create the wealth that eventually percolates down to everyone.

Members of the Liberty and Property Defence League often used the Social Darwinist language of *The Man versus the State* when denouncing anyone who wanted government to be extended beyond the mere protection of life and property. One member of the League, however, censured Spencer on the rather peculiar ground that his theory of evolutionary individualism gave insufficient recognition to the 'cardinal social fact' of inequality, particularly the contribution of exceptional individuals to the advance of society. W.H. Mallock attempted to remove what he considered to be the flaws of Spencerite theory by formulating a 'scientific conservatism' intended to refute, by a combination of logic and empirical evidence, every doctrine that disputed the truths of political economy. Mallock's argument, elaborated in numerous articles and books spanning almost forty years, was that society had advanced from barbarity to civilisation because of the persistent influence of a talented minority whose flair and organisational ability had improved economic and cultural standards for all. What prompted the gifted few to exert themselves for the common advantage was entrepreneurial ambition, the expectation of appropriate rewards for rare talent. Enterprising individuals would be deterred by redistributive policies from exerting themselves, and as a consequence society would slide into cultural mediocrity and economic decline. 'The lesson to be taught', Mallock wrote in *The Limits of Pure Democracy* (1918),

> is that society depends upon the co-operation of unequals – of the few who lead and give orders, and of the many who follow and obey: that this fact reflects itself in the general configuration of society; and that in proportion as the masses of any country neglect it they will, as a whole or sporadically, lose what they have in their efforts to seize more.

His complaint, of course, was that everyone except dogmatic free-marketeers was intent on undermining society's natural command structure.

Mallock's vindication of inequality was similar to that of other individualists, in spite of his criticism of Spencer. His claim to novelty lies in the use he made of his 'scientific' defence of unbridled capitalism to turn socialism on its head. For Marx, according to Mallock, manual labour was the sole source of wealth, and workers were exploited because some of what they produced was hived off as capitalist profit. For Mallock, in contrast, wealth was created by mental labour, and any increase in productive capacity emanated entirely from the economic and social leadership of a gifted elite. The explosion of wealth in nineteenth-century industrial society derived not from the productive energy of manual labour, but from the talent of inventors as well as the acumen of entrepreneurs who grasped the market potential of technical innovations. These people alone were responsible for generating 'surplus value' which, far from intensifying class exploitation, had substantially improved the living standards of the masses. 'Nations now grow rich through industry as they once grew rich through conquest', wrote Mallock in *A Critical Examination of Socialism* (1908),

> because new commanders with a precision unknown on battlefields, direct the minutest operations of armies of a new kind, and the only terms on which any modern nation can maintain its present productivity, or hope to increase it in the future, consist in the technical submission of the majority of men to the guidance of an exceptional minority.

So whereas the socialist message is that the masses are plundered by a predatory minority, the reverse is true: the majority, as Mallock put it in his *Memoirs*, 'are the pensioners of the few'. Once deprived of entrepreneurial command, then, the army of the proletariat would soon slip into penury.

In the early decades of the twentieth century libertarian conservatives continued to argue that the poor would become poorer unless the rich were permitted fully to enjoy the rewards of their entrepreneurial endeavours, and also to berate the collectivist wing of their party for treading a slippery slope to socialism. Occasionally Social Darwinism was used to warn that an encroaching state would impede social progress. Dorothy Crisp, for instance, was horrified that some conservatives were disregarding natural selection in their readiness to endorse misconceived schemes of social amelioration. She was particularly incensed by growing public expenditure on slum clearance, and in *The Rebirth of Conservatism* (1931) predicted that new corporation housing estates would deteriorate into a 'garbage heap' because those

> who sink into slum life are without doubt . . . the weakest and least desirable of the population. To-day the unfit are preserved at the expense of the fit, the deserving pay for the maintenance of the undeserving, and physically, mentally and morally there is a levelling down of the whole race.

The solution lay in heeding the lessons of political economy which taught that society could not prosper, economically or morally, unless individuals bore the consequences of their own faults and misdeeds.

Crisp's book was published in a decade of deep economic recession and massive unemployment. As a corrective to the defects of the capitalist market some conservatives began to advocate an enlarged state, using arguments similar to those of the liberal J.M. Keynes for a mixed economy. The conservative version of planned capitalism is conveyed in the title of an influential book by Harold Macmillan, published in 1938, *The Middle Way: A Study of the Problem of Economic and Social Progress*. The middle way – or 'half-way house', as he sometimes called it – was to be between unfettered capitalism and state socialism. It entailed public ownership of essential industries, government direction of investment, and sufficient expenditure on welfare to establish an irreducible minimum standard of living. Macmillan, who admired Disraeli, presented the middle way as an updated expression of the one-nation ideal, a means of attacking 'most vigorously the grosser inequalities which still divide our democracy with what a conservative Prime Minister was the first to call "The Two Nations"'. Like Ashley and other nineteenth-century patrician Tories, who fretted that without reform the nation would be engulfed by socialism, Macmillan argued that a managed economy would be an antidote to social unrest. Without a more 'orderly capitalism', according to *The Middle Way*, Britain might succumb to the totalitarianism, whether fascist or communist, sweeping through much of the rest of Europe.

The necessities of the Second World War led to the sort of economic planning favoured by Macmillan. There was an upsurge of Disraelian sentiment among conservatives at this time, a feeling that greater effort was needed to eliminate poverty. In 1943 some of them formed the Tory Reform Committee to campaign for full employment in a welfare state, declaring that 'to follow Adam Smith in the age of Keynes is like adhering to the Ptolemaic astronomy after Copernicus'. Only after the defeat of the party in the general election of 1945, however, were most conservatives gradually persuaded of the need for the sort of 'humanized capitalism' advocated by Macmillan and the Reform Committee. In accepting Keynesianism they were, of course, careful to put their own gloss upon it, arguing that the objective of a planned economy was neither social levelling nor the frustration of individual ambition. A 'Disraelian approach to modern politics' – the title of a lecture given in 1954 by R.A. Butler – did not require conservatives to abandon their traditional vindication of inequality. 'Society is a partnership', according to Butler,

> and so underlying all our differences there should be a funda-
> mental unity – the very antithesis of the 'class war' – bringing
> together what Disraeli called the Two Nations into a single social
> entity . . . But if Disraeli provided us with inspiration, he was no
> less prescient in warning of the pitfalls . . . He cautioned us . . . that
> we should seek to secure greater equality, not by levelling the few,
> but by elevating the many . . . It is no part of our policy to repress
> the initiative and independence of the strong. Indeed, unless we
> allow men and women to rise as far as they may, and so allow our
> society to be served by what I describe as the *richness of developed
> differences*, we shall not have the means to earn our national living,
> let alone to afford a welfare state.

This modernised Disraelian strand of conservatism now became party orthodoxy, and for the next twenty years few voices were to be heard proclaiming the truths of political economy.

From the early 1970s, however, a growing number of conservatives urged a right turn from the middle way of economic planning and extensive social welfare. After the election in 1975 of a new Conservative Party leader this momentum to restore a purer form of capitalism became known as Thatcherism, about which there is now an enormous body of literature. As a political project Thatcherism was in some ways startling, vigorously challenging as it did the assumption that conservatives were now permanently resident in a halfway house between individualism and collectivism. In their bid to kill off socialism – by which was meant the post-war settlement put in place by both Labour and Conservative governments – the New Right assailed the institutions of what they considered a bloated and decadent state. Thatcherism was an example of ideological fundamentalism, an acute form of rationalism in politics which wanted society to be reshaped according to a free-market blueprint. The new individualists may or may not have succeeded in burying socialism; but their radical zeal certainly put an end to the assumption that conservatism consists in a Burkean reverence for tradition and a distaste for political upheaval. In one sense, perhaps, the New Right did not break decisively with tradition. There was much talk among them of going backwards to the future – of retrieving, that is, the dynamic spirit of the Victorian enterprise culture in order to restore the British nation to its former glory. But though Thatcherites may have been counter-revolutionary rather than revolutionary, they displayed little respect for a settled way of life in their impatience to dismantle the institutions of what post-war conservatives had hailed as 'humanized capitalism'.

The Thatcherite project was also unprecedented in its political success. In the past extreme individualists, such as members of the Liberty and Property Defence League, had rarely represented the mainstream of conservative thinking. But the New Right – through a network of 'think-tanks' as well as the expulsion from government office of any 'wet' patrician Tory judged not to be ideologically 'one of us' – were soon intellectually ascendant. By the 1980s only stragglers were left on the middle way, and few extolled the virtues of Disraelian conservativism against the 'two nations' approach of the parvenu right. In office through the 1980s, moreover, conservatives did succeed in pursuing a broadly consistent strategy of increasing the scope for capitalist endeavour by rolling back the state from the economy.

Less remarkable than the New Right's political success were its ideas which combined, as had expressions of individualism since Social Darwinism, libertarian and authoritarian elements. Thatcherites advocated a restoration of both freedom and order, an extension of individual choice coupled with a strengthening of the mechanisms of law and order.

The kind of freedom they had in mind was the opportunity for enterprising individuals to accumulate wealth unhindered by government. Post-war Keynesian techniques of economic management, they complained, had led to a massive concentration of state power with little scope for adventure capitalism. Middle-way conservatives and other collectivists had sought a safe haven somewhere between capitalism and socialism. But the middle way had turned into a slippery slope. The effect had been to replace the pendulum of party politics by what Keith Joseph, in *Stranded on the Middle Ground?* (1976), called a 'ratchet' of increasingly interventionist government. Among the manifestations of an overloaded state were punitive taxation to finance excessive public expenditure, high unemployment, inflation, inefficient labour practices, and general economic torpor. The mistake had been to assume that government was capable of eradicating unemployment and poverty by means of economic management and redistributive fiscal policies. 'Making the rich poorer does not make the poor richer', according to Joseph, but it does make the state stronger – and it does increase the power of officials and politicians, power more menacing, more permanent and less useful than market power within the rule of law. Inequality of income can only be eliminated at the cost of freedom. The pursuit of income equality will turn this country into a totalitarian slum.

The solution was to reduce the functions of government to a minimum, recognising that the inequalities arising from a capitalist market are ultimately advantageous to both rich and poor. 'You cannot create a rich society', argued Geoffrey Howe, 'without allowing some individuals to become rich as well.' The expectation of wealth is the carrot tempting an enterprising minority to generate the prosperity from which everyone eventually benefits.

The New Right was fond of contrasting the enervating culture of the welfare state with what one writer has labelled the 'vigorous virtues' of competitive individualism.[10] This is why their project appeared to some extent as a counter-revolution, recalling heroic moments of the past in an effort to drag the nation back to the Victorian golden age of self-sufficiency, thrift, and rugged adventure. But the recreation of this kind of self-help culture was said to require a strengthening of law and order. Among the manifestations of the dependency induced by welfare capitalism, according to Thatcherites, were rising crime rates, promiscuous sex, drugs, unruliness in schools, hooliganism, trades union belligerence, and other forms of 'permissive' behaviour. Hence a call to return to a morality based on self-reliance, decency, and respect for the rule of law. Hence, too, the need for a state which, though limited in scope, was neither weak nor inactive in discharging its responsibility for public order. Under her leadership, Margaret Thatcher announced in 1989, successive governments had attempted both to revive capitalist enterprise and to push back the permissive society:

That's why we've toughened the law on the muggers and marauders. That's why we've increased penalties on drink-driving, on drugs, on rape. That's why we've increased the police and strengthened their powers ... For there can be no freedom without order. There can be no order without authority; and authority that is impotent or hesitant in the face of intimidation, crime and violence, cannot endure.

The economic liberation of individuals, then, had to be accompanied by a restoration of society's traditional structure of command.

CONCLUSION

How should a chapter on conservatism be brought to an end? In his conclusion Vincent Geoghegan asks whether with the collapse of communist regimes the time has come to write socialism's obituary, and at the close of his chapter on ecologism Michael Kenny speculates on the possible development of a comparatively new, still unfixed, political doctrine. Conservatism's future raises fewer interesting questions. The libertarian right may not, as Margaret Thatcher claimed, have won the battle of ideas. But no one seriously suggests, as some do with regard to socialism, that conservatism is exhausted – that having performed its historical mission, so to speak, the ideology may soon be displaced by other styles of thinking. Nor does conservatism, unlike ecologism, seem to contain much evolutionary potential. The dogmas of political economy are not as fashionable among the right as they were in the 1980s during the rage of the counter-revolution, and a few more conservative voices are now heard in favour of the kind of statecraft that facilitates investment and tackles poverty. In future conservatives will probably continue to squabble over the legitimate activities of government, while agreeing about the need for social inequality and a disciplinary state. There are no signs that conservatism is likely either to disintegrate or to evolve in an unprecedented direction.

If speculation about conservatism's future is an unexciting prospect, perhaps we should end on a censorious note. The New Right aroused strong passions among its opponents on the ideological right and left, and there is a temptation to join the chorus of dissent. We could, in the spirit of philosophical scepticism represented by Michael Oakeshott, accuse modern conservatives of drifting from their moorings in pragmatism and historical experience. In this mood we might wonder what a party reputedly suspicious of political blueprints was doing embracing a 'brutopia' of unchecked market forces. Yet such criticism would be historically illegitimate. Conservatism, as we have sought to demonstrate, cannot be equated with traditionalism. It has always been awash with abstractions and convictions, of a vision of how society should be arranged, and of projects either to maintain or to recover ordered hierarchy. The libertarian right of the 1980s, notwithstanding its crusading zeal, was no less an authentic part of the conservative canon as any form of patrician Toryism.

Or one could, if inclined to be censorious from another perspective, conclude by denouncing conservatism as a creed of greed. Perhaps when stripped of its veneer – the patrician rhetoric of social responsibility or the bourgeois endowment of the market with morality – conservativism is little else than a bid by the rich to gain public licence for their exploitation of the poor. But if so the bid has been remarkably successful, and conducted by means of elaborate arguments that require more than the knee-jerk retort 'capitalist ploy' to repudiate them. Conservatism does not, however, often receive the critical analysis it deserves.

I shall therefore conclude with an example of this tendency to avoid rather than confront the assumptions that conservatives make. Central to their vindication of a strong state is the argument that individuals are prone to passionate and unruly conduct. Fear of the destructive potential of fallible human nature explains the 'flog 'em and hang 'em' attitude of some conservatives – their enthusiasm, that is, for such forms of social control as corporal and capital punishment, the prohibition of pornography and sexual heterodoxy, and censorship of what is broadcast and published. Since Burke, conservatives have been inclined to ground their penchant for a 'law and order' state in the Christian doctrine of the Fall. 'Man is inherently sinful', Margaret Thatcher said in the year before becoming Prime Minister, 'and in order to sustain a civilised and harmonious society we need laws backed by effective sanctions. Looking at this country today, I am bound to say that upholding the law is one area of life where I would wish the state to be stronger than it is.' Those critical of conservatism tend to dismiss its account of the human condition as a pretext for the heavy hand of capitalist domination. In doing so they often substitute for conservative pessimism a naive optimism which attributes selfishness and conflict to inadequate institutions rather than the defects of human nature. Now a capitalist society may well encourage predatory behaviour, but it does not necessarily follow that inherent human goodness is awaiting release by post-capitalist structures. From an historical perspective greed and selfishness appear to be ineradicable features of the human condition.

One means of treating conservatism seriously would be not to reject its assertion of human imperfection, but rather to question the conclusion derived from this assumption. Conservatives press the doctrine of fallen human nature into service on behalf of social hierarchy. Their argument is that a minority, through social breeding or entrepreneurial success, become immune to many of the frailties afflicting the bulk of humanity, and so are entitled to police the conduct of those who cannot be relied upon to discipline themselves. But the critic of conservatism might enquire by what twist of logic egalitarian premises are made to justify a hierarchy of sheep and goats. For in its Christian form the doctrine of essential human frailty implies that everyone is selfish as well as possessing potential to transcend corruption. If all are likely to pursue self-interest, then maybe there is a need for political institutions which curtail the activities of those in whom the lust for wealth and power is particularly strong. And if everyone has a potential for altruism, then maybe the primary target of government ought to be such anti-social behaviour as competitive individualism. Perhaps some of conservatism's premises, logically explored, provide a blueprint for political arrangements ensuring a roughly even distribution of resources.

NOTES

1 Anthony Quinton, *The Politics of Imperfection: The Religious and Secular Traditions of Conservative Thought in England from Hooker to Oakeshott*, London, Faber, 1978.
2 R.J. White, *The Conservative Tradition*, 2nd edn, London, Adam and Charles Black, 1964, 1.
3 E.g. J.A. Thompson and Arthur Mejia, eds, *Edwardian Conservatism: Five Studies in Adaptation*, London, Croom Helm, 1988, 1.
4 Kenneth Minogue, *Alien Powers: The Pure Theory of Ideology*, London, Weidenfeld and Nicolson, 1985.
5 S.P. Huntington, 'Conservatism as an Ideology', *American Political Science Review*, 51, 1957, 454–73.
6 Albert O. Hirschman, *The Rhetoric of Reaction: Perversity, Futility, Jeopardy*, Cambridge, Mass., Belknap Press of Harvard University Press, 1991.
7 Michael Oakeshott, *Rationalism in Politics and Other Essays*, London, Methuen, 1962, 58.
8 W.H. Greenleaf, *The British Political Tradition*, Volume 2: *The Ideological Tradition*, London, Routledge, 1983; W.H. Greenleaf, 'The Character of Modern British Conservatism', in R. Benewick, R.N.

Berki and B. Parekh, ed., *Knowledge and Belief in Politics: The Problem of Ideology*, London, Allen and Unwin, 1973, 177–212.

9 Keith Joseph and Jonathon Sumption, *Equality*, London, John Murray, 1979, 100–1.

10 Shirley Robin Letwin, *The Anatomy of Thatcherism*, London, Fontana, 1992.

FURTHER READING

John Weiss, *Conservatism in Europe, 1770–1945: Traditionalism, Reaction and Counter-Revolution*, London, Thames and Hudson, 1977, is a preliminary guide, particularly on conservatism in France and Germany. Dated but unrivalled in its comprehensiveness is Hans Rogger and Eugen Weber, eds, *The European Right: A Historical Profile*, London, Weidenfeld and Nicolson, 1965, with chapters by different authors on most European countries including England, France, Belgium, Spain, Italy, Germany, Austria, and Finland. Roger Eatwell and Noel O'Sullivan, eds, *The Nature of the Right: European and American Politics and Political Thought since 1798*, London, Pinter, 1989, contains five chapters by Eatwell on the nature of conservatism together with chapters by other authors on particular countries including France, Germany, Britain, and America. Perhaps the most eloquent and interesting general account of conservatism, with chapters on Britain, Germany and France, is Noel O'Sullivan, *Conservatism*, London, Dent, 1976, though his characterisation of the doctrine as a 'philosophy of imperfection' inclines him to exclude from the conservative canon writers who properly belong there. More recently the doctrine has been depicted as 'a widening of Burke's indictments not only of the French Revolution but of the larger revolution we call modernity' by Robert Nisbet, *Conservatism: Dream and Reality*, Milton Keynes, Open University Press, 1986. A.O. Hirschman, *The Rhetoric of Reaction: Perversity, Futility, Jeopardy*, Cambridge, Mass., Belknap Press of Harvard University Press, 1991, provides a superb insight into the contours of conservative thinking. Hirschman's approach is to uncover the characteristic rhetorical postures of opponents of reform during the past two hundred years, using illustrations from the counter-revolutionary discourse of the French Revolution, the anti-democratic movement of the nineteenth century and recent polemicism against the welfare state.

There are two books written from different ideological perspectives which are more concerned with the philosophy than the history of conservatism: Roger Scruton, *The Meaning of Conservatism*, Harmondsworth, Penguin, 1980, is a brilliant vindication of authority and inequality with interesting comment on Burke and others within the canon; Ted Honderich, *Conservatism*, London, Penguin, 1991, is a sustained critique of conservative themes.

Arthur Aughey, Greta Jones and W.M. Riches, *The Conservative Political Tradition in Britain and the United States*, London, Pinter, 1992, is an interesting comparative analysis rich in insight. The account of conservatism given in the chapter is elaborated in Robert Eccleshall, *English Conservatism since the Restoration: An Introduction and Anthology*, London, Unwin Hyman, 1990.

With regard to some of the thinkers mentioned in the chapter, the most brilliant study of Burke is probably Conor Cruise O'Brien, *The Great Melody: A Thematic Biography and Commented Anthology of Edmund Burke*, London, Mandarin, 1993. A short, sharp account of Burke's ideas from a Marxist perspective is C.B. MacPherson, *Burke*, Oxford, Oxford University Press, 1980. The story of the group to which Disraeli belonged in the 1840s is told with style by Richard Faber, *Young England*, London, Faber, 1987. Social Darwinism is well treated in M.W. Taylor, *Men versus the State: Herbert Spencer and Later Victorian Individualism*, Oxford, Clarendon Press, 1992; and Kenneth D. Brown, ed., *Essays in Anti-Labour History: Responses to the Rise of Labour in Britain*, London, Macmillan, 1974, contains a chapter on Mallock. On Oakeshott see Paul Franco, *The Political Philosophy of Michael Oakeshott*, New Haven and London, Yale University Press, 1990, and Robert Eccleshall, 'Michael Oakeshott and Sceptical Conservatism', in Leonard Tivey and Anthony Wright, eds, *Political Thought since 1945: Philosophy, Science, Ideology*, London, Elgar, 1992, 173–95. There is now a vast literature on the New Right. Among the more comprehensive books are two by professors of politics: Dennis Kavanagh, *Thatcherism and British Politics: The End of Consensus?*, Oxford, Oxford University Press, 1987, and the conceptually sharper and more interesting Andrew Gamble, *The Free Economy and the Strong State: The Politics of Thatcherism*, Houndmills, Macmillan, 1988; and also two by political journalists: Peter Jenkins, *Mrs Thatcher's Revolution: The Ending of the Socialist Era*, London, Cape, 1987, and the thematically tighter Hugo Young, *One of Us: A Biography of Margaret Thatcher*, London, Macmillan, 1989.

Chapter 4

Socialism

Vincent Geoghegan

PROBLEMS OF DEFINITION

The key problem in defining socialism, as with all ideologies, is that of adequately capturing similarity and difference; showing what unites socialists without minimising the tremendous differences that separate them. Two dangers have to be avoided: 'essentialism' and 'historicism'. Essentialism reduces the richness of the socialist tradition to a few, very general 'essential' or 'core' characteristics. These 'essential' characteristics will be few because once one starts eliminating those many areas over which socialists disagree, relatively little common ground will remain. For example, socialists disagree in their conceptualisations of the state: some see it as a reformable and ultimately beneficial instrument of social change, while others see it as a prop to capitalist society which will eventually wither away. Attitudes to the state cannot therefore form one of the 'essential' elements of socialism. Likewise, since some socialists look forward to the end of private property while others consider it as a necessary feature of any conceivable society, socialism cannot be defined in terms of a 'core' theory of property. As a consequence very few concepts or beliefs will be left to provide the definition of socialism. Those core ideas that do remain will be at a high level of generality; for the more specific one becomes, the greater the risk of resurrecting the major differences that separate socialists. Hence it is true to say, for example, that (except for some very early examples) socialists undoubtedly believe in equality, but when asked what they mean by equality, they have responded with a variety of definitions from equality of opportunity to levelling uniformity. Thus while it is true to say that most socialists do believe in equality, this bald statement conceals more than it reveals. In short, the desire to find common ground uniting all socialists will often result in a rather meagre collection of very abstract 'essential' propositions.

One reaction to essentialism is a flight into 'historicism': namely the reduction of the socialist tradition to mere historical narrative, where an account is given of all those over the centuries who have called themselves, or have been deemed by others to be, socialists. A procession of utopian socialists, Marxists, Christian socialists, social democrats and so forth passes by, leaving little sense of what has brought them all together. Difference is registered by this approach, but any attempt to isolate similarities is all but abandoned, and one is left with a mass of dates, personalities and theories.

Any attempt to provide a definition of socialism that avoids the two dangers of essentialism and historicism is inevitably going to involve an element of compromise. It is, in other words, necessary to have a certain definitional modesty. It will not be possible to produce a definition of socialism that does full justice to similarity and difference; generalities will have to be qualified (as in 'this of course does not apply to socialism brand x'); saving phrases will constantly appear (such as 'most socialists', or 'there was a tendency among socialists', or 'socialists by and large'). So long, therefore, as a degree of flexibility is employed, it will be possible to make general statements about socialism without assuming an underlying essential identity. The philosopher Ludwig Wittgenstein sought to capture similarity and difference with his theory of 'family resemblance'. In an analysis of what united games (board-games, card-games, ball-games, Olympic games), he concluded that they had a series of overlapping similarities and dissimilarities, which united them into a *family* of games. Family members are not identical, but they clearly belong together: 'games form a *family* the members of which have family likenesses. Some of them have the same nose, others the same eyebrows and others again the same way of walking; and these likenesses overlap.'[1] In a similar fashion one can point to overlapping family resemblances in socialism. Wittgenstein argued that no common features could be found in his 'families'; the view taken in this chapter is that, given the compromises mentioned above, it is possible to make general statements about the nature of socialism.

WHAT IS SOCIALISM?

Let us begin at a very general level. Socialists, along with proponents of other ideologies, are engaged in three fundamental activities: they are offering a critique, an alternative, and a theory of transition; that is, they reveal defects in a society, suggest better arrangements, and indicate how these improvements are to be achieved. Of course the relative importance of these activities vary among socialists: some, for example, have a highly developed critique of capitalism, but only a fairly cursory theory of transition, while others may have sophisticated analyses of both, but are unwilling to engage in advanced 'speculation' about a future socialist society.

The critique is usually grounded in some form of egalitarianism. Some early socialists were not egalitarian, some socialists have been egalitarian in theory but not in practice, others have considered equality to be a 'bourgeois' value, and yet others have so defined egalitarianism as to allow a deal of inegalitarianism. None the less most socialists have viewed capitalism, which historically has been their main target, as a fundamentally unequal economic system, concentrating wealth and power in the hands of a minority and condemning the majority to absolute, or relative, poverty and impotence. Socialists stress the unacceptable differences between life chances in such divided societies, and contrast capitalist notions of constitutional and market equality with the widespread inequality found in everyday life. They echo Anatole France's remark that 'The law in its majestic equality forbids the rich as well as the poor to sleep under bridges, to beg in the streets, and to steal bread.'

A second element usually found in the critique is a denunciation of those practices and institutions that undermine or stifle sociability and co-operation. Capitalism is criticised for the isolated, selfish individuals it encourages; too little care is shown for others, who tend to be seen as either irrelevant to one's 'private' sphere, and therefore not worthy of genuine concern, or as competitors, and as such a threat. The result is a stunted individual unable to achieve the humanity that only flows from a genuine community. Socialists agree with the words of John Donne:

No man is an island entire of itself; every man is a piece of the continent, a part of the main; . . . any man's death diminishes me, because I am involved in mankind; and therefore never send to know for whom the bell tolls; it tolls for thee.

A contrast is thus drawn between the rhetoric of community promoted by capitalism, with its images of togetherness and belonging, and the fact of isolation and marginality.

Thirdly, the critique operates with a conception of freedom which makes it highly critical of liberal free-market formulations. The classical liberal definition of freedom as absence of constraint is deemed to be contradictory and shallow. It is contradictory because the liberty of the free market tends to undermine both the freedom enshrined in constitutional rights, and the actual free activity of the individual; poverty flows from free markets and poor people cannot be fully free. The contrast here is between the complacent claim of the advocates of capitalism that it is a free society and the reality of a large measure of unfreedom in such a society; or as David McLellan has paraphrased an old sentiment, 'it was no use having the right of access to the Grill Room at the Ritz if you couldn't afford the bill'.[2] It is shallow in that genuine liberty is not mere freedom *from* external pressures but freedom *to* develop fully as an individual among other free individuals; to be not a mere isolated unit ('free' from all that is most satisfying) but a well-rounded, fulfilled human being, delighting in the free use of all one's faculties.

Thus in their critique, socialists have echoed, and conceptualised in their own particular way, the great rallying call of the French Revolution – liberty, equality and fraternity – rendering it into equality, community and liberty. These values are deemed to be both goals to be achieved and individual attributes. A future society embodying equality, community and liberty would simply not be possible if these values were not in some sense grounded in contemporary humanity. In arguing this way, socialists deploy a variety of empirical propositions and ethical characterisations. Thus while very few socialists would argue that individuals are equal as regards ability, character, and so forth (i.e. possessing *identical* characteristics), most would posit a common humanity composed of human capacities, needs and entitlements. Shylock's words in the *Merchant of Venice* come to mind: 'Hath not a Jew eyes?/ hath not a Jew hands, organs, dimensions, senses, affections, passions? . . . if you prick us, do we not bleed?' The deep inequalities of capitalism are deemed to be an affront to this fundamental level of equality. Likewise, while acknowledging the lack of genuine community in capitalist society, socialists do argue that people are at some basic level social or sociable, or have the ability, or the need to become so. Freedom too, though absent in its full form in capitalism, is held to be a deeply rooted human aspiration or need. Even socialists who are hostile to theories of human nature in which fixed or essential characteristics are assumed, and who stress the changing nature of humanity over history, would none the less recognise the continuing presence of the human capacity for equality, community and liberty. Socialists therefore claim that their critique isn't mere abstract aspiration, but is, rather, rooted in human experience.

The critique is, as we have seen, far from a seamless web. Important differences exist between socialists. What is the status, for example, of the constitutional rights and values of liberal capitalist societies? Many Marxists have considered that the equality, community and liberty offered by such societies is not merely bogus, but actually harmful because it mystifies true relationships and thereby neutralises the revolutionary proletariat; social democrats and democratic socialists, on the other hand, have considered them to be genuine, if flawed gains, which need to be built upon and perfected. Socialists have also weighted these values differently, some emphasising equality and community over liberty (as in certain forms of Asian communism), others liberty over equality and community (as in Western libertarian socialism) and so on. Much of the diversity of the socialist movement arises from these differing emphases.

Tensions between the three values have been identified both within the socialist movement and by critical outsiders. Is it not unfair, it has been argued, to criticise capitalism for failing to combine equality and liberty, when any conceivable economic system is likely to have immense problems in reconciling them? Does not the drive for equality act as a drag on the development of freedom? Are the freedom and equality of the employer to count for nothing? Are not community and liberty also pulling in different directions? Is not a vital component of liberty the right to develop apart from or even against the community? When can the needs of the community legitimately override one's individual liberty? These problems have led many to reject the socialist critique – perhaps capitalism, if not an ideal system, is nonetheless the least worst! They have also prompted many socialists to conclude that some form of accommodation with capitalism, possibly some variant of market socialism, is necessary.

Turning from the socialist critique to the socialist alternative, we are again confronted with great diversity. Socialists have found it impossible to function without an alternative but have embraced the activity with varying degrees of warmth. Thus although an outline of communist society can be reconstructed from Marx's writings, he was worried that speculation about the future would distract the working class from freely creating such a society themselves. William Morris, on the other hand, was an enthusiastic utopian who thought that it was a duty of socialists to show how and why their alternative was superior to capitalism. A strong rationalist current in socialism has given socialists the confidence to pose alternatives. Reason is deemed to be a faculty and a norm, and therefore people can distinguish truth from error and construct a rational alternative to an unsatisfactory (and therefore irrational) reality. Socialism, like liberalism, is heir to that great period of questioning in the seventeenth and eighteenth centuries which most graphically manifested itself in the Enlightenment and the French Revolution. Ideologies such as conservatism which argue that reality is too complex to be adequately grasped by the mere individual (let alone criticised by them) are rejected by socialists as false and repressive. Some socialists, it should be said, do not base their alternatives in rationalism; some have confidence in faculties such as intuition or feeling and develop non-rational (though not necessarily irrational) visions (Sorel's espousal of myth, for example, or the sex/drug-based visions of the US New Left); others look to inspired texts for their grounding, as in certain forms of Christian socialism.

The many and varied alternatives which emerge from this process necessarily reflect the values underpinning the critique. Socialists have favoured redistribution of wealth or abolition of private property to overcome inequality; various forms of co-operative production and radical town planning have been suggested to overcome competition and isolation; and new work and education patterns have been proposed to promote the growth of free individuality. They have varied in degrees of radicalism from reformist amelioration of existing structures to root-and-branch revolutionary transformation, or may take a stages form of a short-term minimum programme leading in time to a more ambitious maximum programme. They are presented in a variety of forms: mani-festo commitments, five-year plans, full-scale utopian blueprints, etc.

A recurring theme is the democratic nature of the alternatives – genuine democracy is seen as embodying the unity of equality, com-munity and liberty: all are equal in a democracy; the democratic will is a communal will; and democracy is grounded in the free choice of the individual. In its earliest days socialism was not democratic – many utopian socialists looked to elites such as intellectuals, philanthropists and statesmen to bring about social transformation. Later socialists, especially those who feared the effect of 'bourgeois indoctrination' on the working class, have also been prepared to modify democracy with more authoritarian elements – the Marxist–Leninist organisational principle of 'democratic centralism', for example. These are exceptions to the predominant conception of socialism as democratic to its core.

Many socialists also claim that their alternatives embody the best of liberalism, liberalism at a higher stage stripped of its association with the worst aspects of capitalism. Eduard Bernstein, for example, when discussing liberalism asserts that 'socialism is its legitimate heir, not only in chronological sequence, but also in its spiritual qualities'.[3] Socialism is seen as providing a climate in which the great, and historically revolutionary, values of liberalism can flourish, unlike capitalism which in practice causes these values to wither. This is what Andrew Gamble means when he writes: 'As a doctrine socialism is not so much a call to reject the principles of liberalism as a claim that it alone can fulfil them.'[4] There are of course socialists who are irredeemably hostile to the liberal legacy both in theory and practice (Pol Pot and the Khmer Rouge, for example) but such intense hostility is an exception. The critique of liberalism and the routine abuse directed towards it by socialists should not be taken as wholesale rejection.

The criticism directed towards socialist alternatives, especially the most radical of these alternatives, recalls the types of argument long levelled at 'utopian' schemes in general; namely, that they are impractical and unrealistic. Often this is couched in terms of theories of human nature: individuals are essentially imperfect as regards intellect and morality and therefore cannot fulfil the sorts of role that socialist society demands. Thus, it is argued, individuals lack the mental ability to plan the immense complexities of a socialist society ('what cannot be known cannot be planned'),[5] and cannot be trusted to act altruistically in such structures; whereas capitalism, by contrast, with its market converting private greed into public utility, merely requires humans, not angels. Such criticism has drawn sustenance from the sorry record of so-called socialist societies from the Soviet Union onwards, despite the claims of many that the socialist credentials of these societies were or are bogus. Friedrich Hayek, one of the most influential critics of socialism, sees the socialist project as based on ignorance and vanity, and doomed to failure due to the inevitable constraints of the real world:

> The intellectuals' vain search for a truly socialist community, which results in the idealisation of, and then disillusionment with a seemingly endless string of 'utopias' . . . should suggest that there might be something about socialism that does not conform to certain facts.[6]

The socialist alternative is thus damned as a factual impossibility.

Socialists clearly disagree in their critiques and alternatives, but it is over the question of transition that the greatest and most intense disagreement occurs. Whereas the alternatives do reflect the values of the critique, the theories of transition may have a more complicated relationship with such values. Many socialists believe that there is a continuity of values from critique to transition to alternative. They argue that the socialist end must be operative in the socialist means. Thus since the goal of socialism includes peace, respect for others, truth, and integrity, these qualities must be apparent in the transition to socialism. This is justified on both ethical and prudential grounds – socialists *should* incorporate their values in the transformation, and are more likely to be ultimately successful if they do so. Other socialists, however, argue that the resistances to socialism are so great in society that the transformation may require the use of methods that, in the interim, fall short of the value system of socialism. Thus the use of violence may be necessary, though the goal is a society without violence; or there may be the need for elite leadership, though a society without elites is desired. The justification is usually in terms of 'political realities', the goal will never be achieved without the use of these 'regrettable' methods – 'one cannot make an omelette without breaking eggs'. The two approaches condemn one another from these perspectives – the latter sees the former as naively idealistic, the former views the latter as cynical and manipulative.

A wide range of transitions has been advocated over the years: among these are general strikes, mass insurrections, parliamentary roads, effected either singly or in concert. Underlying beliefs inform the choice of method. Social democrats have believed that it is possible, through parliament, to turn the state into the cutting edge of socialism; revolutionary Marxists assumed that ruling classes would use any means to cling to power, necessitating the use of violent revolution; ethical socialists believed that fundamental transformations had to occur in the hearts of individuals; Fabians maintained that under the guidance of experts, socialism would gradually but inevitably evolve out of capitalism. Some see the political arena as the main site of transformation, others the industrial; yet others seek to combine the two. Some look for transformation top down, via the state, others from the bottom up, via trades unions, co-operatives and other 'grass-roots' institutions. The variations and combinations make classification extraordinarily difficult.

The moral and practical problems involved in the various theories of transition are themselves multitudinous. Moral questions come spilling out. When is radical political action legitimate? Can the present generation be sacrificed for the good of future socialist citizens? Conversely, is an ethical, reformist strategy a betrayal of the interests of future generations? When is it right to break the law in pursuit of the socialist goal? When can violence be used? Questions on the effectiveness of strategy and tactics are as old as the ideology itself. Who is to be the transforming agency? The working class; a part of the working class; the working class with sections of the bourgeoisie; 'the people'; 'the nation'? What is to be the role of political parties, or of intellectuals? Can socialism be brought about in one country? Who are the enemies of socialism? Does participation in government de-radicalise socialist parties? Socialists have agonised over these questions from the start.

This therefore is a good point to move from consideration of these more general issues to looking at the actual history of socialism. The focus will be on the British experience.

THE EMERGENCE OF SOCIALISM

Socialism emerged with the development of industrial capitalism at the start of the nineteenth century. It is, however, possible to identify precursors in Britain as far back as the fourteenth century, who, while not socialist, are of interest in that: they represent the earliest radical response to the growth of capitalism in Britain; later socialists have declared an affinity with them, so that understanding of the former is assisted by knowledge of the latter; and in a striking fashion, they advocate, embody or discuss beliefs and visions that lie at the heart of socialism and are thus of abiding interest. A good starting point would be the Peasants' Revolt of 1381, which formed part of the complex break-up of English feudalism and the emergence of those social relations that would eventually produce industrial capitalism. In the pages of the medieval chronicler Froissart we can read of the radical cleric John Ball and his sermon to the rebellious peasantry at Blackheath on the proverb 'Whan Adam dalf and Eve span wo was thanne a gentilman', with its image of a golden age of equality before the Fall. By the sixteenth century the capitalist penetration of agriculture was such as to help stimulate a major critical work: Thomas More's *Utopia* (1516). In this work More developed a trenchant critique of private property, and speculated about an imaginary island where property was common, distribution was based on need not wealth, and where 'with the simultaneous abolition of money and the passion for money, how many other social problems have been solved, how many crimes eradicated!'[7] In the following century during the turbulent events of the English Civil War, Gerrard Winstanley proposed political democracy and economic communism, and set up a short-lived 'Digger' colony to put these ideas into practice. 'A man', he wrote, 'had better to have had no body than to have no food for it; therefore this restraining of the earth from brethren by brethren is oppression and bondage.'[8]

The words 'socialism' and 'socialist' began to appear in Britain and France from the late 1820s or early 1830s. The earliest usage of the term 'socialist' was in an 1827 issue of the *Co-operative Magazine*, a journal associated with the man who many see as the founder of British socialism, Robert Owen (1771–1858). Owen's life highlights the Janus face of Britain's Industrial Revolution: from one aspect the tremendous increase in productivity and wealth which enabled Owen, the son of a humble tradesman, to make a fortune as a manufacturer; from the other, the human costs experienced by large sections of the population, which propelled Owen in the direction of philanthropy and socialism. The remedy he proposed rested on a small number of basic ideas which he stubbornly broadcast to whomever would listen, certain that he had discovered the fundamental levers of human happiness. Since for Owen character was determined by the environment, he proposed that the environment be manipulated so as to replace its negative traits with positive ones:

> any community may be arranged . . . in such a manner as, not only to withdraw vice, poverty, and, in a great degree, misery, from the world, but also to place *every* individual under such circumstances in which he shall enjoy more permanent happiness than can be given to *any* individual under the principles which have hitherto regulated society.[9]

Owen attempted to put this theory into practice in a number of ventures: he commenced fairly successfully with a reform of working and living conditions at his New Lanark mill; and much less success-fully in the more ambitious schemes (like the community of New Harmony in the United States) which were envisaged as prototypes for a radically new co-operative form of existence. Owen displayed both a naive rationalism and a deeply engrained elitism. He believed that he could convert conservative governments and landowners, not merely to his minimal quasi-philanthropic enterprises (which could have seemed attractive to ruling circles worried by labour unrest), but to his maximal socialist schemes; ideas of class struggle were alien to his nature. He saw reform in terms of expert planning from above, and ordinary men and women as objects of benevolence rather than as creative subjects.

From the 1830s to the 1880s the energy of the working class in Britain was mainly channelled through movements such as co-operation, trade unionism (in both of which Owen played a role) and Chartism. There was little native development in socialist theory, unless one counts the Christian socialists, a group of predominantly middle-class reformers such as Frederick Maurice and Charles Kingsley, who considered the competition engendered by capitalism to be contrary to Christian principles. Britain did, however, become home to undoubtedly the most influential theorists in the socialist tradition, Karl Marx (1818–83) and Friedrich Engels (1820–95). In his early work (some important texts of which remained unpublished in his lifetime – particularly the *Economic and Philosophical Manuscripts*, 1844) Marx developed a critical synthesis of German idealist philosophy (centred on the work of Hegel), British political economy (including Adam Smith and Ricardo), and utopian socialism (notably the French theorists Fourier and Saint-Simon, and Owen himself). In the resulting new theoretical system a critique of capitalism was formulated highlighting the deleterious effects of aliena-tion, communism was posited as the alternative, and the proletariat were entrusted with bringing about the transition. In his mature work, much of it growing out of his studies in the British Museum, and part of it published in his life-time as the first volume of *Capital* (1867), he produced an anatomy of capitalist society intended to demonstrate that the internal logic of the capitalist mode of production was impelling it towards its own destruction.

Engels' residence in Britain predated Marx's own arrival. In 1845 Engels had produced *The Condition of the Working Class in England* which contained a graphic and horrifying account of the physical and mental suffering inflicted on working people by industrial capitalism. As a member of a German mill-owning family with a factory in Manchester, Engels proved a valuable collaborator for Marx in his studies of capitalism (though the precise nature of the Marx/Engels theoretical relationship is the source of scholarly controversy). Their most influential collaborative political text, the *Manifesto of the Communist Party* (1848), was confident that 'what the bourgeoisie . . . produces, above all, is its own grave-diggers. Its fall and and the victory of the proletariat are equally inevitable.'[10] Engels produced a number of independent texts which developed and popularised (and some would say distorted) what was becoming known as Marxism; after Marx's death in 1883 he was of great importance in the burgeoning Marxist movement. In the wake of the failure of the 1848 revolutions, London had become a centre for exiled revolutionaries, and it was here in 1864 that a body seeking international working-class unity, the International Working Men's Association (the First International) was established; Marx's inaugural address ended with the rallying call 'Proletarians of all countries, Unite!'. This organisation, which lasted until 1876, provided an arena for the development and propagation of socialist ideas, strategy and tactics; and also the forum for a vicious ideological battle between Marxism and anarchism.

During the last two decades of the nineteenth century, in a climate of periodic slump and depression, Britain experienced a socialist renaissance. A number of theorists, most notably William Morris, Eleanor Marx and Edward Carpenter, sought to broaden socialists' concerns to include areas of human experience relatively neglected in earlier theorising. William Morris (1834–96) infused his socialism with insights drawn from his experiences as an artist and art critic. Capitalism, he argued, condemned the bulk of the population to labour that is fundamentally dehumanising; only in a socialist society could genuine creative activity be generalised. He drew on Victorian medievalist notions to compare the days before the triumph of capitalism when 'all men were more or less artists'[11] with current conditions in which the instincts for beauty were thwarted. Lack of fulfilment was not confined to the working class though they were the most abject victims – the aristocracy's idleness and the sham work of the bourgeoisie were part of a pervasive condition of waste and ugliness. He had no inhibitions about depicting a future socialist society, and when the American Edward Bellamy produced an influential, high-tech, centralised utopia, *Looking Backward*, Morris responded with his own *News from Nowhere* (1890), which combined respect for the supposed simplicity and creativity of the past with the political and economic arrangements of the Marxist vision of communism.

Marx's daughter, Eleanor Marx (1855–98), jointly with her lover Edward Aveling, produced work on the relationship between capitalism and the exploitation of women. Socialist feminism had emerged in the days of Owen, and included the Irish socialist William Thompson (1785–1833) and a number of women connected with the Owenite movement whom feminist historians are now beginning to bring to light: Anna Wheeler (1785–?), Fanny Wright (1795–1852) and Emma Martin (1812–51).[12] By the time Eleanor Marx and Aveling came to write 'The Woman Question from a Socialist Point of View' in 1886, the Owenite feminists had been forgotten. This article, which was a review of August Bebel's *Woman in the Past, the Present and the Future*, drew explicitly on the Marxist perspective of this work, and of Engels' *Origins of the Family, Private Property and the State*, to point to the ultimately economic basis of women's oppression in capitalism and to argue that the need for women to organise themselves was a necessary component of the struggle for human emancipation: 'both the oppressed classes, women and the immediate producers, must understand that their emancipation will come from themselves'.[13] In a socialist society (which, like many of the Marxists of the time, they saw as an inevitable, certain event) men and women will communicate as equals; women will have the same educational and other opportunities as men; marriage – in its present commercial form – will disappear; sexuality will lose its burden of shame, and prostitution will vanish. In short: 'there will no longer be one law for the woman and one for the man'.

An even more radical perspective is to be found in the work of Edward Carpenter (1844–1929). His vision of socialism is of a society in which people have not merely overcome economic and political oppression but also the sexual and emotional repression that permeates capitalist society. Carpenter, however, unlike Eleanor Marx and Aveling who spoke of the 'natural horror' people experienced on encountering 'the effeminate man and masculine woman', displayed much greater sensitivity to the diversity of human behaviour and relationships. Carpenter's defence and advocacy of same-sex relationships (a brave act in the wake of the Oscar Wilde scandal) was one aspect of a call for individuals to regain their sensual/spiritual unity. He therefore saw such relationships (which he termed the 'Uranian spirit', emanating from 'the intermediate sex') as a type of vanguard in the struggle against capitalist society: 'the advance guard of that great movement which will one day transform the common life by substituting the bond of personal affection and compassion for the monetary, legal and other external ties which now control and confine society'.[14]

This period also saw the emergence of socialist groups and parties.

One might note the role of Henry Mayers Hyndman (1842–1921), whose contribution lay not in the field of theory (his was a rather undistinguished and highly derivative mixture of Toryism and Marxism) but in the foundation in 1884 of Britain's first modern socialist party – the Social Democratic Federation. Morris, Eleanor Marx and Aveling were all sometime members (Carpenter had some association) and although splits occurred (partly due to Hyndman's high-handedness), a climate was created in which socialist theory, strategy, and tactics could be discussed and, to a limited extent, put into practice.

The year 1884 also saw the foundation of the Fabian Society, an exclusive debating and propaganda group whose cultured and highly individual membership (including George Bernard Shaw, Sidney and Beatrice Webb, Annie Besant, and Graham Wallas) defies easy characterisation. The Fabians were committed to a policy of gradualism, which was evoked in the society's name and motto, part of which read: 'For the right moment you must wait, as Fabius did most patiently, when warring against Hannibal, though many censured his delays.' They stressed steady, piecemeal progress, a gradual replacement of capitalist institutions by socialist ones and eschewed revolutionary, catastrophic conceptions – 'the inevitability of our scheme of gradualness', as Sidney Webb put it. Although committed to democracy, the Fabians were strongly elitist, viewing themselves as an intellectual vanguard; not a mass political party, but a powerhouse of select socialist thinkers, whose role was to inculcate sound scientific views which would promote rational action by a benign state. The second part of the Fabian motto – 'but when the time comes you must strike hard, as Fabius did, or your waiting will be vain, and fruitless' – prompted George Lichtheim to remark that there was no historical record of Fabius having ever 'struck hard', and that 'malicious critics of Fabianism have been known to hint that there may have been something prophetic, or at least symbolic, in this misreading of history'.[15]

THE TWENTIETH CENTURY

In the spring of 1902 Lenin (1870–1924) arrived in London for what turned out to be a year's stay. The previous year Eduard Bernstein (1850–1932) had returned to Germany after spending more than a decade in the British capital. Lenin gained no new insight from his visit – London merely confirmed his views of the stark class division of

capitalism – his commitment to revolutionary Marxism was not affected. Nadezhda Krupskaya, his wife, recalled visits to areas in which
squalid and lavish housing co-existed, where Lenin 'would mutter
through clenched teeth, and in English: "Two nations!"'.[16] Bernstein,
by contrast, was changed by his period of residence and, although Rosa
Luxemburg's remark that 'Bernstein has constructed his theory upon
relationships obtaining in England. He sees the world through English
spectacles'[17] is an exaggeration, it is true that his experience in Britain
was an important factor in the development of his 'revision' of Marxism.
These two men were to be significantly associated with what have been
the two dominant forms of socialism in the twentieth century –
communism and social democracy.

Controversy has long raged on the nature of the relationship
between Marx, Lenin, and Stalin. Whereas anti-Marxist critics portray
a malign trinity, Stalinists arrange the three into a form of revolutionary apostolic succession. Marxist anti-Bolsheviks distinguish the
admirable Marx from the corrupting duo of Lenin and Stalin, while
Bolshevik anti-Stalinists reject any continuity between the monstrous
Stalin and revolutionary founders Marx and Lenin. In the case of Lenin
the debate has been fuelled by the theoretical diversity of his volum-
inous writings and the complexities of his political life. These complications make it very difficult, or even impossible, to portray an essential
Lenin; however, ironically, the very boldness of some of his statements
and acts encourages people to do precisely this (especially when
important interests are at stake). Communism (known also as Leninism
or Marxism–Leninism) was developed under Stalin's aegis, and drew
much of its theoretical sustenance from the events surrounding, and
the ideas expressed in, Lenin's *What is to be Done?* (1902). In this work
Lenin had argued for a tightly disciplined, exclusive party of professional revolutionaries dedicated to bringing socialist consciousness
to, and helping to organise, a working class who, unaided, would
merely develop sub-socialist trade-union consciousness. It was at the
1903 Second Congress of the Russian Social Democratic Labour Party
(held in Brussels and London) that Lenin had eventually managed to
get a majority for his conception against a much broader conception of
the party developed by Martov (Lenin's group thus got the name
'Bolsheviks' or Majoritarians, while Martov's group acquired the name
'Mensheviks' or Minoritarians). This conception became the centre-
piece of Stalinist communism, though used in a way Trotsky had
feared in 1904:

> In the internal politics of the Party these methods lead . . . to
> the Party organisation 'substituting' itself for the Party, the
> Central Committee substituting itself for the Party organisation,
> and finally the dictator substituting himself for the Central
> Committee.[18]

Lenin attempted to combine discipline with democracy in the party's
organisational principle of democratic centralism: relatively free discussion and criticism until a decision is taken when it becomes binding
on the party. The failings in Lenin's own use of this principle were
dwarfed by those of Stalin who merely paid it lip-service; in reality the
democratic element was dissolved. Stalin, via a cult of the leader, came
to dominate party, class, state, and international communism. Drawing
on an idea of Marx, Lenin had, prior to the 1917 October Revolution in
Russia, argued for a temporary proletarian dictatorship after the
revolution in order to root out residual hostile elements. He had,
however, conceived this dictatorship as distinct from the party. Stalin's
equating of the two (anticipated, let it be said, by developments while
Lenin was in power) generated a party state. The party also came to
control the world communist movement via the nominally independent Third International, enforcing the Bolshevik party model and the
latest Moscow line.

  The Communist Party of Great Britain, founded in 1920, for the first
two decades of its existence shared the Soviet party's hostile stance on
'the parliamentary road to socialism'. The Second Congress of the
International (Comintern) explicitly rejected a parliamentary road;
considering that, at best, parliament was an arena for propaganda and
agitation; whereas socialism, as in Russia, was to be brought about
primarily by insurrectionary means. The Communist Party of Great
Britain did, over the years, attract militant elements of the working
class; and in the 1930s, numbers of anti-fascists. It also had internal
factions and oppositional currents. But although the party was able to
foster a lively intellectual culture, including an influential and distinctive school of socialist historians (among others, Christopher Hill,
E.P. Thompson, and Eric Hobsbawm), party ideology, in the hands
of Central Committee/Politburo members such as R. Palme Dutt
(1896–1974), largely consisted of theoretical and policy acrobatics to
shadow developments in Moscow: most dramatic of these was the
rapid *volte-face* on fascism in the wake of the Nazi–Soviet Pact of 1939.
With the death of Stalin in 1953, and in the cold light of revelations of

the grim, inhuman past of Stalinism and the continuing oppressive present (witnessed in the invasion of Hungary in 1956), democratic currents within many Western communist parties became much more prominent. In the 1970s eurocommunism represented an attempt, by principally the French, Spanish, and Italian parties, to develop a strategy that took democratic, parliamentary aspirations into consideration. By the 1980s, time was running out for the world communist movement. The coming to power of Gorbachev in the Soviet Union in 1985, with his watchwords of *glasnost* (openness) and *perestroika* (restructuring), saw a final, doomed attempt to reform Soviet communism from within, which actually led to the complete unravelling of the Soviet system in the USSR and Eastern Europe. In Britain the party – whose journal *Marxism Today* had been part of a desperate search for a reinvigorated Marxism in the 1980s – shattered into hard-line splinters and a 'democratic left' residue which sought to jettison all the remaining baggage of the communist period – and not least, the thoroughly compromised name 'communist'.

In conceiving of the Third International, Lenin had sought a radical replacement for the Second (founded in 1889), which had effectively collapsed amidst the ferocious jingoism at the start of the First World War. Prior to this debacle, however, the Second International had been convulsed by the revisionist controversy; superficially a mere squabble within Marxism but in fact, among other things, a landmark in the development of social democracy. Eduard Bernstein, the most notable exponent of revisionism, developed a critique of a number of Marxist orthodoxies which involved rejecting revolutionary insurrectionism in favour of a gradualist, parliamentary approach. The beast capitalism, he argued, was being tamed: property-holders and shareholders were increasing; small and medium agriculture was growing; wages were rising and prosperity was becoming more widespread. All this was reflected in an increasingly complex class system which belied orthodox expectations of a polarisation between a small, wealthy bourgeoisie and a massive, impoverished proletariat. At the political level, the working class was gradually, through parliament, gaining a say in the organisation of society. In short, Bernstein held that a bloody revolution was not only unlikely but unnecessary. He emphasised present realities and the foreseeable future; and sought achievable, if unspectacular, advances and not some supposed, fanciful millennium. Moreover, the liberal notions of freedom with which he was imbued made political democracy valid in absolute terms, and not merely as a tactic; and further, this democracy enjoined both limitations on majorities and respect for minority rights; proletarian dictatorships were entirely ruled out: 'In this sense one might call socialism "organizing liberalism".'

Much of this type of thinking has informed modern social democracy. The British Labour Party (founded in 1900 as the Labour Representation Committee) has always been a broad church, but this very broadness, insofar as it reflects underlying social realities, has encouraged a social democratic approach among its leadership. According to Ramsay MacDonald the fact that the party was called 'Labour' and not 'Socialist' indicated the parameters within which any sensible left-wing party would have to operate for the conceivable future: 'Under British conditions, a Socialist Party is the last, not the first, form of the Socialist movement in politics.'[19] It was not, of course, German revisionist Marxism but existing native reformist currents, including Fabianism, that provided the main intellectual input into British social democracy, and made most of the running.

Between the two world wars, Labour could point to successes and failures. Its goal of using the existing rules of the parliamentary game to win power was achieved, and the Fabian Sidney Webb could enjoy cabinet office under Ramsay MacDonald. Once in power, however, the party found itself in a double bind: not only did it face the classic socialist dilemma (its state role was to stabilise society, and therefore capitalism, while its party role was to overcome capitalism) but this dilemma was aggravated by both its unwillingness to depart from a narrow constitutionalism and by its desperate desire to be seen as a 'respectable' party. The world economic depression brought matters to a head in 1931, when Ramsay MacDonald formed a National Government with Tories and Liberals to introduce cuts in pay and unemployment benefit demanded by international bankers – but opposed by important sections of his own party. The ensuing election saw the Labour vote plummet, leaving the party in opposition for the rest of the decade.

In the period of economic prosperity between the 1950s and the early 1970s, the 'revisionism' of Anthony Crosland (1918–77) represented a highly optimistic reformulation of the social democratic case. It was a theory appropriate to a reformist practice – Labour social democracy had given up the idea that socialism was fundamentally distinct from capitalism, in favour of the notion of the interpenetration of the two. Crosland argued in *The Future of Socialism* (1956) that in Britain, 'Capitalism has been reformed almost out of recognition'. There was now a caring and effective state, strong trade unions, businesses increasingly run by socially aware managers rather than bloated plutocrats, and the likelihood of continuous and largely crisis-free prosperity. The existence of private ownership of the means of production was no longer to be seen as a barrier to socialism; remaining inequalities and social injustices could be removed in the context of a mixed economy and a parliamentary democracy – thereby reconciling equality with liberty and efficiency.

With the collapse of economic prosperity in the 1970s, Croslandite optimism became unsustainable. The New Right onslaught, enshrined in government from 1979, left the Labour Party badly split. The social democrats, too, split. A resurgent left drove frightened social democrats like Shirley Williams and David Owen out of the party altogether, and into attempts, via the Social Democratic Party, at restructuring the centre-left in Britain; ultimately, most regrouped with their natural ideological allies in the Liberal Party. The social democrats who remained in the Labour Party were influential in seeing off the challenge of the left, and in drafting the essentially social democratic manifestos with which the party (unsuccessfully) fought the elections in this period.

Distinct from communism and social democracy a third stance, democratic socialism, can be identified. Not all commentators would accept the validity of this procedure. Anthony Wright, for example, has been sceptical about the distinction between social democracy and democratic socialism, viewing it as a largely untheorised piece of Labour left rhetoric:

the distinction ... was not accompanied by any serious attempt to explore the theoretical pedigrees of these traditions in order to establish what distinction (if any) there actually was, apart from the fact that one sounded more muscular than the other.[20]

Bernard Crick,[21] on the other hand, subsumes much of what would be considered social democratic into a very broad category of democratic socialism, including, among others, Anthony Crosland, Ramsay MacDonald and Beatrice and Sidney Webb. Undoubtedly problems do exist in maintaining this distinction. Can one describe as a democratic socialist someone who patently did not use this term as a self-description? Furthermore, how is a history to be written of a tradition that was not really aware of itself as a tradition? There will also be the inevitable boundary disputes as to where social democracy ends and democratic socialism begins. Nonetheless the distinction is worth persevering with, for it does help to illuminate genuine points of difference in the socialist movement.

Democratic socialism can be seen as trying to steer a third way between communism and social democracy; an attempt to synthesise the best elements of the two other traditions, while rejecting the objectionable features of both. Democratic socialism shared with communism (or more precisely, with the Marxist core professed by the adherents of communism) a similar analysis of the basic anatomy of capitalism. Democratic socialism therefore criticised social democracy for its naive reading of capitalism – for its blindness to entrenched interests and the inherent instability of the system. This, it argued, issued in a shallow liberal conception of the institutions and personnel of exploitation and oppression. On the other hand, democratic socialism shared with social democracy a thorough-going critique of the authoritarianism of communism – the rhetorical praise for, but actual stifling of, genuine participation at all levels of society. Democratic socialism could therefore be seen as a form of synthesis of these two strands or traditions: namely an attempt to combine a real move towards socialism with authentic democracy. In the British context this involved a combination of radical social analysis with genuine respect for the strengths of the liberal constitutional system.

Within the British Labour Party, a fierce attack on social democratic assumptions was precipitated by the 1931 crisis. The whole episode served to confirm to democratic socialist critics just how capitalist interests could successfully protect themselves against a Labour government – a situation which called for a hard look at traditional Labour views. This stance was adopted by a body within the party called The Socialist League and in the writings of one of its leading members – Harold Laski (1893–1950).[22] Laski's work provided a critique of both social democracy and communism. In Democracy in Crisis (1933), he argued that vested economic interests prevent the people from advancing from formal political control to real economic and political power. Using Marxist conceptions of state and society, Laski rejected the thesis that the great institutions of society (the courts, the press, the educational system, the armed forces, etc.) were genuinely neutral, as opposed to merely formally so; they were firmly in a bourgeois camp which showed every willingness to resort to whatever means were required, including violence, to protect its privileged position. Laski feared that people's understandable frustration would lead to violent revolution, resulting in either defeat and chaos, or in the establishment of a Soviet-type dictatorship which would be essentially alien to British liberal-democratic traditions. Instead he hoped that a future Labour government would push through a thorough socialist transformation. However, the crisis of 1931, and the rise of fascism, had demonstrated how ruthless capitalist interests could be; and thus a radical Labour government would have to be prepared to make a significant departure from traditional constitutional practice to protect its policy: it 'would have to take vast powers, and legislate under them by ordinance and decree; it would have to suspend the classic formulae of normal opposition'.[23] This theme was reiterated by another prominent Socialist Leaguer – Sir Stafford Cripps – who envisaged a Labour government placing before Parliament 'an Emergency Powers Bill to be passed through all its stages in one day' which would allow rule by ministerial orders 'incapable of challenge in the Courts or in any way except in the House of Commons'.[24] The Laskian perspective graphically demonstrates both the character of, and the problems inherent in, British democratic socialism. A radical (in Laski's case, Marxist) analysis of capitalism is combined with a profound belief in the continuing utility and validity of liberal-democratic values and institutions; yet these latter can only be preserved by actions that would appear, to many, to be a flagrant violation of liberal democracy. Laski himself was on the National Executive of the Labour Party, and, due to the complexities of Labour Party organisation and certainly not to any hegemony in the party, found himself Chairman of the Labour Party during Labour's 1945 landslide election victory. The new government rapidly found its party chairman's radical criticisms an embarrassment, resulting in Attlee's famous rebuke that 'a period of silence on your part would be welcome'!

A more recent expression of democratic socialism can be found in the work of Tony Benn (b. 1925). Reflecting on his time as a Cabinet minister in the 1970s, he recalled a Cabinet meeting at which Anthony Crosland reluctantly accepted the humiliating terms set by the International Monetary Fund as the price for assistance; this, Benn argued, displayed the utter bankruptcy of Crosland's social democratic vision of a humanised capitalism: 'That was the moment when social democratic revisionism died in the Labour Party. It was killed, not by the Left but by the bankers.'[25] Of particular concern for Benn is Britain's imperfect democracy – its formal inadequacy, covert checks, and external constraints – all major obstacles to the achievement of socialism. Formal problems include 'the unfinished business of 1688', for example, the lack of a written constitution, the powers of the House of Lords and the residual personal prerogatives of the monarch plus new impositions such as the growth of ministerial and prime ministerial government at the expense of parliament. To this is added the effect of powerful vested interests, the civil service, judiciary, armed and security services, media, city, and others who directly and indirectly sabotage socialist initiatives. Finally there is the external pressures from the USA, international capital, and, a particular *bête noire* of Benn's, the EEC. Like Laski, Benn wishes to see the election of a government committed to a radical socialist agenda. Legitimate extra-parliamentary activity includes:

1   the right of the labour movement to organise itself to promote a Labour victory at the polls;
2   the right to limited civil disobedience where ancient and inherited rights are threatened; and
3   the right to protect a Labour government from a coup by force if necessary.

If the Labour Party is to be successful it must reform its own internal structure, particularly in the area of inner-party democracy; higher levels of the party must become accountable to lower, and all must become accountable, whether in power or opposition, to the electorate. It is therefore none too surprising that Benn's brand of democratic socialism has won him few friends among the great and the good in the Labour Party. He has viewed this growing marginality as an opportunity to speak out, untramelled by party institutional constraints.

CONCLUSION: THE END OF SOCIALISM?

The collapse of communism has raised the question not simply of the continued viability of social democracy and democratic socialism, but of socialism itself. There is much talk of the end of socialism. This assertion partly derives from a false assessment of the supposed strength of socialism in the past. Earlier rhetoric has encouraged this assumption. Loose claims such as 'Marxism is the ideology of a large fraction of the planet' and 'socialist parties have at last come of age' concealed the facts that comparatively few 'citizens' of communist states did hold Marxist beliefs and that committed socialists formed only a small fraction of the electorate voting socialist. The 'end of socialism' approach therefore rests in part on the inaccurate image of a great edifice collapsing. However, one truth which does help give credence to 'the end of socialism' claim is that there has indeed been a crisis of belief and confidence among sections of the traditional formulators of socialist ideology – the intelligentsia. Broader intellectual trends have helped stimulate this crisis. Influential post-modernist theory has poured scorn on comprehensive theories of historical change and on universal values, thereby undermining many of the traditional bases of socialist theorising. The abject failure of 'actually existing socialism' in the Soviet Union and East Europe, and the scramble for capitalist relations of production have also taken their toll – the bitter Soviet joke: 'What is socialism?' – 'The long road from capitalism to capitalism' hits a nerve. The undoubtedly true claim that such societies were not socialist prompts more questions than it answers. Furthermore, world recession has provided a conducive climate for 'realist' economic theories, popularised in Margaret Thatcher's homely, 'good housekeeping' analogies. Where socialists have gained or held on to power, it has usually involved a significant downplaying of their socialism. It is also in many people's interests to fan the flames of self-doubt: after all, might not journalistic clichés concerning 'the death of socialism' help to create a genuine fatality?

A counter-view is that socialism is not dying but changing. Like all long-established ideologies, socialism has had a protean quality. These changes have always encouraged premature obituaries for the whole ideology: the 'failures' of the utopian socialist communities, the defeat of the revolutionary wave of 1848, the collapse of the Second International in 1914 seemed, to some, to sound the death-knell of socialism itself. In each case socialism re-emerged, having learnt valuable lessons from its trials and tribulations. Why should the era of the collapse of communism prove finally fatal? Will not new forms of socialism emerge which are more appropriate to changed conditions? Though it is difficult to speculate on these possible new forms, three areas readily spring to mind. Firstly, as the drawbacks and failures of New Right free-market nostrums become increasingly evident, socialist energy is increasingly exploring ways of combining markets and socialism, avoiding the pitfalls of the New Right and the Old Left. Secondly, questions of citizenship are also becoming of interest to socialists. How are political and civil rights to be combined with social rights in a new citizenship? Finally, the relationship between socialism and ecologism will surely prove fertile territory.

It is, of course, possible that socialism might so change that it ceases to be socialism. We may be witnessing the beginning of a major redrawing of the ideological map, where the traditional ideologies and ideological divisions are replaced by entirely new patterns. The economic, social, and intellectual landscape may have so changed that conventional distinctions between 'left' and 'right' have lost their rationale. In such a regrouping, the various elements of socialism may disperse into new combinations. The image here is not of the 'death' of socialism, nor of a mere change of shape, but of a fundamental deconstruction and reconfiguration of socialist values and beliefs.

NOTES

1 Ludwig Wittgenstein, *The Blue and Brown Books*, Oxford, Blackwell, 1972, 17.
2 David McLellan, ed., *Marx: The First 100 Years*, Oxford, Fontana, 1983, 145.
3 Eduard Bernstein, *Evolutionary Socialism*, New York, Schocken, 1961, 149.
4 Andrew Gamble, *An Introduction to Modern Social and Political Thought*, London, Macmillan, 1981, 100.
5 Friedrich Hayek, *The Fatal Conceit: The Errors of Socialism*, London, Routledge, 1988, 85.
6 Ibid., 85–6.
7 Thomas More, *Utopia*, Harmondsworth, Penguin, 1965, 130.
8 Gerrard Winstanley, *The Law of Freedom and Other Writings*, Harmondsworth, Penguin, 1973, 295–6.
9 A.L. Morton, *The Life and Ideas of Robert Owen*, London, Lawrence and Wishart, 1962, 73.
10 Karl Marx and Friedrich Engels, *Selected Works*, London, Lawrence and Wishart, 1968, 46.
11 A.L. Morton, ed., *Political Writings of William Morris*, London, Lawrence and Wishart, 1973, 61.
12 See Barbara Taylor, *Eve and the New Jerusalem: Socialism and Feminism in the Nineteenth Century*, London, Virago, 1983.
13 Eleanor Marx Aveling and Edward Aveling, 'The Woman Question

from a Socialist Point of View', *The Westminster Review*, LXIX, January and April 1886, 21.

14 Edward Carpenter, *Selected Writings*, Volume 1: *Sex*, London, GMP, 1984, 238.

15 George Lichtheim, *A Short History of Socialism*, Glasgow, Fontana, 1975, 65.

16 N.K. Krupskaya, *Memories of Lenin*, London, Panther, 1970, 65.

17 Quoted in David McLellan, *Marxism after Marx*, London, Macmillan, 1979, 23.

18 Leon Trotsky, *Our Political Tasks*, London, New Park Publications, n.d., 77.

19 Quoted in Bernard Crick, *Socialism*, Milton Keynes, Open University Press, 1987, 70.

20 Anthony Wright, *British Socialism: Socialist Thought from the 1880s to 1960s*, Harlow, Longman, 1983, 24.

21 Crick, *Socialism*.

22 Laski has been called a member of 'the socialist intellectual trinity between the wars' (Isaac Kramnick and Barry Sheerman, *Harold Laski: A Life on the Left*, London, Hamish Hamilton, 1993, 249) – the other two being G.D.H. Cole (1889–1959) and R.H. Tawney (1880–1962). This is not to suggest that there was much unanimity between the three: Cole underwent a complex ideological development which included the espousal of Guild Socialism, while Tawney's Christian or ethical socialism has often been appropriated by Labour social democracy. Rather the 'trinity' image suggests the visibility of the three, and their influence on British left-wing thinking of the time.

23 Harold Laski, *Democracy in Crisis*, London, Allen and Unwin, 1933, 87.

24 Quoted in Frank Bealey, ed., *The Social and Political Thought of the British Labour Party*, London, Weidenfeld and Nicolson, 1970, 137–8.

25 Tony Benn, *Parliament, People and Power*, London, Verso, 1982, 33.

FURTHER READING

General

The classic history of socialism is G.D.H. Cole, *A History of Socialist Thought*, London, Macmillan, 1953, 60, although its five volumes only go up to 1939; while a fine concise history is provided by George Lichtheim, *A Short History of Socialism*, Glasgow, Fontana/Collins, 1975. Good introductions to the basic themes of socialism are: R.N. Berki, *Socialism*, London, Dent, 1975; Bernard Crick, *Socialism*, Milton Keynes, Open University Press, 1987; and Anthony Wright, *Socialisms: Theories and Practices*, Oxford, Oxford University Press, 1987. An old history of British socialism, which is very good on origins, is Max Beer, *A History of British Socialism*, London, Bell, 1929; an illustrated one-volume edition was published by Spokesman in 1984. A modern history can be found in John Callaghan, *Socialism in Britain since 1884*, Oxford, Blackwell, 1990.

Texts

A wide range of British extracts, with a useful introduction, can be found in Anthony Wright, *British Socialism*, London, Longman, 1983. On individual authors: Robert Owen, *A New View of Society and Other Writings*, Harmondsworth, Penguin, 1991; Karl Marx and Friedrich Engels, *Selected Works*, London, Lawrence and Wishart, 1968; William Morris, *Political Writings of William Morris*, London, Lawrence and Wishart, 1973; Edward Carpenter, *Selected Writings*, Volume 1: *Sex*, London, GMP, 1984; G.B. Shaw, ed., *Fabian Essays in Socialism*, London, Fabian Society, 1889; V.I. Lenin, *Selected Works*, London, Lawrence and Wishart, 1969; Eduard Bernstein, *The Preconditions of Socialism*, Cambridge, Cambridge University Press, 1993; C.A.R. Crosland, *The Future of Socialism*, London, Cape, 1956; Harold Laski, *Democracy in Crisis*, London, Allen and Unwin, 1933; Tony Benn, *Arguments for Socialism*, Harmondsworth, Penguin, 1980.

Commentaries

For Owen and Owenism see J.F.C. Harrison, *Robert Owen and the Owenites in Britain and America: The Quest for the New Moral World*, London, Routledge and Kegan Paul, 1969, and Gregory Claeys, *Citizens and Saints: Politics and Anti-Politics in Early British Socialism*, Cambridge, Cambridge University Press, 1989. From the vast literature on Marx, Engels and Marxism three good introductions are: George Lichtheim, *Marxism*, London, Routledge and Kegan Paul, 1961; David McLellan,

The Thought of Karl Marx, London, Macmillan, 1971; and Lesek Kolakowski, *Main Currents of Marxism*, 3 vols, Oxford, Clarendon, 1978. William Morris is served by E.P. Thompson, *William Morris: Romantic to Revolutionary*, London, Merlin, 1977; Edward Carpenter by Chushichi Tsuzuki, *Edward Carpenter 1844–1929: Prophet of Human Fellowship*, Cambridge, Cambridge University Press, 1980; and Eleanor Marx in two volumes by Yvonne Kapp, *Eleanor Marx*, London, Virago, 1979; for the Fabians there is A.M. McBriar, *Fabian Socialism and English Politics 1884–1918*, Cambridge, Cambridge University Press, 1966.

A good commentary on Lenin is provided by N. Harding, *Lenin's Political Thought*, London, Macmillan, 1983, and on Bernstein by Peter Gay, *The Dilemma of Democratic Socialism: Eduard Bernstein's Challenge to Marx*, New York, Collier, 1962; for Crosland see David Lipsey and Dick Leonard, eds, *The Socialist Agenda: Crosland's Legacy*, London, Cape, 1981; for Laski, see Isaac Kramnick and Barry Sheerman, *Harold Laski: A Life on the Left*, London, Hamish Hamilton, 1993; and for Benn, see Jad Adams, *Tony Benn: A Biography*, London, Macmillan, 1992.

Chapter 5

Democracy

Richard Jay

[D]emocracies have ever been spectacles of turbulence and contention; have ever been found incompatible with personal security and the rights of property; and have in general been as short in their lives as they have been violent in their deaths.

James Madison, in A. Hamilton, J. Madison and J. Jay,
The Federalist, 10 (1786), London, Dent, 45

The only cure for the evils of democracy is more democracy.

Al Smith (unsuccessful Democratic candidate
for the US Presidency in 1928) quoted in P. Green, ed.,
Democracy, New York, Humanities Press, 1993, 99

INTRODUCTION

In contemporary political debate, the idea of democracy is associated with two sharply contrasted ideological themes.

The first of these endows the politics of nation-states in western Europe, North America and Australasia with a unique moral and historical status. It celebrates what are variously termed Western or liberal democracies – or, more controversially, simply 'the democracies' – as pillars of freedom and fair government, generators of economic prosperity, and havens of peace, tolerance, and security in an otherwise dangerous and unstable world. The fragile character of these regimes has often been emphasised: the call to protect democracy from internal subversion, terrorism, international communism and other enemies is not unfamiliar. During the late 1980s, however, a triumphalist mood gripped large sections of intellectual and public opinion. World-wide trends towards greater political liberalisation and democratisation culminated in the collapse of the West's main rival, the Soviet Union. In an unprecedented display of 'People's Power', it was argued at the time, communism had been rejected throughout eastern Europe in favour of the political and economic freedoms associated with Western-style democracy. Reflecting upon this in a notorious essay, Francis Fukuyama announced 'The End of History'.[1] Historic ideological rivalries, he claimed, were giving way throughout the world to a recognition of the universal status of the liberal-democratic state.

Within liberal-democratic states themselves, however, there had emerged a second powerful theme strongly critical of their democratic credentials. On the one hand, it was claimed, ordinary citizens, and even the political leaders they elected, were becoming increasingly powerless in the face of wide-ranging social and economic changes – the globalisation of economic activity, the proliferation of unelected agencies at national and supranational level, the decay of traditional organisational and community bases for influencing decision-making. At the same time, ordinary citizens had developed increased expectations about the prospect of exerting control over their own lives, participating in the wider world of which they were part, and influencing key decisions. Alienation, disillusion with professional politicians and normal politics, and the search for alternative channels through which to exercise control over events were the inevitable consequences, therefore, of what was fashionably termed the growing 'democratic deficit'. This analysis pointed beyond the current structures of liberal democracy towards more radical conceptions of democracy and political participation.

DEMOCRACY AND IDEOLOGY

The absence of a common perspective upon central political concepts is a familiar one in this book. But the idea of democracy presents us with a particular difficulty. Many authorities are highly sceptical of characterising it as a distinct ideology at all, with the consequence that it is rarely accorded separate treatment in studies similar to our own.[2] Indeed, the absence of the '-ism' suffix of our other chapter titles should alert us to the fact that it denotes something rather different.

One aspect of this is that the primary use of the term is to identify, not a distinct system of ideas, but a particular form of government, or a way of taking collective decisions. Furthermore, the origins of the concept lie in a wholly different historical era and political culture from those in which the other ideologies were formed. 'Liberalism', 'fascism', 'feminism', and so on are modern labels coined for programmatic philosophies associated with major political movements which have emerged over the last two hundred years since the French Revolution. 'Democracy', by contrast, derives from the political discourse of ancient Greek city-states, especially that of Athens, in the fifth and fourth centuries BC, where it denoted a particular kind of regime, or political formation. It meant, literally, 'rule by' or 'power of' 'the people' – more accurately, perhaps, 'the common people'[3] – a definition developed later by the United States President Abraham Lincoln as 'government by the people, of the people, for the people'. The Greeks conceived of democracies as regimes in which citizenship, access to public office, and participation in the public debates and decisions of the Assembly were widely shared among 'the many' ('hoi polloi'), rather than being exclusively the preserve of 'the few' ('oligarchy'), the nobility ('aristo-cracy'), 'the one' ('monarchy') or an arbitrary ruler ('tyranny'). One clear difficulty arises from this background. Greek democracy was 'direct' democracy. In these small-scale, face-to-face, almost tribal, communities, individual citizens attended the Assemblies in person, voted on legislation as well as electing key state officials, and were annually eligible in rotation for appointment by random selection to other civic positions. These arrangements are a far cry from modern indirect or representative democracy, where the conduct of public affairs is entrusted to a minority of periodically elected politicians and a large professional bureaucracy, and ordinary citizens play a limited political role largely as spectators. This contrast clearly poses a problem: do we have here two different, but equally valid, conceptions of democracy? Or do modern systems simply not meet up to authentic democratic standards?

A second, rather different approach, emphasises the fact that, in today's world, democracy is almost universally accepted as a good thing. Ideologies, after all, purport to represent competing visions of the world, whereas, so it is often said, 'we are all democrats now'. This was not always so, as the quotation from Madison which heads this chapter suggests. Until round about the turn of the twentieth century, the weight of political and intellectual opinion was tilted decisively against the virtues of popular self-government. The common people were widely held to be too foolish, or too distracted by their immediate personal cares, to be politically competent. Democracy substituted quantity for quality, counting heads in place of attending to standards of right or truth, equality in place of natural hierarchies. A host of ancient Greek authorities, like the philosopher Plato, could be quoted to explain how appalling the brief experiment with democracy in ancient Athens had been, and how men of intellect, breeding and substance had been marginalised when politics fell into the hands of the unrestrained, uneducated mob.

Whatever the validity of these views, the total dismissal of democracy has today generally fallen out of fashion. The people are a permanent force in politics. By proclaiming the democratic credentials of their movement, policy or regime, political leaders aim to accupy the high moral ground. The question is no longer whether democracy is, in general, desirable, but what is the best or most authentic form, and whether political practice accords with democratic principle. During the years of the Cold War, debate flourished over whether the combination of representative government and capitalist economics in the West, or Soviet-style 'people's democracies' of the East, with their managed economies and one-party states, were more democratic. In the 1960s, the Canadian Marxist academic C.B. Macpherson initiated a fashion for explicating different *models* of democracy,[4] which have proliferated in the hands of subsequent writers. The American scholar Russell Hanson was moved to comment on the historical evolution of an idea that 'As the *value* of democracy became transcendent, its *meaning* was lost in the cacophony of different interpretations . . . '.[5] The implication of this stance is that the term has become a victim of ideological disarray, a legitimating principle without a common reference, if not, indeed, a mere rhetorical flourish in the war of political words.

Let us see, though, if we can establish some lines to avoid such extreme scepticism.

At the most general level, we may say that a democrat is one who rejects the belief that political legitimacy attaches to any exclusive group or caste because of their special talents, status or hereditary background. Legitimate authority springs, rather, from 'the many', the people. They alone are entitled to determine what political role they shall play, and who shall be held to speak in their name. The old adage *vox populi, vox dei* – the voice of the people is the voice of God – sets out this idea in an extreme form,[6] though we also need to explore what are the channels through which this voice is to be expressed, and what legitimises it as the authentic voice of the people. The source of today's democratic ideas lies in the challenge posed in early modern Europe to the dominant medieval belief in a hierarchical social order endowed by God for the better governance of his people, and its replacement with an understanding of social and political life as a human creation and activity designed to meet humanity's natural wants and civil interests. Since then, the cause of democracy has been advanced in terms of a number of differing principles and conceptions of political life, most of which are contentious, and which locate the idea of democracy within an ideological debate.

THE PURPOSES OF DEMOCRACY

In our earliest record of a debate about forms of government provided by the ancient Greek historian Herodotus, a committed democrat, Otanes by name, is made to say the following: 'The rule of the many . . . has . . . the fairest of all names, to wit, equality; and further it is free from all those outrages which a king is wont to commit.'[7] This sets out a link between democracy, equality and protection against the abuse of power – what in modern times we would call 'liberty' – but one that raises a number of problems.

Liberty

Whereas equality in relation to the making and application of law – *isonomia* – appears to have lain at the heart of ancient democratic ideas, it is the rhetoric of 'liberty' that provided the main thrust behind democratic claims in early modern times. And here we can identify at least two contrasting conceptions of liberty which have shaped modern thinking about the relationship between citizens and the state.

One has been called the *liberal*, or, perhaps less confusingly given the complex meaning of liberalism (see Chapter 2), the *protective* conception; the other is that of *civic republicanism*.

Liberal views of government arose in seventeenth century Europe and essentially treated the state as a mechanism for safeguarding the personal security, private rights and civil liberties of its members. They rested upon the belief that society was composed of autonomous, and largely rational, individuals whose main concern was the conduct of their personal religious, domestic and commercial affairs. Individuals

entered into a political community and placed themselves under
external authority for the limited end of protection against unwarranted
intrusions by others. Involvement in public affairs was a matter of
voluntary commitment, to be undertaken by those with special qualifications. Civic republicanism, by contrast, had been formulated during
the earlier Renaissance period. Its roots lay in the free commercial city-
states of northern Italy and north-west Europe, where it drew inspiration from the political cultures of the classical Greek and Roman worlds.
Rather than treating government primarily as a means of serving
private ends, it endowed the idea of a free state with positive moral
value as the expression of the common life and culture of its citizens,
celebrating their patriotic commitment to its public welfare as a positive
virtue. Personal liberty, and the fate of family, friends, and fortune,
were held to be bound up in the liberty of the state as a whole. As the
price of liberty was eternal vigilance, so a free state required active
engagement in public life, and personal commitment to acquire and
deploy the necessary moral and political qualities of good citizenship.

These two ideas intertwined in seventeenth- and eighteenth-century
European thought. They underpinned the emergence of British constitutional government, and provided the ideological impetus behind the
two great political upheavals of what came to be called the Age of
Democratic Revolutions, the American War of Independence (1776), and
the French Revolution (1789). Neither doctrine endorsed a thorough-
going form of democracy. They performed, rather, the negative function
of undermining the legitimacy of paternalistic and authoritarian principles of government, and the positive one of replacing them with
principles of self-government. In doing so, they extruded into modern
democratic thought a number of antinomies or tensions which remain
with us today. One, for instance, revolves around whether the central
value of democracy lies in safeguarding private rights, or in advancing
the public interest. Another is that between individualistic and collectivist (or, in the currently more fashionable term, communalistic)
accounts of the democratic state: are we to understand 'the people' as a
mere aggregation of separate persons with different, perhaps even
incompatible, aims? Or do they constitute an identifiable political
community with a distinct personality and purpose? A third lies
between the conception of the good citizen as a passive respecter of law
and the rights of others, and that of the active citizen engaged in the
public life of the state. These issues have often been seen to involve
questions about political size and complexity. Civic republicanism was

rooted in the idea of a homogeneous, small-scale, civic body of like-minded citizens, and it is arguable that, of these two visions, it is only the liberal perspective that is appropriate to today's large and heterogenous nation-states.

Equality

I have developed somewhat the significance of the idea of liberty. What, though, of equality? The pursuit of democracy is often linked directly to the pursuit of political equality. 'One man, one vote' (or, today more acceptably, 'one person, one vote' – universal suffrage) is widely regarded as the bedrock of democracy. Alongside it are the equal rights to stand for public office, and to public benefits arising from membership of the state. But it is arguable that this formal recognition of equal citizenship bears little relationship to what traditionally has been meant by equality in a democracy. The Greek philosopher Aristotle, for instance, treated democracy as a form of sectional class rule – 'rule by the poor' – who used their access to the political process, not to ensure fair and impartial government, but as an instrument of collective economic advancement. This was precisely what writers like Madison and other advocates of liberal and republican government feared. In a famous essay written in the 1820s and 1830s, *Democracy in America*, the French liberal writer, Alexis de Tocqueville (1805–59) reflected upon the cultural shift from the idea of liberty to that of equality which he observed in the rapidly democratising society of the United States, and the threat, as he saw it, that this posed to the liberal foundations of popular government.

Many radical democrats, in turn, have tended to dismiss the significance of formal equality in favour of substantive equalities which represent both the prerequisites of genuine democracy and the objectives of public policy in a democratic community – equal power, equal political resources, equal leisure time to pursue the political life, equal economic resources. One jaundiced early twentieth-century critic lamented that, 'In the hands of a democracy, taxation should be made the means of redressing . . . inequality . . . the preponderant class voting and spending money which another class are obliged to pay.'[8] As we shall see later, though, this general engagement in egalitarianism has become increasingly complex. Socio-economic class membership is no longer recognised as the sole fracture line within contemporary societies. Recognition is being extended to distinct cultural and ethnic groups, and there is an increasing understanding of the complex relationships of inequality and deprivation between, say, men and women, Afro-Caribbean, Asian and native white citizens, and other minority groups. Equal recognition and treatment for all arguably entails moving beyond simply individual equality of opportunity, or the levelling of social and economic goods. Instead, it entails the distinct recognition of groups and communities, with, perhaps, complex arrangements to ensure that all have a fair say and a fair share in society's deliberations and benefits.

Other public ends

These concerns with liberty and equality do not exhaust the case for democracy, which is also one for good, efficient and stable government. The classic proposition that, where hard decisions are to be taken, two heads are better than one easily extends to provide a rationale for widespread consultation and participation. The eighteenth-century philosopher Jean Jacques Rousseau (1712–78), for instance, saw democratic assemblies as forums in which that elusive commodity, the common good, might, through the wisdom and good sense of ordinary people, be pursued, and then given recognition through the expression of the general will. One of the most important calls for extending political rights in the nineteenth century came from reformers anxious to call 'the democracy' into political life in order to outweigh and overawe privileged social groups who blocked the state's capacity to formulate policy in 'the public interest'. The liberal economist J.A. Hobson delivered an eloquent assault upon non-democratic government.

> Dictatorship or oligarchic rule is always thrice cursed. It curses him who rules, by the poison of absolute power. It curses him who submits to such a rule by the loss of liberty that it involves and by the resulting injury to personality. And it curses government itself by depriving it of the contribution of the common man . . . . In order to be well-governed, the governed must themselves take part in government.[9]

The argument from personality, as Hobson puts it, or perhaps better 'human dignity', was given equally eloquent expression by the eighteenth-century philosopher William Godwin (1756–1836).

Democracy restores to a man a consciousness of his values, teaches him by the removal of authority and oppression, to listen only to the suggestions of reason, gives him confidence to treat all other men with frankness and simplicity, and induces him to regard them no longer as enemies against whom to be on guard, but as bretheren whom it behoves him to assist.[10]

The belief that democracy is associated with peace is one of its strongest appeals. Democracy, after all, replaces government by force with government by consent. Madison's statement at the head of this chapter represented an orthodox view of the inherent turbulence and violence of popular politics, but it is one that democrats have disputed. With Rousseau, in particular, arose the belief that war and conflict arise, not from the people, but from the failure to endow the people with a role in the life of the state. The German philosopher Kant, writing in the same era as Godwin, believed that war was primarily the outcome of dynastic and imperial ambitions, and that a world populated by free republics would curb international conflict: indeed, war between what we would commonly call democratic states is in fact extremely rare.

Votes and elections

In truth, though, democracies have very often originated in violence and revolution – the English Civil War of the seventeenth century, the French Revolution, and the American War of Independence, for instance. Today we are inclined to distance ourselves from these traumatic events, and identify the core of democratic politics with the idea of peaceful political change through the ballot box. Free elections and universal suffrage lie at the heart of democracy. President Abraham Lincoln sought to clarify this at the start of the American Civil War in 1861, when he stated that the greatest task of the American republic since its foundation was

to demonstrate to the world that those who can fairly carry an election can also suppress a rebellion; that ballots are the rightful and peaceful successor of bullets; and that when ballots have fairly and constitutionally decided, there can be no successful appeal back to bullets . . .[11]

This remains a continuing challenge for democratically-based regimes. Minority groups with strong ideological commitments and a deep sense of injustice may be tempted to resort to revolutionary violence or terrorism against them, ostensibly in the name of popular liberty. They invite the state to abandon what they claim is its thin veneer of reverence for democracy, and to reveal the iron fist which lies at the core of state power. This dilemma currently manifests itself in Northern Ireland, where the Republican movement has sought its aim of a united Ireland through a combination of constitutional means and armed struggle. The democratic logic of this is widely contested, and many appeals continue to be made for Republican leaders to 'choose, for all time, between the Armalite [rifle] and the ballot box. Either they are democrats or revolutionaries, not both.'[12]

Radicals, however, would argue that, even where the resort to violence is illegitimate, this should not delegitimise forms of direct action where normal political processes ignore or fail to satisfy powerful claims and grievances. The ballot box conveys the seductive belief that people exert power, whereas in fact the extension of the franchise has been as much a means of curbing and absorbing democratic demands as of meeting them. Civil rights marches, sit-ins, demonstrations, industrial strikes, extra-parliamentary lobbying – all these methods, which political establishments are likely to condemn, belong, not just to the historical process of creating modern democracy, but to its continuing vitality. For they place issues on the political agenda which might otherwise not appear, and they stimulate active political participation. At the same time, as one supporter of the democratic legitimacy of direct action has ruefully observed, those who issue such calls from the political margins are always likely to be challenged by a pertinent question: *Who voted for you?*

Modern democracies, as we observed, are markedly different from ancient Greek democracy where citizens made a much more direct and extensive contribution to collective decision-making, but where the citizen body was invariably restricted to native free-born male warriors, and where women, slaves, and resident immigrant labour were confined entirely to economic and domestic functions. Morever, even in modern times, the view of the franchise as a basic right has only recently displaced one that treats it as a privilege associated with contributing arms or taxes to the state, or with qualities of personal competence and rational judgement identified by professional qualifications, economic independence, or educational achievement. Victorian Britain assumed that the interests of women, the propertyless, recipients of charity, and non-white subjects of the Empire were adequately represented by their employers, husbands, or appointed officials. Blacks in the deep South of the United States, having been liberated from slavery in the 1860s, only overcame electoral obstacles as a result of the civil rights movement of the 1960s. Swiss women had to wait for the vote until the 1980s, South African blacks until 1994.

It is questionable, though, whether our modern belief in the right to vote either as a fundamental human right, or as one arising from mere residence in a state – that is, as a necessary correlative of the duty to obey the laws of the land – provides all that is required. Democratic government, even more than its competitors, it may be argued, needs citizens who are responsible, reasonable, and aware if the Madisonian slide into disorder is to be averted. Much of the historical rhetoric of democracy has been devoted to minimising the problem. The people, it is said, are inherently wise and commonsensical; their interests are universal, not sectional; their inherent virtue will materialise once the chains of oppression are lifted from their shoulders. Vigorous assertions of 'people's power' are welcomed as healthy and life-enhancing against the dead, stultifying hand of 'the system'. Those of a more sceptical disposition have tended to advise greater caution. For some writers, curbing popular enthusiasm by diverting it through organisational and constitutional channels represents the answer. The Liberal politician Robert Lowe presented another line when he observed that 'We must now educate our masters' after the 1867 Reform Act had enfranchised a large working-class constituency. Education in citizenship has been a perennial theme in twentieth-century discussions. In his essay *On Representative Government*, John Stuart Mill (1806–73) argued that the acquisition of the vote by both labour and women would of itself have an educative effect, stimulating electors to acquire in the long run a fuller understanding of public affairs. Yet he was sufficiently cautious also to recommend interim measures. He argued for multiple votes for the educated and professional classes rather than one person, one vote; proportional representation to fragment a working-class electoral majority; and a professional executive arm of government capable of controlling the independence of the popular chamber.

Achieving sensible outcomes and raising political consciousness is also traditionally held to be the function of debate and discussion, hence the importance of parliamentary chambers and free speech. Some recent writers have appealed to a distinct model of 'deliberative democracy'[13] to highlight the idea that the democratic process is not confined simply to registering personal preferences, but stimulates rational argument aimed at remoulding ideas, searching out common ground and dispelling hostility and distrust before the decisive, and divisive, act of voting takes place. A.D. Lindsay, the idealist philosopher, was one of many writers to articulate a communalist philosophy of democracy on this basis: 'What matters', he claimed, 'is not primarily what anyone wills, but the discovery of the spirit of the common life and what it demands . . .'[14] Such an emphasis upon process rather than outcomes imposes strong demands upon the time, energy and skills of ordinary citizens, and it is at least arguable that many might prefer snappier ways of reaching decisions than the prospect of engagement in interminable debate.

What is popular sovereignty?

The central principle that drove democratic demands along during the nineteenth century was that of the sovereignty of the people. At one level, this simply asserted the modern idea of government by consent, an act of authorisation by the people of their governing institutions. 'We the People of the United States . . . ordain and establish this Constitution' are the words opening that historical document enacted in 1787. More precisely, however, it attributed to 'the people' an inherent unity, and endowed them with the supreme unquestioned authority that was claimed by contemporary absolute monarchs. But what originally attached to 'the one' posed particular conceptual problems when it was attached to the common people – that rag-bag army of 'the many', the masses, the common people, the plebeians, the Third Estate. A shared identity tended to exist less in practice and more in the imaginings of theorists or the rhetoric of politicians claiming to act 'in the name of' the people. More dangerously, where unity was absent, the temptation to create it, if necessary by authoritarian and repressive means, always existed. The radical Jacobins who assumed the leadership of the French Revolution in 1792 are, in particular, accused of having set the precedent for the use of force and terror to impose the 'people's will' upon political dissenters and a recalcitrant pluralist society. The concept of popular sovereignty, indeed, is deeply suspect among those to whom the idea of liberty means the sovereignty of the individual, and most constitutional regimes with the exception of the USA locate sovereignty, not in the people, but in the constitution itself, or the key representative institutions (e.g. parliamentary sovereignty).

This suspicion of the concept has tended to be enhanced by its association with the principle of majority rule. While majoritarianism, resting as it does on treating all voters equally, appears to be the essence of democracy, it has always generated fears of majoritarian tyranny and the suppression of minority rights. Both de Tocqueville and J.S. Mill were horrified by this prospect. The practical and moral case for identifying 'the people' with the majority, and treating the majority view as decisive, has always carried most conviction where oppressive minorities deny effective rights to the majority, or where society reveals sufficient fundamental consensus and tolerance for minorities to accept that they will receive fair treatment, or might later convert members of the majority to their view by reasoned argument. In societies deeply divided on religious, class or communal grounds, the simplistic application of majority rule without safeguards of minority rights has invariably had a polarising effect, and proved disastrous for the maintenance of a democratic style of politics.

Representation

While representative government is, in one form or another, the universal form of democracy in the modern world, it remains, for many, an imperfect instrument. Looming over modern debates has been the example of ancient direct democracy – for some writers a terrible warning of fractious disorder, but for many radicals an inspiration and a possible template for new democratic forms. Many modern states, indeed, combine representation with features of direct democracy – referenda and plebiscites on important single issues, and opportunities for the recall or mandatory re-selection of elected representatives. Today's communications revolution opens up the prospect of many new ways of registering public opinion on contentious issues. The combination of television with other home-based electronic media allows the rapid dissemination of complex information, easy access to points where preferences can be registered, and the possibility of a speedy succession of votes on a range of issues. The next development beyond the television shopping so popular in the United States, it is claimed by some observers, will be 'tele-democracy'!

Proponents of a more radicalised democracy have always, though, sought even more direct forms of engagement than these. The public meeting, or factory-gate gathering, with their face-to-face debate and decision-making by a show of hands have often been seen as commanding greater legitimacy than the individual decision-making of the secret ballot (though they are invariably, also, the arenas most easy to manipulate and intimidate by powerful elites or activist minorities). Additionally, there are arenas beyond the sphere of electoral politics where more direct democratic decision-making is possible – in the family, schools, neighbourhood and community groups, the workplace, and in a clutter of small, self-generated voluntary groups and associations. How successfully citizen participation in matters of local importance satisfies demands for a role in the big political issues of the day is, though, open to question. Further, does such direct engagement not tend to discriminate in favour of the active, the energetic, the obsessively committed, those with economic security and leisure time, and against the more marginalised and those with other commitments? A number of feminist writers, for instance, have recently begun to question simplistic commitment to 'direct democracy', on the grounds that it skews the opportunity for participation towards males unencumbered with domestic and other commitments.

Some form of representation may therefore be inevitable: but what kind? Should our representatives be selected from territorial constituencies, as is currently the case with elected lower chambers, like the British House of Commons, in most countries? Or should the constituencies not, as corporatist theories propose (and as is partly the case with some upper houses like the Irish Senate), be defined in functional or institutional terms, with representation from collective interests such as organised labour, farmers, proprietors, consumer groups, churches? This, it has been argued, is far more meaningful in modern societies, where people's identity is far less bound up with their geographical locality and more with their social location, than it was in earlier times. Should not, indeed, decision-making bodies mirror the social background and identities found in society at large? The British Labour Party has traditionally complained that the low proportion of working-class MPs makes the House of Commons unrepresentative. In 1993, to a chorus of disapproval, the party attempted to increase the number of women in parliament by applying quotas to the selection of parliamentary candidates. Within many European countries, and increasingly in America and Britain, democratic representation has become connected to the concept of proportionality. To achieve fairness in decision-making, it is often claimed, elections and appointments to decision-making bodies should mirror the balance of social constituencies in the larger society, with women and minority ethnic and religious groups all gaining their 'fair share' of places. In the United States, this has begun to be increasingly contentious, because of its association with what is claimed to be an increasingly repressive culture of 'political correctness', hostile to individuality and personal achievement.

One way of dealing with these problems of representation is to focus instead upon expanding the forms of accountability which we mentioned earlier – by making elections more frequent, or, mandating representatives and subjecting them to recall. Yet, while highly democratic, these mechanisms may well cut across the need to ensure competence, consistency and impartiality in public decision-making. The British political tradition, for instance, embodies a long-standing doctrine that individual MPs should represent, not merely their constituents, but the public at large, being charged with responsibilites for serving the wider national interest. Edmund Burke, from a conservative perspective, and John Stuart Mill, from a liberal one, both advocated that MPs should be selected precisely for their wisdom and independence of judgement, not for their subservience to the views of their electors.

Democracy, capitalism and socialism

Eighteenth-century thinkers had pondered deeply on whether the emergence of a commercial society based upon the pursuit of private gain was compatible either with the social solidarity associated with republican government or with the public commitment required of active citizenship. The weight of ancient opinion was that it was not. But this essentially aristocratic idea gradually came under pressure as trade and capitalist accumulation became central features of the modern state. Political life was subjected to increasing embourgeoisement, and liberal individualism gained the upper hand. The development of critical socialist ideas, however, ensured that the original debate did not disappear, but was reconstituted in another guise.

Currently, as we have seen, the dominant view in Western societies supports a close association between democratic states and capitalist economies. Historically, it is argued, their development has gone hand in hand. Where economic free choice has been subordinated to systematic collective state planning, it has been at the price of democracy. One reason proposed for the link is that capitalism generates multiple centres of power, wealth and interest, which underpin diversity and competitive politics, blocking the central monopolisation of power and resources. The free market itself, Enoch Powell, among others, has said, is a supremely democratic device, registering individual preferences and aggregating them into social decisions through the price and market mechanisms in a highly subtle way. Capitalism is claimed, also, to create a sense of personal autonomy and independence, a central democratic value. Likewise, economic competition is a healthy incentive to innovation and flexible thinking, a barrier against regimentation and the conformity of the totalitarian state. At the heart of both capitalism and democracy is the idea of free choice, and democracy suffers wherever the attempt is made to subordinate the variety, tensions, and spontaneous processes of capitalism to an overarching vision of social equality, justice or order.

Socialist writers, by contrast, while acknowledging original linkages between liberalism, capitalism and democracy, would claim that the historic development of democratic institutions has entailed subjecting the operations of liberal capitalism to social and political regulation. Capitalism encourages concentrations of private political power, generates inequalities between economic winners and losers, and operates through economic laws which cannot be subjected to collective choice and control. It accentuates the distinction between the private and the public realms, and the values of competition and consumerism rather than public commitment and responsibility. By contrast, democracy goes hand in hand with some form of socialism. Both are concerned to ensure the accountability of private power to the general public, the self-management of society's common affairs, and the pursuit of common, collective goals.

I have looked at some of the important concepts traditionally associated with democratic thought. I now want to locate democratic ideas in an historical context to illustrate how the ideas were linked to changing contexts and political programmes – i.e. how they functioned ideologically – and to comment, briefly, upon relationships between democratic ideas and and democratice practice.

DEMOCRATIC IDEOLOGY: A BRIEF HISTORY

Democratic ideology is concerned with articulating the claims of the people to political power, and exploring the appropriate arrangements for its legitimate exercise and accountability. The historical bearers of democratic ideas, and the grounds on which democrats have based their case, have, however, varied: 'the people' have not been an historic constant, nor have their grievances and aspirations. And the transition from early modern agrarian societies, through the period of industrialisation, to today's so-called post-industrial societies has meant a substantial change in the understanding of what democratic politics entailed.

Radical democrats and Whigs

Modern democratic ideas were formed against the background of the emergence of liberal ideas in the seventeenth century. These ideas articulated the perspective of enlightened sections of the landed and commercial classes. Concerned primarily to establish constitutional restraints upon an overbearing royal executive, and to accommodate deep religious differences, the main writers of the time were not democrats, though they rooted political authority ultimately in doctrines of natural ('human') rights, the basic equality of man (if not necessarily of women) and the consent of the people.

The term 'democracy' first seems to be used in the constitution of the American colony of Rhode Island in 1641, which was declared to have a 'Democratical or Popular Government'. Within a few years of this, the Leveller movement in England was proposing a new 'Agreement of the People' to safeguard the birthright of free Englishmen and settle the constitutional question thrown up by the English Civil War. The Levellers sought a democratic republic, and appealed to the fashionable principles of natural rights to make their claims for political rights. Such rights might be exercised by those of independent mind and means, who could neither be bribed nor bullied into conferring their votes other than according to their conscience. Their proposals for annually elected parliaments, abolition of the House of Lords, the separation of Church and State, freedom of religious conscience and worship, manhood (or at least a small property) franchise, and a devolution of more power to local parish councils, together with a range of other guaranteed protections against the abuse of state power, provided a programme that was to reappear time and again over the next two centuries as the platform of democratic political forces.

These events in America and England closely paralleled each other.

Both were partly driven by the culture of dissenting protestantism, which elevated the independence and autonomy of the individual conscience, and rejected hierarchical ecclesiastic institutions in favour of egalitarian religious communities. They expressed, also, the economic and social aspirations of smallholders and traders in the face of the vigorous expansion and all-embracing power of big landholders and state-backed commercial corporations, and the aristocratic predominance in government. Expropriation and redistribution of wealth were not integral to this programme, though the removal of legal and contractual relationships which artificially preserved economic monopolies against free competition and free sale were of importance: these were to be property-owning democracies, where the 'little man' was to be protected in his freedom and independence against what later generations were to call the 'plutocrats'. These ideas gradually became disseminated in urban Britain among the small traders, craftsmen, cobblers, printers, weavers, and other forms of skilled labour, and were articulated by agitators such as Tom Paine in the years leading up to and beyond the revolutions in America and France inspired by the doctrine of the Rights of Man. The last great popular movement directly driven by the Leveller demand for mass political rights and political reconstruction was the Chartist movement which flourished briefly in the 1840s.

Establishment Whigs and Liberals were deeply suspicious of such autonomous political activity among the people. The franchise, they believed, should remain a privilege linked to indications of rationality and competence, or a stake in the country associated with the ownership of taxable wealth. They were also deeply enamoured of the idea of the balanced constitution. Civic republican thought, in particular, retrieved from ancient writers like Aristotle, Polybius, and Cicero ideas about the political arrangements that might counterbalance tendencies toweards either absolutism or class rule by the poor. British Whigs articulated the idea of a constitutional balance among the 'King, Lords and Commons' as the essential feature of British political life. In America, the Founding Fathers contrived the 'checks and balances' embodied in the United States constitution to curb the power of both the president and the popular assembly. Whigs not only took a pluralistic position on constitutional arrangements; they perceived civil society as an array of different interests and bodies – local communities, landed and commercial interests, religious bodies – which it was the task of representative institutions to accommodate and harmonise into a single nation. The great danger, as Madison famously warned in *The Federalist*, was the emergence of 'factions' – parties sharply divided on class lines, which would provide a recipe for civil war and the appropriation of property. This, he felt, could be curbed, not by recreating the small-scale homogenous republics of ancient times, but by incorporating the thirteen American colonies into a single republic in which variety and diversity would provide a counter to political polarisation.

The central political strategy of the Whigs, when faced with popular demands, was to seek to absorb the people within 'the pale of the constitution', appropriating the rhetoric of democracy while still containing it within orderly channels. Within this context, the beginnings of parliamentary reform in Britain during the early nineteenth century created a new breed of politician whose role was to widen the political arena, mediating between the world of established parliamentary politics and that of extra-parliamentary agitation and the promotion of single-issue politics. Daniel O'Connell, for instance, created in Ireland during the 1820s the first modern civil rights movement with the aim of securing Catholic representation in parliament, and for the next two decades alternated between parliamentary activism and mass agitation to gain further reforms for Ireland. For few of these leaders was democratic government itself a central political objective or issue of principle. Rather, democratic practice, in the form of widening political participation and consciousness among the masses, was a spin-off from the need to secure audiences and political clout for special interests or moral causes.

The revolutions in France and America established popular principles far more firmly in these countries than in Britain, but with very different implications. In America, the tradition of small-town politics and freehold proprietorship which survived throughout New England was bolstered by the continuous spread of free labour in the westward expansion of the rural frontier. Independence, rugged individualism, self-sufficiency, and hostility to big East Coast bankers and merchants, along with fear of the expansion of the southern slave plantations, sustained popular democratic ideology. Thomas Jefferson vitalised the radical spirit which had faded in the years immediately after the creation of the new republic in 1786 with the foundation of the Democratic Party, and under the presidency of Andrew Jackson between 1828 and 1836, virtually complete white male suffrage was achieved. In the rapidly growing cities, democratic politics created popular political machines like Tammany Hall in New York which, though often deeply corrupt, provided access to public jobs, housing, and welfare. Moreover, labour unions, though forming themselves in a hostile climate, soon found channels of access into the relatively open structure of politics and government. In the late nineteenth century, while their European counterparts were being seduced by the novel ideas of collectivism and state socialism, large sections of the labouring classes in America continued to articulate political demands for a fairer society in terms of traditional radical democratic ideology.

The consolidation of popular politics in America proved a rich and fertile field for European commentators. The French aristocrat Alexis de Tocqueville's brilliant conceptualisation of American life, *Democracy in America*, explored the emergence of a new egalitarian mass culture – homogeneous, conformist, antagonistic to individuality, moral leadership, and creative energy. His – somewhat partial, it must be said – observations profoundly affected J.S. Mill, as he set about devising political formulae and institutions that might contain the impact of mass democracy in Britain. Equally significant was the study by the British Liberal James Bryce, in *The American Commonwealth* (1888), which, among other things, explored the seedy world of the new urban party machines and caucuses, and showed that political corruption, rather than being swept away by democracy, was becoming institutionalised within it. In Britain in 1877 the first national political machine, the Liberal Federation, had been founded, an event which confirmed what was for many commentators the dispiriting fact that democracy, rather than posing a united popular front against the factionalism and partisanship of aristocratic and bourgeois politics, was in fact giving rise to the consolidation of mass-based competitive organisations.

In France, the revolutionary tradition gave rise to a somewhat different account of popular democracy. During the eighteenth century, Rousseau's *Social Contract* had brought the idea of a unitary democratic republic to its logical conclusion. Against the liberal idea of a large-scale nation-state founded on security of property and commercial activity, he presented an ideal of the small-scale popular republic, guided by a shared political consciousness aimed at the common good – what he termed the 'General Will' – which was expressed by the direct engagement of all citizens in the political life of the Assembly. In order that citizens should place common interests over personal and factional interests, he advocated public adhesion to a state religion, regulation of private moral behaviour, legislation to sustain broad equality of personal property and wealth and the inculcation of patriotic sentiments into the populace. These ideas played an important role in the French Revolution. The zeal with which the Jacobin leadership attempted in 1792–4 to suppress political opposition, and subordinate the complex world of French society to a single idea of the General Will through dictatorship and terror, has ever since given support to accusations that radical democracy is, by its nature, authoritarian, even totalitarian, for it favours conformity and uniformity at the expense of individuality, de-legitimises deviation from the popular will as sectionalism and self-interest, and bestows legitimacy upon self-appointed leaders who claim to understand the 'real interests' of the people better than they do themselves. The General Will, it has often been said since the days of Napoleon, frequently manifests itself in politics as the will of a General.

Many writers, in consequence, identify two distinct courses traversed by democratic traditions. One, an Anglo-American tradition, heavily influenced by liberal constitionalism, has the pluralistic idea of 'unity in diversity' (*e pluribus unum*, the motto of the USA) as its central theme – the other is a revolutionary French republican tradition, in which the unity and homogeneity of the people is expressed in the idea of 'the one and indivisible republic'.

The latter tradition, it is argued by many writers, has been transplanted into the official state ideologies of many modern one-party authoritarian populist regimes. Arguably, they shaped the ideas later formulated by Karl Marx about the dynamics of revolutionary class politics, in which the working class is perceived as acting in unison to dismantle the structures of bourgeois society and supplant sectional divisions with communal harmony. Vladimir Lenin pressed this one step further to provide a rationale for the 'democratic centralism' of the elite Communist Revolutionary Party in the Russian Revolution of 1917, violently overthrowing the freely elected Provisional Assembly, and imposing in its place 'the dictatorship of the proletariat', i.e. of the party leadership. Both the Peoples' Republics of eastern Europe, set up by the Soviet government after the Second World War, and many Third World single-party regimes established during the late twentieth century in the wake of national independence sought legitimacy in terms of these ideas. They grounded their democratic credentials in the successful overthrow of *anciens régimes* or oppressive colonial domination, appealing to the primacy of equality over personal liberty, and locating the dominant party as the true representative of peoples from among whom divisive class and sectional interests had been purged. Whether it is fair to blame Rousseau, with his nostalgia for small, static rural communities, for the sins of modernising authoritarian and totalitarian regimes remains a moot point. But as C.B. Macpherson argues, this model of democracy has a strong moral and aesthetic appeal in the face of the fragmentation, selfishness and inequality which many observers detect in modern Western states.

Democracy and the public interest

In the early part of the nineteenth century, sections of the middle class, particularly among professional administrators and experts in social and economic policy, attempted to associate themselves with democracy and identify a strategy for its development which was neither outrightly collectivist, nor linked purely to what they perceived as the outdated negative programme of petty-bourgeois radicalism. Jeremy Bentham (1748–1832) and James Mill (1773–1836), for instance, disengaged the case for democracy from its association with natural rights and republican constitutionalism, and founded it upon utilitarian premises. They perceived government as an instrument for serving the public interest and maximising public welfare. This they associated primarily with building the infrastructure necessary for private economic actors to take rational economic decisions in a modern, free-market society, and setting out public regulations and provisions, such as relief during unemployment and old age, where markets failed to deliver. Since, however, all individuals, they believed, were driven by self-interest, government could not pursue these objectives impartially where ruling classes and, in Bentham's words, 'sinister interests' predominated in public life. Only a foundation of equal voting rights could guarantee honest and impartial government, and ensure that all interests were equally recognised when legislators and public servants totted up the costs and benefits of different policy options. Democracy on this view therefore represented, not government by the people, but an effective system of public accountability to private citizens.

Bentham himself was attracted in later years to the radical programme of annual elections and a single legislature (though he backtracked on the principle of equal votes for women). Both he and James Mill, however, felt that greater political rationality resided within the 'middling rank' of society, and Mill, to the amusement of many contemporaries, was to argue that, so closely did the interests among the various sectors of society coincide, the electorate could be confined to propertied males over the age of forty. Moreover, many of the administrative reforms later carried out in their name, such as the introduction of the poor laws, were deeply resented among the working class. But their main significance lay in establishing a programme for the democratic state which imbued publicly accountable administrative elites and scientific experts with a political mission – that of identifying common strategic interests that straddled class barriers, subjecting over-mighty private interests to public control, and engineering social policy to maximise public welfare and maintain social unity.

In Britain, this philosophy of government became increasingly pervasive throughout the nineteenth century, and in the early twentieth forged a close liaison with social liberalism and managerial centralists in the Labour movement such as the Fabians. At the same time in America, the Progressive movement, led by former president Theodore Roosevelt, was articulating a similar call for *The New Democracy*. This was the title of a key progressivist manifesto, published in 1909, which called for active government to enhance the welfare of ordinary citizens, regulate the growing power of giant economic conglomerates and corporations, control the financial system, and weed out the corruption and inefficiencies of machine politics. The culmination of this move towards public responsibility came with the New Deal presidency of F.D. Roosevelt between 1932 and 1945, when a generation of college-educated planners, managers, and economic experts was introduced into the weak, fragmented machinery of American federal government, and initiated a dramatic programme of active government directed towards countering economic depression and mass unemployment.

Socialism, conservatism and democracy

Throughout most of the nineteenth century, socialists and conservatives were deeply critical of democracy. Socialist intellectuals in the main argued that the pursuit of merely political reforms giving the masses access to representative bodies was a distraction from the real task of effecting a fundamental transformation of moral and social relations. Writing in the 1840s, Karl Marx (1818–83), the most important theorist of revolutionary socialism, had believed that even a democratised bourgeois state was unable to provide an effective vehicle for pursuing the interests of the masses. Nor indeed, as many advocates of political reform believed, could it provide the means of harmonising differing interests in the face of the inequalities of capitalist society. Faced with growing social and economic problems, the labouring classes would increasingly be driven to politicise their industrial struggle against capital in a revolutionary form, and formal political democracy would disintegrate under the pressures of class conflict. The revolutionary working class, bearing the new universal ideas of socialism and communism, would usher in a society that transcended the old class divisions, destroy the rationale of the state as a mechanism of class rule, and mark the reappropriation of a genuinely self-governing community of equals.

As Geoghegan observes in Chapter 4, many later socialists rejected this analysis. The ideologists of social democracy declined to treat the ballot box and the electoral process as mere formalities. Rather than dismissing political rights as of no significance, they actively organised to consolidate the power of the working class at the polls and, in elected legislatures, to collaborate with 'bourgeois' political parties and state bureaucracies to secure a wider range of social and economic rights for the members of the working class. Their programmes were collectivist, not individualistic. They sought either state intervention to protect the economic interests of industrial labour against capital, or legal protection for their own collective bodies – the trade unions and co-operative societies – in the name of working-class solidarity.

By the mid-twentieth century, states had evolved, in Britain, Scandinavia, and other parts of Europe particularly, which embodied new conceptions of democratic politics. 'Social democracy' acknowledged the traditional role of national representative institutions as a 'forum of the nation' devoted to the accommodation of divergent interests. Yet it understood the function of this accommodation to be that of building legitimacy for the systematic erosion of unjustified social inequalities. Ultimately, said those who retained an essentially instrumental view of electoral politics, this process would evolve into a new socialist society that could afford to dispense with orthodox representative institutions. The more pragmatic increasingly came to reject the view that the legitimacy of parliamentary politics depended upon its capacity to deliver socialism, and to believe that electoral and parliamentary decisions provided a final arbitration of the legitimacy of the socialist programme.

Conservatives, likewise, despite a suspicion of the political competence of the masses which is instrinsic to their philosophy, have increasingly accepted the democratically expressed will of the people as a final arbiter. Throughout the nineteenth century, those liberals who shared similar doubts and qualifications were inclined to rely upon two devices to curb the possible excesses of popular government: constitutional protection of minority and private rights; and education to improve the level of voter rationality. Many conservatives, however, who recognised the irresistibility of democracy, or felt that the masses could be made to see that their economic and social grievances arose from liberal economic and social policies, adopted a more robust attitude to the possible relationship between the establishment and the masses. Lord Randolph Churchill, for instance, the father of Winston, and the *enfant terrible* of the Conservative Party in the 1880s, formulated the principles of a new 'Tory democracy': '"Trust the People"', he proclaimed. '. . . I have no fear of democracy. Modern checks and balances are not worth a brass farthing.'[15] Tory democracy was concerned to involve the people in the traditional institutions of the nation, not to lead them along the path of social and political transformation.

> The Tory democracy is a democracy that believes that an hereditary monarchy and hereditary House of Lords are the strongest fortification which the wisdom of man, illuminated by the experience of centuries, can possibly devise, not for the protection of Whig privilege, but of democratic freedoms . . . which adheres to and will defend the Established Church . . .

Crucial to this perspective on democracy was a faith in traditional institutions to engage the respect of the masses, the instinctive leadership capacities of a paternalistic social elite, and the natural deference of the working classes – classes which, because of their inherently conservative instincts, Benjamin Disraeli had once termed 'Angels in Marble'.

The persistence of deference into the age of democracy has not been the sole factor that has, in the event, restrained the inherent levelling and egalitarian thrust of democratisation in the modern world: judicious propaganda, appeals to national solidarity, and electoral pragmatism have all served to reconcile conservatism to democracy and *vice versa*. So, too, has the general bureaucratisation of political parties: 'Who says organisation says oligarchy', as the sociologist, Roberto Michels, commented in a famous early twentieth-century study of the emerging hierarchical structures in social democratic parties. However, British conservatism led the way, later followed by continental Christian Democratic parties, in forging a philosophy capable of surviving the advent of universal suffrage.

Democracy institutionalised

The basis of modern democratic politics was laid in the years immediately after the First World War. For the first time, competitive political parties secured mass electoral bases, and regimes began to call themselves democratic. Within a number of years, some of the more vulnerable had tumbled to the onslaught of totalitarian, nationalist and old-fashioned authoritarian politics. Economic and political turbulence, widening social divisions, rapid mobilisation and politicisation of untutored electorates proved too much. The understanding and commitment of much intellectual opinion was also weak: the ideological certainties and moral absolutism of fascist and communist movements had a stronger appeal than the compromises, accommodations and seeming ineffectiveness of government by pragmatic party politics. Other regimes survived; and in the period after the Second World War, new schools of thought started to explore the secret of their success, and to offer lessons for new democracies elsewhere.

The most significant development was the growth of an intellectual consensus that democracy was no longer an ideal, nor a second best to other utopias, but a political fact. Democratic theorising shifted from its earlier associations with radical change, constitutional theory or an ideal of popular self-government, towards a realist analysis of how successful democracies worked, and, in many cases, to an endorsement of their practices: 'Democracy *is* the good society in action', claimed the American political scientist S.M. Lipset. The burgeoning social sciences generated information that, in the main, appeared to confirm what was in effect a traditional Whig theory of politics. Three propositions received general assent. One was that large sections of the mass electorate lacked the qualities necessary to sustain democratic politics. They possessed limited knowledge of, or interest in, political affairs; held irrational and incompatible beliefs; and they lacked the necessary tolerance and readiness to compromise. To that extent, a fair degree of mass political apathy and non-engagement was highly desirable. A second was that democratic systems were primarily maintained by the consensual relationships among political and social leaders – elites –

whose understanding of, and commitment to, the rules of the democratic game were far greater than that of their followers. A third was the virtue of a rich and healthy plurality of organisations, identities, and cross-cutting allegiances within the infrastructure of civil society. Such networks provided powerful barriers against the instability and psychological disorientations of mass society, and the depradations of the totalitarian state.

How, then, if the people did not rule, were democracies governed? A number of models were developed which sought to capture the essential features. One focused upon patterns of *oligarchic party competition*. In *Capitalism, Socialism and Democracy*, published during the Second World War, the economist Joseph Schumpeter claimed that capitalism and socialism were nineteenth-century systems which were giving way to the professional management of a mixed and regulated economy. Democracy differed from other systems in that it had free electoral competition among oligarchic political parties, and was 'an institutional arrangement for arriving at political decisions in which individuals acquire the power to decide by means of a competitive struggle for the people's vote'. Politicians, Schumpeter claimed, were like businessmen, dealing in votes, and bidding for an electoral mandate to govern with as little direct hindrance from the electorate as possible. It was a picture that looked suspiciously like the British system, as the power of Parliament declined in relation to that of party leaders, ministers and their civil servants. A second model – that of *pluralism* – was forged in the more open, fluid and amorphous context of American politics. It focused rather more attention upon the rich array of pressure groups and secondary associations acting within the public arena to affect policy. These gave active citizens wider opportunities for participation and influence; they represented a diffusion of power inimical to centralised authority and majority tyranny; and they encouraged compromise and accommodation in decision-making. Whether these groups were always accessible to ordinary citizens, or had equivalent resources to exert comparable political influence, proved to be a rather controversial issue. A third model – that of *corporatism* – suggested that pluralist models understated the extent to which some interests were clearly more powerful and important to government than others, and were actively involved in the governing process. Corporatist writers pointed to the centrality of the triangular partnership in a number of European countries between organised labour, business, and government. This was integral to managing an advanced economy. It generated a consensus over the distribution of the social product, and ecouraged collaborative class relationship aimed at the common goal of economic growth. Finally, the *consociational* model of democracy offered an account of stable government in European societies deeply divided on religious, ethnic or ideological grounds. This emphasised the crucial importance of strong political leadership in controlling the affairs of the different communal blocs, and close elite collaboration, including power-sharing or 'grand coalition' executive arrangements, to ensure a fair allocation of public resources among them.

These models revealed differences between American images of diffused power and European ones of its centralisation. But the common theme was an identification of democratic politics with the collaborative relationships among leaders of powerful organised vested interests. Electors, rather than being regarded as integral to the democratic process, were marginalised: the public at large seemed of little consequence; considerations of stability seemed to override issues of freedom, equality and the public interest.

The breakdown of democratic consensus: participation and ungovernability

In the late 1960s and early 1970s, fundamental features of the post-war democratic world came under sustained attack from two directions.

On the one hand, *radical participationists* associated with what was loosely termed the 'New Left', attacked elitist theories for ignoring the source of democratic ideas – the demand for ordinary citizens to have influence over, and to participate in, decisions that affected their lives. Wider opportunities for participation were called for, and the active engagement of formerly apathetic citizens encouraged. The closed political shop was declared open. The call for greater participation was made primarily on behalf of social groups marginalised by the political process: blacks in the United States; gay rights and women's movements; students and young activists in the labour movements; minority parties like the Liberals in Britain, nationalist parties and Green parties. Participation was, though, demanded not merely within the organisation of the state, but the organisations of civil society: family, school, college, workplace, trade union, neighbourhood community, and so on. 'The personal is political', the slogan closely associated with feminism, gave clear expression to a view that traditional distinctions drawn between the 'private' and the 'public' worlds were inherently artificial. All social relationships formed a seamless web, and the principles operating in one impinged upon the rest. Democracy should not, therefore, be treated as a mere form of government, but rather understood as a universal culture, which required all human relations to be conducted on a basis of equality and active engagement. These themes emphasised the importance both of direct democracy and of direct action as legitimate and effective forms of political practice – not just as means of exerting power, but as forms of self-development and education.

Cutting completely across these views were *neo-liberal* and *neo-conservative* theories associated with the 'New Right' which strongly influenced the Thatcher governments of the 1980s in Britain. For them, the main problem of modern democracy was one of *ungovernability*, arising mainly from an excess of participation. It was believed that many current economic and social problems – including the accelerating growth of public expenditure and inflation, and rising taxes – arose from excessive expectations on the part of democratic electorates, uncontrolled expansion in the public bureaucracy, and the capacity of organised groups, not least the trade unions, to hold governments to ransom. Industrial squabbles and strident competitive demands upon the public purse proved able to drive government economic policies off course. This was accompanied by a decline in political authority. Increasing party competition encouraged party leaders to inflate their electoral promises without spelling out the consequential costs. The remedy, it was argued, for these destabilising forces was to be found in a new political strategy, that of depoliticisation. Voters' expectations of what governments could provide were to be deflated. Those functions of the state that could better be provided by private agencies, enterprises or individuals would be disbursed: collectivism was to be replaced by the market-place. And the authority of government was to be strengthened against pressures from the electorate and its own bureaucracy.

After participation?

The clash between these two views, and the impact of the Conservative governments of the 1980s, have continued to stimulate a wide-ranging debate about the purposes and future of democratic politics in Britain and elsewhere. The ideas of the New Right have largely triumphed, but not without raising substantial charges of authoritarianism from radicals, trade unionists and even the mainstream centre of politics. Social democracy, and the old balance of power in industry and the state, have been overturned. The promise of radical social change held out by the advocates of participation has been confounded. On the political left, a new regouping of political forces and intellectual arguments has been proceeding. The declining promise of socialism, and the need for Labour and Liberal politicians to find new ground from which to challenge the dominance of conservatism, have stimulated interest in political reform.

One area of debate is over the character of Britain's unwritten constitution, and the adversarial character of its electoral and parliamentary politics. An 'elective dictatorship' was how Lord Hailsham described the system in 1976. In 1988, the Charter '88 group was formed to campaign for a written constitution. This would involve the reform of Parliament and the electoral system, devolution and a stronger local democracy, a Bill of Rights, and other mechanisms. All of these would be designed to modernise an antiquated political system increasingly unsuited to managing national affairs in the age of democracy, to define and contain the power of government, and to encourage a consensual, rather than a confrontational, style of politics.

A second issue is concerned with the concept of citizenship. The debate about participation has increasingly been channelled into one about the relative merits of active and passive conceptions of citizenship (see above, p. 123) . A further substantial issue is the extent to which the rights of citizens embrace social rights – that is, whether it is the responsibility of the community as a whole, represented by the state, to ensure the delivery of universal social benefits and standards of welfare to its citizens. In the post-war world, this was widely accepted. It was given philosophical expression by the social theorist T.H. Marshall, in a book published in 1949 entitled *Citizenship and Social Class*, where he represented the newly founded welfare state as the culmination of an evolutionary historical process involving the progressive expansion of our conception of citizenship from the promotion of civil to political and finally social rights. This view is now suspect, not least as an account of history, but mainly because of its open-ended fiscal implications, and because it is accused of having detached individual rights from the personal responsibility and correlative duties to society that good citizens should display. John Major's Citizens' Charter, for instance, is concerned, not with distributive issues of social justice and the level of public welfare, but with the quality of service to consumers of public services, and it aims to promote a view of citizen–state relations that is much closer to that of an economic exchange or contractual relationship. Against this, the political left, faced with the declining appeals of class politics and the language of socialism, has resorted to encouraging a fuller conception of citizenship that will support the case for protecting public services, and harness together the disparate claims of under-privileged, marginalised or undervalued groups for their 'rights' – racial and cultural minorities, women, the unemployed, the aged, and so on.

A final aspect of these new concerns is the role of political parties. The development of democracy as a form of government has been intimately bound up with the growth of party politics and their role in mediating between citizens and the state. Parties, however, according to the new democratic theorists, are under challenge. Modern citizens are increasingly disinclined to identify with party labels, or with the great clashes of religious and class identity that gave rise to modern democratic debate. They are more instrumental and sceptical in their judgements on political leaders. They are far more willing to initiate autonomous political action, and to channel their energies into campaigns and movements that capture their personal imagination and interest – what commentators have called 'new social movements'. Political life is therefore set to become far less organised from the top down, and far more based upon a pluralism of initiatives from below.

It is fair to say that these views have yet to secure wide popular support. They mainly extrapolate from the values and concerns of the educated professional middle classes, and minority groupings, who increasingly set the tone of political debate in the media and radically inclined political movements. In the 1980s, substantial efforts went into political reconstruction on the left under the banner of a new democratic movement – 'rainbow coalitions', aimed at creating majorities out of minority causes and groups, were the political flavour of the decade. It remains unclear as yet whether the basis of a new form of politics is being laid down.

CONCLUSION

It would be comforting to conclude on an optimistic note, to say that faith in the democratic way of life has never been stronger than at the current moment in history, and that one could look forward to its further extension throughout the world. Evidence from recent years might well seem to support this view. Democratic principles provide a widely accepted touchstone of political legitimacy; movements dedicated to building democratic societies have proliferated; many militaristic and authoritarian regimes have yielded to democratic successor states. The ideologies of liberalism and conservatism have come to terms with popular government, while the traditional language of socialism has, in recent years, virtually been displaced on the 'progressive' left wing of politics by terminology and concerns drawn from the classic traditions of democratic thought – citizenship, civil society, pluralism, popular sovereignty. A number of correctives need to be applied to this picture.

One is that such optimistic views of democratic progress have more than once been dashed aside: the inter-war period shows how vulnerable states may be to economic dislocation, racial and national assertiveness, and the growth of chiliastic movements of the left and right. Today, in Europe – west and east – we can see these familiar scenarios emerging, placing similar pressures upon the democratic process. If we move beyond these regions to the chaotic states of sub-Saharan Africa, or the clash between Islamic religious fervour and shaky authoritarian states in the Middle East, the picture appears even less rosy.

Secondly, there is no consensus still upon what lies at the heart of the democratic project, and therefore what principles and practices democrats are to promote. Is it to ensure the direct exercise of the people's sovereign will, fairer competition among political parties, consensual elite accommodation, an enrichment of the institutional life of civil society, or the deconstruction of centralised authority and a systematic empowerment of society's marginalised, alienated, and oppressed? All these remain intellectually plausible candidates. Nor is it yet clear that the recently recreated partnership between economic liberalism and political democracy, which has driven the political agenda over the last two decades, is either inherently stable or has achieved widespread acceptance. The disintegrating fabric of increasingly privatised, individualistic and fragmented societies may well, as orthodox left-wing opinion suggests, point towards either a renewed collectivism or increasingly authoritarian government.

Finally, the scope for endowing ordinary people either with effective power to take key decisions affecting their lives, or to ensure that decision-makers are accountable, is growing constantly narrower. The globalisation of economic, cultural and social processes, the consolidation of world-wide business conglomerates, and the development of interdependent relationships through vast networks of inter- and supra-international organisations, proceeds at an ever faster pace, creating structures and forces far beyond the capacity of ordinary citizens to influence, and increasingly beyond the control even of sovereign states. Indeed, the very concept of sovereignty, and hence of popular sovereignty, is increasingly meaningless. Contemporary theorists like David Held have talked of the consequential need to project our democratic aspirations beyond the nation-state. But this may be just as unrealistic as the hope expressed by Rousseau over two hundred years ago that economic and social 'progress' could be reversed, and that humanity would learn to live on simpler terms in small, free republics where genuine popular self-government could obtain.

NOTES

1 F. Fukuyama, 'The End of History?', *The National Interest*, 16, 1989.
2 E.g. Andrew Vincent, *Political Ideologies*, Oxford, Blackwell, 1992.
3 *Demos* originally referred to a rural territorial unit, like the 'commune' of medieval Europe (and France today), from which the concept of 'communism' derives.
4 C.B. Macpherson, *The Real World of Democracy*, Oxford, Oxford University Press, 1966.
5 'Democracy', in T. Ball, J. Farr and R. Hanson, eds *Political Innovation and Conceptual Change*, Cambridge, Cambridge University Press, 1989.
6 See Francis Lieber, 'Vox Populi, Vox Dei', *On Civil Liberty and Self-Government*, Philadelphia, J.B. Lippincott, 3rd edn 1877.
7 *History*, New York, 1928, 177.
8 W.E.H. Lecky, 'Old Age Pensions', *Historical and Political Essays*, London, 1908, 300.
9 J.A. Hobson, *Democracy*, London, John Lane, 1934, 76–7.
10 *Enquiry concerning Political Justice*, volume 2, Toronto, 1946, 119.
11 Quoted in B.E. Brown, *Great American Thinkers*, volume 2, New York, Avon, 1983, 64.
12 Editorial, *Belfast Telegraph*, 31 December 1993.
13 D. Miller, 'Deliberative Democracy and Social Choice', in D. Held,

ed., *Prospects for Democracy*, Cambridge, Cambridge University Press, 1993.

14 *The Modern Democratic State*, London, Oxford University Press, 1943, 241.

15 R.J. White, ed., *The Conservative Tradition*, London, 1964, 228–30.

FURTHER READING

Among an enormous recent literature, the most useful general texts are: J. Lively, *Democracy*, Oxford, Blackwell, 1979; A. Arblaster, *Democracy*, London, Open University Press, 1987; D. Held, ed., *Prospects for Democracy*, Cambridge, Polity Press, 1993; G. Duncan, ed., *Democratic Theory and Practice*, Cambridge, Cambridge University Press, 1983; K. Graham, *The Battle of Democracy*, Brighton, Harvester Wheatsheaf, 1986; G. Sartori, *The Theory of Democracy Revisited*, Chatham, N.J., Chatham House Publishers, 1987; R. Dahl, *Democracy and its Critics*, New Haven, Yale University Press, 1989. P. Green, ed., *Democracy*, New Jersey, Humanities Press, 1993, is a collection of short readings.

The following focus particularly on different forms or 'models' of democracy: C.B. Macpherson, *The Real World of Democracy*, Oxford, Oxford University Press, 1966; D. Held, ed., *Models of Democracy*, Cambridge, Polity Press, 1987; D. Held and C. Pollitt, eds, *New Forms of Democracy*, London, Sage, 1986; J. Drysek, *Discursive Democracy*, Cambridge, Cambridge University Press, 1990; P. Hirst, *Associational Democracy: New Forms of Economic and Social Governance*, Oxford, Polity Press, 1993.

On the complex relationships between liberalism and democracy, and the idea of citizenship: C.B. Macpherson, *The Life and Times of Liberal Democracy*, Oxford, Oxford University Press, 1977; B.S. Turner, *Citizenship and Capitalism*, London, Allen and Unwin, London, 1986; D. Heater, *Citizenship: The Civic Ideal in World History, Politics and Education*, London, Longman, 1990. For participatory and radical critiques of liberal democracy: C. Pateman, *Participation and Democratic Theory*, Cambridge, Cambridge University Press, 1970; B. Barber, *Strong Democracy: Participatory Democracy for a New Age*, Berkeley, University of California Press, 1984; C. Mouffe ed., *Dimensions of Radical Democracy*, London, Verso, 1992.

For the 'governability' of democracy: M.J. Crozier, S.P. Huntington, J. Watanuki, *The Crisis of Democracy*, New York, New York University

Press, 1975; C. Offe, *Contradictions of the Welfare State*, London, Hutchinson, 1984.

Relationships between democracy, markets, and business corporations are considered in: D. Usher, *The Economic Prerequisite to Democracy*, Oxford, Blackwell, 1981; D. Miller, *Market, State and Community*, Oxford, Clarendon Press, 1990; C. Pierson, *Beyond the Welfare State?*, Cambridge, Polity Press, 1991; R. Dahl, *A Preface to Economic Democracy*, New Haven, Yale University Press, 1986. On the relationship with feminism: S. Rowbotham, 'Feminism and Democracy', in Held and Pollitt, eds, *New Forms of Democracy*, London, Sage, 1986; C. Pateman, *The Disorder of Women*, Cambridge, Polity Press, 1990; A. Phillips, *Engendering Democracy*, Cambridge, Polity Press, 1991. For a flavour of debates within Eastern Europe: J. Keane, *Democracy and Civil Society*, London, Verso, 1988; P.G. Lewis, ed. *Democracy and Civil Society in Eastern Europe*, London, Macmillan, 1992. On the impact of information technology: I. McLean, *Democracy and New Technology*, Cambridge, Polity Press, 1990.

Chapter 6

Nationalism

Richard Jay

Where the sentiment of nationality exists in any force, there is a *prima facie* case for uniting all the members of the nationality under the same government, and a government to themselves apart. This is merely saying that the question of government ought to be decided by the governed.

> J.S. Mill, *Representative Government*, London, Dent, 1910, 360–1

We have created our myth. The myth is a faith, it is a passion. It is not necessary that it be a reality. It is a reality by the fact that it is a good, a hope, a faith, that it is courage. Our myth is the Nation, our myth is the greatness of the Nation! And to this myth, to this grandeur, that we wish to translate into a complete reality, we subordinate all the rest.

> Benito Mussolini (1922), quoted in H. Finer, *Mussolini's Italy*, New York, 1935, 218

INTRODUCTION

The term 'nationalism' conveys a number of different meanings. Often it denotes a state of mind,[1] a consciousness manifested by members of a group that they belong to a particular nation, an awareness of sharing a common culture or identity, a sense of fellow-feeling towards those recognised as co-nationals. This may involve public displays – exhibitions of group solidarity against outsiders, a display of exclusive emblems and symbols, the singing of patriotic songs, the pursuit of national interests in preference to other interests and values. Some writers associate nationalism with a universal human need to 'belong' or 'identify'; some with nasty psychological attitudes towards out-groups. Others, by contrast, have treated the 'nation' as a distinctive and singularly modern political phenomenon. Nationalism involves the historic proclivity over the last two hundred years for redrawing the map of the world to establish states with a recognised seat in the General Assembly of the United Nations. Nationalism also, however, often carries with it negative overtones, sometimes of the most subjective kind: *my* enthusiasm for the English team is merely decent patriotism, but *those* football hooligans exemplify the nastiness of nationalist bigotry. In the mid-1990s, it is all to easy to associate nationalism with ethnic hatred and the killing fields of Bosnia and Northern Ireland.

While these accounts all point to important different dimensions to the subject, an exploration of nationalism as *ideology* requires us to narrow the field of inquiry somewhat. We can look at it as a body of ideas from two perspectives.

Nationalism can be treated, first, as a *universal* claim about the legitimation of the modern state. It was, as one famous account puts it, 'a doctrine invented in Europe at the beginning of the nineteenth century' which 'holds that humanity is naturally divided into nations, that nations are known by certain characteristics which can be ascertained, and that the only legitimate type of government is national self-government'.[2] This programme was intimately linked to the philosophical and political ideas of the late Enlightenment, and to the tumultuous events of the French Revolution and the succeeding wars between 1789 and 1815. It posed a fundamental challenge to predominant modes of thought which grounded political authority in heredity, divine right or natural law, but which made little explicit connection between the idea of a political community and national identity or national territory. Nationalism, however, posited the 'nation' as the locus of political right. The nation commanded primary political commitment and allegiance, and its freedom, unity, integrity, and purity provided the basis of political action. It required the structures of confederacies, principalities, 'stateless' feudal and tribal domains, and empires to be redrawn in accordance with these new requirements, and established a specific political model – that of the *nation-state* – as a universal norm.

By the end of the nineteenth century, this doctrine had become enshrined in a general *principle* – that of the right of all nations to self-determination. In this form it was accepted in the aftermath of the First

World War by the victorious powers at the Versailles peace negotiations and by the new revolutionary leadership in Russia as one of the foundation stones of a new European political order. Since then, it has been incorporated into the Charter of the United Nations. This locates nationalism, at one level, within a corpus of broadly liberal and democratic principles, but does not guarantee that nationalists will necessarily further these ends. The political complexion of the United Nations is, to say the least, varied. And in the 1930s, Adolf Hitler appealed to the principle as a means of securing German unification 'so as to unite all the most valuable racial elements in the nation . . . for the purpose of raising the German nation . . . to a dominating position'.[3]

Secondly, nationalists set out *particular* claims in discourses about their own nations. Here we are dealing, not with national*ism*, but a multiplicity of national*isms*. Nationalists not only articulate a universal message – what some authors might call a 'meta-narrative' – but also narratives tied to the specific and unique circumstances of the nation whose cause they espouse. These identify its legitimate boundaries and membership, and set out its claims. They trace its history, the key dates in its development, its enemies, allies, patriots, martyrs and traitors. Its culture, character and traditions, what values it stands for, are articulated, as well as its future goals – perhaps even, to use a popular phrase from nineteenth-century America, its 'manifest destiny'. The intelligentsias of nationalism have tended to comprise few great philosophers, but more than their fair share of poets, musicians, antiquarians, and linguists, who have explored and created the cultural artefacts that allegedly give meaning to the life of the nation. It is in this area that nationalism appears, not as a principle that may be rationally affirmed, but as something irrational, bound up with feelings, emotions and passion.

The most important forces stimulating nationalist ideas can, perhaps, be summed under three headings: the idea of the nation-state; the principle of popular sovereignty; and Romantic theories of culture. I shall consider each of these in turn.

THE NATION-STATE

The historical formation of the nation-state antedated the development of the formal doctrines of nationalism. Throughout western Europe in the late medieval period, dynastic rulers and political grandees began to consolidate territorial control, to preside over increasingly integrated economic, taxation and legal systems, and to inculcate greater homogeneity of religious, linguistic, and cultural forms between the dominant elites and wider sections of society. This process of political and cultural integration, or 'nation-building', led men and women to begin to conceive of themselves in terms of a national identity defined by their political allegiance, rather than in terms of the communal, ethnic or tribal origins from which they came – as 'English' or 'French', not Saxons, Gascons, or Northumbrians.

The consequences of such nation-building processes were, and are, complex. First of all, they set in train competitive relationships with other states. Nation-states in Europe proved to be robust political experiments in cultural, military and economic terms. There were immense advantages to be gained in stealing a march on neighbouring states, and powerful incentives for neighbours to flatter their opponents by imitation. The French Revolution dramatically accelerated this process of nation-building by mobilising the people against internal and external enemies, disseminating patriotic rhetoric, rebuilding governing institutions, creating citizen armies and primitive forms of national economic and social planning. Strategists in neighbouring countries of very different political persuasions were stimulated into reacting. The Prussian military reformer August Gneisnau said of the French Revolution that it had

> set in motion the national energy of the entire French people. If other states wish to re-establish the balance of power, they must open and use these resources. They must take over the results of the Revolution and so gain the double advantage of being able to place their entire national energies in opposition to the enemy and of escaping from the dangers of revolution.[4]

Not only are there external dialectical processes which create imitation, there are also internal ones. As the sociologist Ernest Gellner has argued, the consolidation of 'official' cultures – a national language of government, a core educational curriculum, established religions, a 'great tradition' of national literature – creates second-class citizens of these who cannot, or will not subscribe to it, or who are blocked from doing so. Grievances arising out of self-perceived oppression or marginalisation will stimulate men and women to treat their cultural identity, not as the mark of Cain, but as a badge to be worn with pride. Self-exclusion, isolation and separation, as well as dialogue and the search for cultural accommodation and equal treatment of different traditions, stimulate political action. And it may, though not always, become a focal point around which claims for self-determination may be made.

Finally, these relationships set up complex patterns between ideas of tradition and modernity. The 'Janus-faced' quality of nationalism, as it is often called – the capacity to look both to the past and to the future – is intrinsic to its very nature. The dynamic power of the modern nation-state is such that the cultural gap between peoples – what the Victorians, with their robust view of the world, termed 'levels of civilisation' – can rapidly widen. The unqualified defence of tradition is rarely successful and stimulates attempts to harness the new and the old together. The secret of success lies in summoning up the ancient tribal gods to sanctify adopting the weapons of the oppressor. Appealing to what is primeval and primordial is hailed as the bedrock on which the nation is to rise again.

THE SOVEREIGNTY OF THE PEOPLE

One writer has claimed that nationalist ideology is little more than 'the application to national communities of the Enlightenment doctrine of popular sovereignty. The rest of nationalist ideology is rhetoric.'[5] Though oversimplified, this correctly identifies one inspiration behind modern nationalism in the liberal and radical principles of the eighteenth century which founded the legitimacy of government upon the rights of the people and government by consent. The *Declaration of the Rights of Man and of Citizen* (1789) identified the 'people' with the 'nation', stating that 'the principle of sovereignty lies in the Nation', while the revolutionary ideologist, the Abbé Sieyès, claimed:

The Third Estate embraces everything belonging to the nation. In every free nation, and every nation should be free, this is the only way of ending differences concerning the constitution. Not by turning to the notables, but to the nation itself.

The appeal to nationality in this sense can be looked at in two ways. Firstly, it embodies an extension of the view held by eighteenth-century republican thinkers, like Rousseau, that the liberal individualist theories of government developed by John Locke and others failed to account for the allegiance and bonds of solidarity that members of a political community did, and should, feel towards each other and the state itself. The cement that bound society together was 'patriotism', they believed. But if patriotism was to be a reality, it must involve, not only loyalty to the state, but the enrichment of emotional ties among those who are to be bound together in the new common enterprise of the democratic community. Secondly, at the pragmatic level, those who took up the cause of liberty were invariably minorities in a sea of indifference, rural ignorance, and hostile, imperial states. Those who advocated political rights in these circumstances necessarily had to weld together popular alliances that cut across existing political and social divisions to counterbalance the power of their rulers. A vital part of this was defining a wider identity which embraced and transcended differing social classes, ethnic groups, tribes, and religious congregations. This was the 'nation' – all those, that is, who, irrespective of their divisions, stood for the cause of the people.

Secular radicalism appropriated, but rarely invented, the language of the nation, which had historically been applied to the 'political nation' – the 'notables' in Sieyès' phrase – whom tradition endowed with authority. And conservatives were not slow to reconceptualise this language in the context of defending established principles of government against their opponents. Edmund Burke, for instance, challenged the French revolutionary idea by identifying the English nation as an historically evolved community of unequally located classes, organised around its traditional leaders and constitution. Disraeli made clear that the People and the Nation were entirely distinct: 'Nations in a state of dissolution become a people', he stated. Once the concept of the nation had been identified, that is, the question of who provided its legitimate representatives and leadership became open to debate. Neither the left nor the right had any inherent monopoly over the rhetoric and symbols of national identity, and the idea of the nation, therefore, became ideologically contested.

ROMANTICISM

The relationship between nationalism and the concept of *culture* is a controversial one. Some writers would differentiate sharply between ideologies of *political nationalism*, whose aim is to secure political rights and citizenship, and *cultural nationalism*, which is concerned with protecting or promoting cultural symbols and values. But the line is not clear cut. In a broad sense, nations are human associations defined in cultural terms. Culture is a badge of identity. Nationalism in general associates peoples, cultures and states as part of an integral whole. It is cultural clash, generated by political and economic change as well as by changes in ideas, language, and consciousness, that partly lies behind it. But there are also those who have a professional stake in creating or manipulating cultural artefacts – theologians, poets, musicians, artists, writers, linguists, priests. And it is their concern that has given rise to a different set of themes within nationalism.

In the mid-eighteenth century, fashions in cultural and intellectual life began to change dramatically. A reaction set in both to the contemporary philosophies of materialism, rationalism and utilitarianism, and to the ornate, contrived styles of high culture, exuberantly displayed in the great courts and houses of Europe. This issued in the cultural and philosophical movement that came to be termed Romanticism. Romanticism emphasised the heroic rather than the conventional; the soul rather than the body; the emotional and instinctive; the heart, not the head. Its targets were the spiritual barrenness of the 'machine age'; the crushing of individuality by conformity; the soulless structure of the utilitarian state; the ethical limitations of secular, materialistic doctrines embodied most strikingly in the new 'dismal science' of political economy. Authenticity was to be found in nature and the mores of ordinary folk. The language of the people – or, if it was fragmented or incomprehensible, what linguists could cobble together as a coherent literary vernacular – was replete with new meaning and significance. History and tradition were more valuable guides to authentic action than universal reason. Virtue was to be found in the past, whether in primitive communities, the pagan Dark Ages, or the civilisation of the medieval world before modernity came along to corrupt and corrode it.

The original breeding ground for cultural nationalism was Germany. Its progenitor, Johann Gottfried von Herder (1744–1803), deeply resented the increasing adoption by Germany's social elite of the French language, Parisian fashions, and, as he saw it, the shallow philosophies of the French Enlightenment. These were displacing the great traditions of philosophy, theology, and literature conveyed in the German language. Every language, he believed, embodied the distinct spirit of a people (the *Volkgeist*), and every people had a distinct contribution to make to human civilisation. Just as God was One, but his manifestations were many, so the human race He had created was a unity based on diversity. Linguistic and cultural erosion or domination (even in relation to the Slav peoples, so despised in Herder's native Prussia) were thus contrary to God's will in creating 'nations' as natural units of humanity. When French armies defeated Austria and Prussia in 1806–7, philosophers like Johann Fichte (1762–1814) in his *Addresses to the German Nation* identified this doctrine with a political programme. The distinct culture expressed through the German language could be preserved only by unification of those who spoke it within a state that could match that of France.

Nationalism was in a unique position to harness the Romantic spirit. In the freedom and life of the nation could be found a repository of moral values and emotional commitment, filling the gap vacated by traditional religious faith. The nation provided a spiritual power against materialism and secularism, and a source of commitment in a sceptical and apathetic age.

As cycles of intellectual fashion have come and gone since the early nineteenth century, so a succession of neo-Romantic, post-Romantic, and post-modernist movements have resurfaced, reinvigorating the association between culture and politics, personal and collective identity, and the nature of the state. The 1980s and 1990s have proved to be such a time: modernistic philosophies of unlimited economic growth, abstract planning and technocratic manipulation have been subjected to sustained intellectual assault. The politics of identity is once more fashionable.

But cultural nationalism has always revealed great variations and deep ambivalence. One is the relationship between 'high' and 'low' culture – the language of the 'real' people, and that which is projected on to the public stage. W.B. Yeats, the leading figure of Ireland's literary renaissance in the 1890s, for instance, condemned 'the more ignorant sort of Gaelic propagandist, who would have nothing said or thought which is not in country Gaelic'.[6] Cultural nationalism often breeds moral absolutism and poor political judgement: 'I could never be bothered wi' [John] MacCormick', said the revolutionary Scottish poet, Hugh MacDiarmid, of his fellow nationalist. 'He believed in practical politics and had no time for art and culture. Art and culture means everything to Scotland. Practical politics, as everybody knows, is rubbish.'[7] Finally there is a tension between the kind of cultural pluralism espoused by Herder and cases where a belief in the values implicit in one's own culture becomes the basis of oppression.

THE CONCEPT OF THE NATION

Nationalists, therefore, have presented the nation as a focus of human life to serve a wide array of political projects: political mobilisation, democracy, defence of the realm, economic growth, the conservation of tradition, spiritual regeneration, *inter alia*. What, then, is a nation? How is it to be differentiated from other kinds of human community?

First of all, to call a people or community a nation is not merely to describe it, but also to *recognise* its legitimacy as an autonomous political actor. The United Nations comprises the states of those peoples whose sovereignty and right to self-determination are acknowledged by the international community. National minorities may be held to have rights; but, as the United Nations Charter affirms, these are minority rights, not rights to self-determination. The complete denial of nation-hood involves resorting to a different set of concepts: we refer, not to nationalism, but to communalism, tribalism, sectarianism, or ethnic politics. Nations, therefore, are not *mere* ethnic groups, but actual or potential political communities. What, though, makes them ripe for such status? What makes the appeal to self-determination legitimate?

The nineteenth-century French writer Ernest Renan took one view: the nation was 'a soul, a spiritual principle', possessed of a conscious-ness akin to 'a daily plebiscite of the people'. This account carries the republican theory of active citizenship to an absurd conclusion, but makes the point effectively that the acquisition of national self-consciousness and a national personality is central to nationalists' overall objectives. In reality, since few peoples reveal such psychic unity, most nationalists have to deal with humbler clay. They seek, amidst the complex interactions and relationships of human societies, lines and fissures to provide the definitive, objective criteria of nation-hood. For some nationalists, there have appeared 'natural frontiers' – seas, mountains, rivers, forests, which demarcate the limits of potential nation-states. Others search out objective social criteria – the possession of a common language, a shared historical experience, one-time polit-ical autonomy, religion, racial origins, economic integration. In setting out their political stall, nationalists invariably seek to press the claims of longevity – the nation's origins in a great, though now sadly deceased, civilisation, or primordial origins lost in the mists of history, now being revived after aeons of forgetfulness or repression. The bulk of modern scholarship would suggest, however, that, even where modern nations have their roots in the past, they come into existence as nations because nationalists themselves conjure them intellectually out of a confused mass of historical and anthropological data. Nations, as one writer has put it in a famous phrase, are *imagined communities*.[8] The problems arise when these images and visions overlap and clash. When, in nineteenth-century Europe, nationalists set about applying the principle of self-determination to peoples as a solution to the evils of political and cultural oppression, they found themselves facing problematic questions. Had, for instance, geography formed the basis of a distinct Irish island nation? Or did the archipelago of the British Isles not constitute a single proto-nation? Did the division between industrialised, Protestant Ulster and the rural, Catholic South create two nations? Was the decay of the Irish language the sign of the end of a nation, or an inspiration to build a nation once again? Were the South (Yugo-) Slavs, who spoke a similar Serbo-Croat language, but differed between Roman Catholic and orthodox religions, one nation, two nations or part of the wider pan-Slav nation? This changed the nature of the debate. The denial of freedom to nations had been diagnosed as the source of the problems of the age. It now appeared that the pursuit of self-determination presented, not the solution, but a new problem potentially more intractable than the old. This was 'the national question': how were these competing claims to be decided?

One way of doing so would seek to differentiate between two kinds of nationalism – 'good' nationalism and 'bad' nationalism, 'progressive' or 'reactionary'. In the main this has tended to be associated with two contending conceptions of the nation. On the one hand lies what we may call the 'civil' nation, identified as a body of equal citizens, whose communality is defined by a civic culture that is pluralistic, tolerant, and based upon either the recognition that individuals have rights irrespective of their racial, ethnic, or cultural origins, or upon giving all cultural groups equal legitimacy. This is a political, or territorial, conception of the nation. On the other hand lies what we may call the 'ethnic' nation, defined primarily in terms of a pre-political ethnic or cultural identity, where political membership is held to be enjoyed, not irrespective of, but as a result of, sharing common historical or genetic roots.

Many writers have offered different labels to help us explore these two conceptions: the difference between 'risorgimento' and 'integral' nationalism, 'liberal' and 'tribal' nationalism, 'open' and 'closed'.[9] Some writers link the difference in the development of Europe between the 'Western' nations, which historically enjoyed access to a 'high' national culture rooted in European civilisation as a whole, and 'Eastern' nations, with essentially narrow, localised peasant cultures. Others have contrasted the 'organic' or evolutionary development of political identity in the early nation-states with the contrived attempts at nation-building in more recent times. Classical Marxism tended to contrast the 'progressive' character of 'bourgois nationalism' which, in forging modern states and economies, allowed politics to move on to the higher stage of working-class solidarity across national boundaries, with the populist, and potentially reactionary, nationalisms thrown up by what Engels called 'ethnographic monuments'.

These represent abstract conceptions of the nation. In reality, as we shall see, it has never been entirely possible to differentiate sharply between the dark and the light side of nationalism. However, it is an important distinction, which helps us to illuminate some of national-ism's later problems.

THE IMPACT OF NATIONALISM

In this section I shall consider the impact of nationalism in three different arenas, and from three different viewpoints. The first part examines how far Europe, which invented the idea of the nation-state, proved able to effect it in practice. The second examines the marriage of European nationalism with anti-Europeanism in parts of the world where European imperialism impinged. The third examines the re-emergence of nationalism within modern democratic states, focusing upon the British Isles.

European nationalism

The optimistic assumptions that lay behind nationalism in early nineteenth-century Europe were best expressed by the Italian Giuseppe Mazzini (1805–72). Mazzini was born into a land whose common political identity had disappeared with the Roman emperors and whose petty states, though nominally under Austrian tutelage, were a play-thing of international power politics. The revolutionary nature of Mazzini's 'Young Italy' and 'Young Europe' organisations was a characteristic response to the authoritarian politics of his day, and his writings inspired many nationalists elsewhere. In them were expressed the spirit of Romanticism, democratic ideas and conceptions of social progress derived from thinkers such as Saint-Simon. Mazzini called for Italian unity. He believed that national self-determination would bring Europe peace, prosperity, freedom, co-operation, and progress, and he based his demands upon

> a historical and philosophical conception: the substitution of feudal monarchy by the principle of popular sovereignty . . . a necessary step towards association, and the apportionment of collective work; the constitution of the immense sum total of moral, intellectual and economic forces . . . to co-operate towards the betterment of the whole human family and the increase of collective wealth.

In the nation, Mazzini believed, people fulfill a duty of service to other human beings and to God, whose guiding hand he saw working in the world: 'Neither Pope nor King; only God and the People will open the way of the future to us.' Both were guarantors of peace and co-operation. War arose from feudal barbarism, but God had providentially shaped the world in terms of 'natural frontiers' within which nations could live according to their true identities. These clearly demarcated a single Italian nation (though Mazzini found diffiiculties in defining natural boundaries elsewhere). A united Italy also had a civilising mission:

> And just as to the Rome of the Caesars . . . there succeeded the Rome of the Popes . . . so the Rome of the People will succeed them both, to unite, in a faith that will make Thought and Action one, Europe, America, and every part of the terrestrial globe.[10]

Mazzini believed that national identity was inherent, and that all national claims are compatible. His conception of a nation was that of a large territorial unit, possessed of a flourishing cosmopolitan civilisation, with long historical traditions. And he felt that the 'national awakening' was a revolt against oppressive and conservative political regimes. All of these beliefs were flawed.

In 1848, the year of revolution, liberal nationalist movements all over Europe challenged the established European system, and almost everywhere were defeated. The events had a threefold significance. Firstly, the initiative for building nations passed in important parts of Europe from the political left to the right. The later German Chancellor, Prince von Bülow, commented on this change:

> It was the Liberals who first expressed the idea of German unity and spread it through the people .... The goal could not be reached by the course which they followed. Then Conservative policy had to step in, in order, as Bismarck expressed it, to realise the Liberal idea by means of Conservative action.[11]

Realpolitik, war and diplomacy replaced revolutionary idealism as the basis on which new nations such as Germany and Italy entered the European state system.

Secondly, the nationalisation of states was accompanied by sustained attempts to create national economies through economic protection. Free trade and *laissez-faire* economics, as Friedrich List (1789–1846) had earlier claimed in a call for German protectionism, came to be seen, not as a universal principle, but as a policy which sustained Britain's headstart in economic development. Rapid industrialisation accentuated class conflict, and the political function of nationalism increasingly became that of binding nations together against radical and socialist politics.

Thirdly, successful nationalisms began to assume that they had a civilising mission to the world. This was, as we can see from the earlier quotation, implicit even in Mazzini's views. Nations pushed out their frontiers, within Europe and throughout the world, intensified their programmes of acculturisation, and, as the British politician Joseph Chamberlain said, 'learned to think imperially'. The equality of national status conceptualised by Herder, already under stress, was turned upside down, and European nations came to see it as their duty to disseminate a higher culture to less civilised peoples.

Finally, the attempt to forge new liberal nations in Europe did not always create civil societies in which national and cultural minorities could take their place. Instead, it stimulated further national awakenings. At the interstices of the great European empires in eastern Europe and the Balkans lay a patchwork quilt of peoples living in areas where boundaries were unclear and contested, and whose religious, linguistic, and cultural identities mingled and overlapped. The 1848 revolutions showed the potential for many of these peoples to be mobilised by fanatical priests, populist bigots, and unscrupulous dynasts against liberal ideas. J.S. Mill lamented that 'the sentiment of nationality so far outweighs the love of liberty that the people are willing to abet their rulers in crushing the liberty and independence of any people not of their race or language'. But even what appeared on the surface to be enlightened liberalism could rebound. In 1867, Hungary gained autonomy within the Habsburg Empire, and established a liberal constitution with a national minority policy that wholly confused ethnic and territorial conceptions of the nation: 'All citizens of Hungary form a single nation – the indivisible, unitary Magyar nation – to which all citizens belong irrespective of nationality.'

The mobilisation of peoples under these circumstances has subsequently ensured that these regions of Europe are a tinderbox of war and conflict. The Victorian liberal historian Lord Acton, and a group of socialists generally termed the 'Austro-Marxists', writing on the eve of the First World War, both adopted the view that applying the principle of national self-determination in these areas was both impracticable and potentially disastrous. Acton sought a liberalised monarchy, the Austro-Marxists a socialist state, but both believed that the only equitable and stable outcome involved recognising the diversity of cultural and communal identities as integral elements of a pluralist state. History swept these views aside. The assassination by a Serb nationalist of the Austrian Archduke Ferdinand in 1914 precipitated European war among the great powers. After 1917, the old European empires were disbanded, and new successor states such as Yugoslavia, Czechoslovakia, and Poland were created, but it proved impossible to satisfy three competing principles for a new European peace: the right to self-determination; the protection of minority rights; and curbing the size and power of the 'restless' nations such as Germany and Italy. Fascism was able to exploit all these tensions to its advantage, bringing Europe towards the Second World War in 1939.

Since the end of the Second World War, two experiments have been conducted in Europe which reflect the belief, held by Acton, that the ethnic state is unrealisable, dangerous to liberty, tempted by the counter-productive strategy of economic self-sufficiency, and is the generator of war. One, the European Union, emerging out of pragmatic economic and social collaboration, and founded on the broadly liberal and democratic principles of the civil state, is a success. Inevitably, movements towards political integration meet the resistance of special economic and political interests. Moreover, it stimulates precisely those local, patriotic, and national sentiments whose purpose it is, in the long run, to erode. Substantial questions of identity are increasingly posed by new conceptions of 'Europeanism' and European citizenship. Yet the marriage of nations and supra-nationalism has, so far, proved to be a rocky but effective one. The second experiment was the Soviet empire. In theory, this was founded upon the international solidarity of the proletariat across national frontiers, but, in reality, a centralised imperial state ruled over a vast multi-ethnic, multi-national system by divide-and-rule, repression of some nationalities and collaboration with local national elites. When, in the 1980s, President Gorbachev sought to liberalise this system from the top down, it fell apart into a host of independent states, many of them increasingly racked with minority ethnic conflicts and wars. (Former Yugoslavia, an independent system, revealed the problem in its most dramatic form.) The Soviet failure exposes two significant aspects of nationalism. One was that ethnic identities, stimulated in the nineteenth century, could not simply vanish into forms of cross-national proletarian solidarity. The second is that, when the structure of empire fragmented and political leaders scrambled for control in its successor states, the mobilisation of national symbols and rhetoric, and appeals to national solidarity, proved to be the most attractive and effective form of politics. Even the most enlightened attempts to replicate Western civil societies proved vulnerable to national minority claims, as President Havel found when he was compelled to accept the separation of Slovakia from the Czech Republic.

Anti-colonial nationalism

In the late eighteenth and early nineteenth centuries, European ideas about the organisation and legitimacy of the national state spread beyond their homelands, first among European settlers ('colonial nationalism'), and then to indigenous peoples brought under, or threatened by, European control ('anti-colonial nationalism'). In the Americas, Australia, and southern Africa, settlers have broken away, by negotiation or revolution, to establish self-governing states, and to begin the task of investing them with distinct national identities and projects. Just as dramatic was the revolt of non-European peoples, mainly during the period between the 1940s and 1980s, against the great nineteenth-century European empires in Asia and Africa. Nationalism in Europe had been in large measure the response of different peoples to their neighbours: outside, it was harnessed predominantly as a response to Europeans (including, of course, the United States). This simplified the task of nationalist intellectuals, since what the nation was *for* could be elided into the task of defining what it was *against*.

In the colonies, for instance, stark cultural and racial differences clearly differentiated a small alien elite and the indigenous populations. As Julius Nyerere, later leader of Tanzania, noted, 'Africans all over the continent without a word being spoken, looked at the European, looked at one another, and knew that in relation to the European they were one.' This was misleading. Africa is a patchwork of different tribal, linguistic, cultural, religious, and racial groups. But it was a convenient falsehood which latched on to colour as the crucial distinction. Moreover, it could – just as misleadingly, given the political and social inequalities of African and Asian societies – be related to a dominant power relationship: as one Arab nationalist put it, imperial rulers treated all 'natives' with 'spiritual arrogance, racial haughtiness, social aloofness, and paternal authoritarianism'. These relationships between colonist and colonised were given philosophical expression by Franz Fanon (*The Wretched of the Earth*) and Albert Memmi in the context of political conflict in French North Africa. Both explored the warped psychological relationship of mutual suspicion and mutual dependence which colonialism established, depriving both sides of their humanity, and eventually forcing those who have been colonised to expel their masters as a means of liberation.

Formulating conceptions of the nation in the less-developed world has often posed difficult problems. In some Asian countries like Japan, China, and India, which had long histories of political integration and rich indigenous cultures, nationalists had traditional symbols which they could mobilise against Europeanism, and have turned them into strong modernising nations. But European diplomats had often imposed centralised administrations upon fairly arbitrary territorial units. National opposition tended, therefore, not to be articulated in cultural terms, but in terms of the secular principles of 'decolonisation' and 'majority rule' around which all oppositions could rally. The 'nation' in such instances became defined by leaders of the independence movements and the post-independent states primarily as those who happened to have been enclosed within the colony's boundaries. But what of internal cultural variations? As in the European case, the legitimacy of minority claims against the integrity of the new states tended to be vigorously dismissed as communalism or tribalism, even, in the words of an Iraqi Ba'ath Party document, as 'the disorders of bourgeois, feudal, tribal and sectarian realities'.

Also as in Europe, where pan-Slav and pan-German movements had appealed to broad cultural groupings which spanned what were interpreted as artificial frontiers, so elsewhere new identities were sought on a larger scale. This was always easier for self-perceived exiles engaged in the politics of far-away countries to imagine than for those at home close to political realities. The Negritude movement, which sought to create a black or African personality, was forged by black intellectuals in Paris: pan-Africanism was orignally an invention of black Americans fighting discrimination in the United States, which only later was adopted by indigenous African leaders to encourage political collaboration across the continent. In the Middle East, and beyond, the last forty years has seen a sustained battle between two 'pan-' movements – secular Arab nationalism, appealing to linguistic and cultural criteria of nationhood, and an increasingly assertive revivalist Islamic movement appealing to religious values. The Iran–Iraq war of the early 1980s was not just a clash between states, but between two revolutionary figures, the Ayatollah Khomeini and President Saddam Hussein, each of whom aspired to assume the leadership of ideological movements with the power to mobilise millions of followers in the region.

The most distinctive feature of anti-colonial nationalism, however, was the association of nationalist aspirations with ideologies of socialism, Marxism, and communism. In Europe, the socialist left and nationalism were invariably at loggerheads. Both were competing for the newly politicised electorate. The left appealed to international working-class solidarity, and offered socialism as a unifying force across ethnic frontiers. Outside Europe, the relationship was more ambiguous. Revolutionary Marxists certainly denounced 'bourgeois' nationalism as a force that promised to replace the tyranny of the colonist with that of privileged indigenous elites. But the ideologies of the left were able to ally with populist challenges to colonial regimes, and performed three major functions. First, Marxist and other theories of imperialism offered a powerful set of intellectual arguments. According to these, modern European civilisation was founded upon capitalism, a materialistic system devoted to the soulless task of economic accumulation. Imperialism arose out of capitalism's need for new markets, resources or areas of investment. By exploiting the less developed parts of the world, it sustained the domestic rate of profit, and created surpluses with which to stave off social discontent at home. This, secondly, not only offered a way of explaining the 'backwardness' of colonised peoples in terms of the inherent injustices and corruption of European civilisation, but, given the views held by most orthodox socialists, pointed the way, not back into traditional rural values, but forward into a modern ethically based world system. Individual nationalist leaders could present themselves and their people as participants in a universal movement – 'anti-colonialism', 'anti-imperialism', the 'national liberation struggle' – a revolt of the oppressed everywhere, not as a localised movement bent on narrow ethnic self-determination. Finally, radical socialism, and particularly the Russian Revolution, offered what appeared to be a viable alternative to the chaos and destruction of liberal capitalism – economic modernisation through collective planning, the one-party state, and a rhetoric of communal solidarity that could be integrated with traditional indigenous communal institutions and values of village life: African socialism, Arab socialism, even Islamic socialism formed ingenious ideological hybrids out of tradition and modernity.

The fate of post-colonial states has been very varied. Some lucky few have prospered and live at ease with themselves. Most are in a condition of increasing turbulence. One aspect is that the radical ideology that pointed to the solidarity of the oppressed has failed as much outside as inside Europe: states have taken their different routes to nation-building, and the idea of the common interests of the 'third' or 'underdeveloped' world has proved to be a pure abstraction. A second is that the clash between tradition and modernity has become more intense. Economic aspirations for European and American living standards have been stimulated. Economic modernisation and development have therefore, in a sense, become the nationalism of such states, with the consequent impact upon traditional modes of life. Yet this also stimulates, and perhaps can only be conducted under the aegis of, what are, apparently, outmoded, traditional, anti-European beliefs. In recent years, Islam has perhaps provided the more powerful cultural force against Europeanism. It is ascetic, indigenous to the Middle East and areas of southern Europe and Asia, rich in history, ideas and memory, and with a strong messianic streak. It has attracted even black leaders in the United States because it allows them to create a separatist culture distinct from the white man's gods of liberalism, materialism and Christianity. Its rise is testimony to a major intellectual shift in recent years against Western values, which has the power to destabilise international affairs and the order of existing secular state formations.

Minority nationalism in the developed democracies

The intellectual and political orthodoxy of the years after the Second World War treated nationalism as historically dated and morally unacceptable. 'Nation-building' was regarded as a painful, once-for-all historical process, still in train in the new states formed out of former colonial territories, but largely completed in the mature democracies and the USSR. The idea of the ethnic state was an anachronism which had burned itself out in the authoritarian fascisms, racism, and ethnic pogroms of the pre-war and wartime period. At the top of the political agenda was democracy, which the political classes perceived as a system for distributing economic prosperity fairly among different classes, regions and cultural groups. The bases of movements that continued to assert nationalist claims – in Ireland, Flanders, French Canada, Scotland, and the Basque and Breton regions, among others – were perceived to lie in relatively stagnant rural regions, which bred ideologies tied to conservative, mainly Roman Catholic, religious and communal values. The principle of national self-determination recognised by the United Nations was applied, not to endow peoples with the right to redraw national frontiers, but as a diplomatic device to underpin existing state formations.

All this changed in the 1960s and 1970s. Minority movements acquired new intellectual and political vigour. Economic theories of anti-imperialism, internal colonialism, and uneven development drawn from the Third World and applied to local conditions created radical political fringes. Theories of culture were fashionable, and directed attention at long-ignored discrepancies within states. Rapid post-war modernisation brought the shock of the new to peripheral areas, displacing traditions and creating new social groups with rising expectations, better education and increased mobility. Frustrations arising out of cultural marginality, or simply arrested promotion into positions of status and power dominated by the post-war provincial establishments, were channelled into an alternative kind of classless, oppositional politics.

Could these new claims be accommodated? Could they be dismissed by 'progressive' opinion as merely the last stand of old and outdated cultural absolutisms, antagonistic to modernity? Or did they represent something more acceptable, and perhaps even desirable, in a world that increasingly associated diversity and pluralism as integral elements of democracy – a claim for the recognition of *difference*, where there existed the possibility of negotiating a democratic accommodation among various traditions? In 1977, Tom Nairn, the Scottish Marxist-turned-nationalist, in *The Break-Up of Britain*, presented the most striking pose in this debate. For him, the United Kingdom, in its post-imperial, post-colonial phase, could no longer sustain accommodations among the various nationalities. Differential economic performance – 'uneven development' – was revitalising regional and cultural identities and pointing them towards the separatist, or radical devolutionary, option.

What is Britain?

The orthodox image of Britain is that of a long-established political identity, focused upon the supremacy of the Westminster Parliament as the forum of the nation, and recognising the diversity of nationalities and cultures represented within the unity of the Kingdom. Different party ideologies may view this differently: Liberals emphasise diversity and decentralisation; Conservatives the elements of continuity, authority and unity; Labour those of working-class solidarity and the capacity of the central state to deliver uniform economic and social benefits throughout the Union.

These images, however, are not exhaustive, nor without their complications. Those on the (significantly termed) 'Celtic fringe' would argue that much of the traditional sense of Britishness derived from images of Englishness – standard pronunciation, a literary canon, sights of the white cliffs of Dover, honey for tea, and the crack of leather on willow on an English summer's afternoon. A succession of Romantic and neo-Romantic movements have imbued the national culture with rural nostalgia, feudal longings and reverence for tradition. England's green and pleasant land, however, was built on the economic foundations of commerce, financial speculation, and industrial muscle. And modernising movements, like the National Efficiency movement early in the twentieth century, which have sought to update Britain's scientific and entrepreneurial skills, to replace the aristocratic culture of leisure and amateurishness with one of professionalism and drive, have faced an uphill battle.

The Union, too, was always, in a sense, a Protestant union forged against external Catholic powers, and the subversive potential of Catholicism within. Not only, in the end, did this mean that Catholic Ireland fled the British family of nations, but secularisation has left traditional national institutions like the Church of England in an increasingly anomalous role. Finally, the Union went hand in hand with empire, images of British martial spirit and military success, and a faith in the British as a governing race, dispensing the benefits of political liberty, civilisation, and culture. Most of these traditional conceptions are under threat. The end of empire has undermined much of the instrumental rationale for maintaining the Union. As in France and Germany, immigration has established black minorities which challenge traditional identities. Is Britishness tested by possession of British citizenship, or, as Lord Tebbitt once suggested, by which side you cheer for in the test match?

These trials indicate two different directions for the future. One, which has had the higher profile over the last two decades, and has been driven by the Conservative right represented by Enoch Powell, Lady Thatcher, and now John Major, is towards a tighter and narrower definition of Britishness. This involves reinvigorating an idea of conservative nationhood – one built around the revival of 'Victorian values' of traditional family morality, economic freedom, pre-war educational standards, law and order, defence of the Union, and patriotic resistance to foreign bullies, not least to Brussels and the idea of a federal Europe. The other view challenges the antiquated nature of British institutions, its emphasis on centralisation, unity and orthodoxy rather than equality and diversity, which looks to partnership not national solidarity, and outwards towards participation in a wider Europe rather than backwards to the relics of a dead imperial culture. Which will prevail remains to be seen.

Ireland

Irish nationalism was a political force even before the French Revolution, and has one of the richest of ideological traditions. It also reveals a deep ambivalence, which reflects a complex historical relationship between Britain and Ireland, and between different political forces on the island itself.

On the one hand stands the project of an Ireland that is a modern, secular (or pluralist) society based on equality for all irrespective of religion, origins or culture. The roots of this tradition lay in a liberal colonial nationalism developed during the eighteenth century within the Anglo-Irish ruling elites and among middle-class Protestants, the descendants of earlier settlers from Britain. Their image of an Irish Protestant nation, distinct from but still related to Britain, was radical-ised in the 1790s by the United Irishmen who envisaged the extension of civil and political rights to the indigenous Irish Catholic population, and the foundation of a separatist republic based on equal citizenship that would embrace, in the words of Wolfe Tone, the leader of the unsuccessful revolution of 1798, 'Protestants, Dissenters and Catholics'. These liberal and republican ideas soon supplanted more traditional monarchical principles within the Catholic political classes, and shaped the formation of popular national politics over the following century. The mobilisation of Catholic Ireland around a series of economic, religious, and political grievances, however, served to fragment the country, both between Protestants and Catholics, and between the rapidly industrialising northern counties of greater Protestant settle-ment and the poorer, more traditional rural south. In addition, calls for equal citizenship within the United Kingdom became ambiguously tangled up with calls for devolution or separation. Protestant leaders increasingly argued that, irrespective of nationalist claims, this would result in a Catholic state for a Catholic people, equipped with symbols alien to British Protestant culture. The emergence of unionism led, in the period 1920–2, to the partition of Ireland, with a 26-county Free State (later Republic) established containing a preponderant Catholic major-ity in the South and a six-county Northern Ireland within the United Kingdom, containing a substantial Catholic minority.

The second feature of Irish nationalism helps to reinforce Protestant apprehensions. In the inter-war period, the post-revolutionary leader-ship of the new Irish Republic forged a political culture for the state. Though founded upon British liberal parliamentary institutions, it was shaped by a cult of revolutionary violence inherited from the period of internal war between 1916 and 1922. Reflecting the close association that had emerged throughout the nineteenth century between Catholic voters, the Catholic Church and nationalist politics, it gave a special constitutional status to the Church, and legitimised deeply conservative social and moral values expressed within contemporary, ultramontane Catholicism. It set out to replace the cultural and economic dependence of the colonial past by creating an economically self-sufficient, rural-based state revolving around the Gaelic language and culture. And it made irridentist claims for sovereignty over the lost six counties of the North. This exclusive, but aspirational, nationalism, justified on majorit-arian principles, provided the justification for northern Unionist leaders to consolidate a statelet in which the Catholic minority remained largely second-class citizens.

The revolutionary tradition has played a crucial role in all this. This tradition is traced from Tone to the Easter Rising of 1916 and the subsequent Anglo-Irish war. It continues to be used by the modern-day Sinn Fein/Irish Republican Army to legitimise a campaign of revolutionary terrorism aimed at removing British authority in Northern Ireland and ending partition. The Easter Rising leaders declared that:

> In every generation the Irish people have asserted their right to national freedom and sovereignty; six times during the past three hundred years they have asserted it in arms. Standing on that fundamental right . . . we hereby proclaim the Irish republic as a sovereign independent state. . . .[12]

Like them, modern republicans appeal to a story of British conquest and colonisation; dispossession from the land and discrimination against the native Catholic population; of famine and forced emigration; forcible Anglicisation and the repression of discontent – and through all this, a continual, often muted, fight-back by the Irish people for equality, dignity, and freedom. It inherits two ideological themes. One is a populist, Jacobin radicalism tinged with vaguely socialist ideas of class struggle, and deployed against both British 'imperialism' and the Irish establishment which has abandoned the interests of the 'people'. Left-wing nationalists, heirs to the Irish Marxist James Connolly (1868–1916), also see the unresolved national question as the perpetuation of neo-colonialism, and a barrier to the emergence of 'normal' class-based loyalties. The second is a powerful religious myth, deployed most effectively by Padraig Pearse, the leading ideologist of the 1916 Rising, of death and resurrection, the successive crushing of Ireland's will and its re-emergence, Phoenix-like, from the ashes.

The belief that victory in the struggle for Irish freedom is inevitable is supported by the view that the partition of Ireland runs counter to reason and nature, and is designed to deny the Irish people as a whole the right to self-determination. Ireland, it is claimed, is an integral island territory, its people a single people until British colonialism introduced an alien minority. Even then, under British tutelage it was always treated as a single administrative unit. Partition was an arbitrary act, designed to protect selfish British interests, and to create an artificial northern statelet with a built-in loyal Protestant majority. This has

entrenched ancient sectarian antagonisms and prejudices in a discriminatory system against the local Catholic minority. Their second
class status will remain, it is claimed, whatever the efforts at reform,
until the constitutional status is changed.

It has been possible for nationalists to regard northern Protestants as
simply a somewhat recalcitrant national minority because Unionists
have neither acquired, nor indeed in the main wanted to form, a clear
and distinct national identity. This has, rather, been defined primarily
by what they opposed – minority status in an Irish Catholic majority
state ('Home Rule is Rome Rule'), the subordination of a distinct
economic system to that of the South, and separation from their kinsfolk
on the mainland. They have largely been content simply, therefore, to
define themselves in a very abstract way as 'British', or, in political
terms, as Unionists, or 'loyalists' to the Crown. Some would accept an
essentially 'Irish' cultural identity, others would proclaim the moral
superiority of the Ulster Protestant heritage, and some would aspire to
a non-sectarian regional identity. The right to self-determination has
never, in the main, been put forward as a political demand. Rather it is
a principle that has been thrust upon them since 1922 by British
governments and Irish nationalists as a way of defining Northern
Ireland's constitutional status within the United Kingdom as a con-
ditional one; and it has been accepted by Unionists as the main
democratic obstacle to the threat of being shunted without their consent
into a single all-Ireland state.

Protestants may once have espoused, and indeed, for much of its
history, led, Irish political nationalism. Few do so today. The history of
cultural nationalism is revealing here. Protestant radicals initiated the
exploration of Irish peasant culture, and Protestants were in the
forefront of the Young Ireland Romantic movement in the 1840s which
sought to contest the modernisation of Ireland and its increasingly
sectarian politics. By reviving a declining language and culture, they
aspired to make it 'a nation once again' rather than an increasingly
divided, fragmented country. These ideas, however, provided an identity and status mainly for a declining Anglo-Irish intellectual elite and
the new Catholic bourgeoisie and failed to win over the robust Presby-
terian culture of Ulster. As they were popularised by cultural leaders
in the Gaelic League and Sinn Fein before the First World War, they
were penetrated by absolutist cultural stereotypes, calls for the complete de-anglicisation of Ireland and the constitution of the nation on
racial terms. It was Douglas Hyde, the Anglo-Irish founder of the Gaelic

League (1893), who declared that 'in spite of the little admixture of Saxon blood in the north-east corner, this island is and will ever remain Celtic at the core'.[13]

There has been a sustained attempt in recent years to reconstruct images of Irish nationhood. Revisionist historians have exposed the one-sidededness of the traditional themes of absolute antagonism between England and Ireland, native Catholic Irish and Protestant colonial intruder: instead, complex patterns of conflict and collaboration emerge. The vision of Irish nationhood as a single cultural and political unity is under challenge. In the 1970s, leaders of constitutional nationalism like John Hume of the Social Democratic and Labour Party (SDLP) and Garrett Fitzgerald set out to reconstruct both the case for unity and its character. Unity was to be accomplished, not by force, demography or the inevitability of history, but because of pragmatic economic co-operation between two peripheral economies within the emerging European Community, and a mutual recognition that the anachronistic politics of the North hindered social progress. The basis of unity was to be consent, freely given, to a new state that would be pluralistic, based on federal principles, and recognise the equal status and power of the different traditions. In the late nineteenth century, Irish writers explored a growing tension in the vision of respectable Irish society – whether it should look for its future beyond England to a broader European civilisation, or to the native traditions of the West of Ireland. After half a century of the latter, modernisers in Irish society now seek to redefine Ireland as a modern, Western liberal democracy, its future firmly located in the European Community, a wider framework within which domestic antagonisms can be accommodated and resolved. Many lay Catholics and secularists seek reform of a culture in which women's rights and individual freedoms have traditionally taken second place to traditional moral values. In 1990, the election of the liberal barrister Mary Robinson as President appeared to mark the advent of a new Ireland. Within Northern Ireland itself, a growing consensus among government, liberal Catholics and liberal Protestants points towards attempting to reconstruct ethnic politics in a non-antagonistic form by institutionalising mutual recognition of the 'two traditions'.

Liberalising the language of nationalism is one thing – decon-structing a long-standing consolidation of economic, social, cultural and political controversies along ethnic–national lines, especially when they are reinforced by communal and political violence, quite another. One side's liberal initiative is very often perceived by the other as an act of aggression which fails to recognise its fears and aspirations. Nationalism continues to remain as much a part of the national question as its solution.

Scotland

Ethnic and cultural issues have traditionally in Scotland been over-shadowed by economic and social grievances and justifications for regional self-government. Scottish political leaders in the nineteenth century successfully mobilised the new democracy around Conservat-ive and Liberal (later Labour) principles, with each party being pre-pared at different stages to acknowledge regional differences and the case for local administrative devolution. The Scottish National Party (SNP) was formed in 1934. Its main grievance was the collapse of Scotland's prosperous Victorian economy, a shift of ownership and control of local resources south of the border, indifference at West-minster, and the unwillingness of the Union parties fully to represent the interests there of the Scottish people. Many of its early adherents were vigorous campaigners for Scottish culture, the Gaelic language, and the traditional values of rural life. But the founder, and main driving force, was John McCormack. Like many of those attracted to the Liberal-orientated Home Rule movement before the First World War (and, indeed, those who have been among the more vigorous representatives of the party in recent decades), McCormack was a convert from socialism, who believed that Scotland's left-wing major-ities and 'progressive' political ethos could never be effective while England continued to send Conservative majorities to Westminster. The party's last period of resurgence in the 1970s launched an attack upon the failure of post-war planning mechanisms, the lack of local accountability of the Scottish Office and its bureaucracy, and the fact that the local economy had been made even more vulnerable by unsuccessful attempts to stimulate growth through external invest-ment. The discovery of North Sea oil in the 1960s provided the key weapon. This, said nationalists, was 'Scotland's oil'. Rather than the profits being diverted into the pockets of international capital and the British Treasury, they could now become the foundation for Scottish regeneration and political autonomy.

Scotland's political culture has been profoundly influenced by three factors associated with the Act of Union in 1707. Many nationalists argue that union was accomplished dishonestly, and that what was intended as an equal partnership turned into English dominance. But it engaged Scotland directly in the benefits of British imperialism. It preserved the essentials of a Scottish, bourgeois, civil society in the form of separate legal, educational, and economic arrangements, and, in the period after the Second World War, a large state sector engaged in the delivery of public services. And it also established a partnership between the modern, anglicised, commercial Presbyterians of the Scottish lowlands, and the British state, when the Jacobite Rebellions of 1715 and 1745 unleashed the forces of the Catholic, Gaelic-speaking feudal clans from the underdeveloped highlands. Traditional Scotland was subsequently brutally destroyed or isolated in a decaying, though periodically rebellious, culture in the islands of the West. The age of democracy, therefore, found, unlike Ireland, no vast peasant masses to be mobilised behind traditional symbols, interests and the old religion, but commercialised agriculture and a flourishing industrial and commercial world. Moreover, a combination of unionist statecraft and the imagination of Sir Walter Scott neatly channelled the nineteenth-century cultural revival and the Romantic movement into the preservation of the Union and the promotion of tourism. Nationalists have invariably rejected the status-ridden pastime of games, dancing, regimental marchpasts and cultural displays as simply 'Tartan Toryism'. Radical, populist cultural nationalism, expressed, for instance, by the communist poet Hugh MacDiarmid, gained few converts.

In the 1980s, the SNP's star waned, and the party divided over economic policy, the European Community and the choice between devolution and independence. This decay, however, has been accompanied by a substantial growth in Scottish national consciousness. Conservative governments since 1979 have been accused increasingly of governing Scotland without legitimacy or consent, and they have been cut to a tiny minority of seats. They have, it is claimed, used the country as a laboratory for novel policies like the poll tax; imposed economic strategies that have devastated the economy; and dismantled a public sector upon which a large, representative sector of Scottish society depends. In this context, the SNP's agenda has, in effect, been taken up by the Labour and Liberal parties, and sections of the Scottish establishment. The Constitutional Convention, established in 1979, and boycotted by Conservatives and SNP, set out to build a new national consensus around a pragmatic case for self-government. In place of traditional rhetorical attacks against England and the English, a new language is evolving. In this, the Union is presented as an increasingly anachronistic structure, lacking the flexibility to change and adapt to a world of greater economic and cultural diversity. English conservatism is a brake upon progress. As in Ireland, Scotland is reopening links with Europe which antedate the era of centralisation at Westminster. The political climate in Brussels is far more in tune with Scottish needs and aspirations – recognition of regional identities; social partnership in industry; a vigorous public sector for social improvement and economic development. There has been a revival of cultural life. Scottish political independence may be a long way away, if, indeed, it ever comes. But an independent national consciousness appears to be in the making which challenges traditional sentimental and ideological ties with London.

Wales

By contrast with Scotland, culture has traditionally been at the heart of Welsh nationalism. Plaid Cymru was founded in 1925 to resist the erosion of a civilisation based upon the use of the Welsh language, its poetry and music. Its founder, J. Saunders Lewis, was profoundly influenced, as was Sinn Fein in Ireland, by the neo-Romantic conservative ideas of the European right in the early part of the century, such as the French *Action française*. Lewis rejected materialism, secularism, the growth of urban life, and class politics. As his colleague, J.F. Daniel, said in 1937, 'it is in the poetry of Taliesin and Dafydd Nanmore far more than in the Special Area Acts or Five Year Programmes that the salvation of Wales is to be found'. Modernity deprived humans of true moral virtue, he believed, which was associated with the simple life of the countryside and the small towns characteristic of North Wales, but was being fundamentally eroded with the industrialisation and systematic anglicisation of the South Wales valleys and ports.

Lewis was a convert to Catholicism, and his image of nationality was one familiar in conservative Catholic thought – nostalgia for medieval and Renaissance Europe, where a plurality of scholarly cultures had flourished within a common Christian civilisation until the age of the nation-state had dawned to tear this sophisticated social fabric apart. His was 'Not a fight for Wales' independence, but for Wales' civilization.' With the advent of the European Community, however, much of whose ethos has been shaped by Catholic Christian Democratic thought, this image has seemed far less anachronistic.

In the nineteenth century, democratic opposition to Wales's Anglican, and anglicised, elite had been expressed through the radical wing of the Liberal Party. A genuine nationalist movement emerged with Plaid Cymru's call for a revival of the Welsh nation when Liberalism declined as a national party, the language went into virtually terminal decay, and a Labour Party based upon the industrialised South assumed a dominant role. Pragmatically, Saunders had no desire for Welsh independence if that meant subjection to secular socialism. As in Scotland, the fate of nationalism and Labour have been bound up together. In the 1960s and 1970s, Plaid began to accuse Labour of having become an establishment party, and increasingly unable to find answers to problems of de-industrialisation and the vagaries of investments from outside the country. Plaid was able to expand beyond its narrow, philosophical cultural nationalism, and assume a more radical political role. Cultural radicals targeted, sometimes with direct action, the penetration of North Wales by tourism, English residents and visitors with second homes, whose incomes raised the price of housing, and whose children were expected to be taught in English in the schools. On the wider front, it adopted more secular demands for regional economic improvement and development, and increasingly adopted the language and concepts of social democracy.

The 1979 referendum on Welsh devolution revealed little support, and proved to be disastrous for Plaid's subsequent electoral fortunes. With a Conservative government in power, Labour soon resumed its role as the party of opposition. Unlike Scotland, however, the main enemy of nationalism has proved to be Conservative Secretaries of State for Wales. The role of the Welsh language in the public life of the province has been given official recognition, to the point where, in some areas, a distinct English-speaking backlash can be detected. English economic policies have been moderated by a regional administration which has seen its task as that of identifying distinct Welsh interests, and representing Wales to Whitehall, rather than the reverse. This has not stopped the virtual destruction of south Wales's traditional industries. Nor, indeed, has it clearly invigorated a new vision of national life and purpose. Wales appears to remain too fragmented, with too many forces linking it to England, to create, as yet, a shared national vision.

CONCLUSION: THE END OF NATIONALISM?

The idea of the united, culturally homogeneous nation-state, dedicated to the common welfare of its members, and engaging their full loyalty and commitment, is one which has exerted a powerful hold over the political imagination during the last two hundred years. It has appeared both to serve important instrumental purposes, and to meet profound emotional needs. The organisational power of the nation-state has provided means of economic modernisation, political mobilisation, and popular resistance to imperial domination. It has also offered a focus of meaning and purpose, an almost transcendental embodiment of communal solidarity, for peoples under threat from mysterious and apparently uncontrollable forces associated with deep-seated global changes.

According to many commentators, however, the age of nationalism, and with it that of the nation-state, is over. At least in the more advanced areas of the world, the nation has served its historical purpose of transporting peoples from traditional to modern societies. In the process, it has fully revealed the dark side of its nature – racial exclusiveness, militaristic imperialism, and ethnic purification. Beyond the primitive simplicities of national solidarity, the closed mind-set involved in an exclusive identification with 'people like us', lies an era of openness, toleration, and global understanding.

This thesis is subject to a number of problems. One is that it has all been said before. As early as 1784, the German philosopher Immanuel Kant[14] gave expression to a widely shared belief among Enlightenment intellectuals that reason and self-interest would guide modern nations and republics beyond parochial divisions towards a common world political order. Rather than representing the end of the era of political and cultural divisions, however, Kant's essay appears as a fundamental misreading of the immanent politics of the age: his faith in universal reason was soon to be sidelined by the rapid proliferation of nationalist reconstruction in the wake of the French Revolution.

This relationship between the universal and the particular, the inherent tension between the global and the parochial, has persisted. The world today is spanned by international bodies and agencies – the UN, the World Bank, defence alliances like NATO, charitable and campaigning bodies like Oxfam and Amnesty International. Economic corporations operate world-wide. The information revolution, in the form of satellite communications, gives expression to the idea of a single global village. All of these appear to highlight the anachronistic status of the idea of the sovereign nation-state. As often as the age of nationalism has been pronounced dead by subsequent generations of 'progressive' intellectuals, so often have different peoples asserted their distinctive rights, cultures and interests against the pressures towards international integration and cosmopolitanism. It is not at all clear that this complex, contradictory process is likely to resolve itself in the near future.

NOTES

1 H. Kohn, *Nationalism: Its Meaning and History,* revised edn, New York, 1965, 9.
2 E. Kedourie, *Nationalism*, London, Hutchinson, 1985, 9.
3 *Mein Kampf,* Boston, 1943, 479.
4 H. Seton-Watson, *Nations and States*, London, Methuen, 1977, 445.
5 Quoted in B. Shafer, *Faces of Nationalism*, New York, Harcourt Brace Jovanovich, 1972, 64.
6 Quoted in F.S.L. Lyons, *Ireland since the Famine*, London, Fontana, 1973, 244.
7 I. McLean, 'The Rise and Fall of the SNP', *Political Studies*, 18, 1970.
8 B. Anderson, *Imagined Communities*, Verso, London, 1991.
9 P. Alter, *Nationalism*, London, Arnold, 1989, ch. 1.
10 G. Mazzini, 'To the Italian', *The Duties of Man and Other Essays*, London, Dent, 1907.
11 *Imperial Germany,* London, 1914, 139.
12 Proclamation of Poblacht na h-Eireann (Provisional Government).
13 *Revival of Irish Literature and Other Essays*, London, 1894, 131.
14 'Idea for a Universal History from a Cosmopolitan Point of View', in L.W. Beck, ed., *Kant on History,* Indianapolis, 1963, 23.

FURTHER READING

Good general discussions are contained in P. Alter, *Nationalism*, London, Arnold, 1989; E.J. Hobsbawm, *Nations and Nationalism since 1780*, Cambridge, Cambridge University Press, 1990; H. Kohn, *The Idea of Nationalism*, London, Macmillan, 1967. For a hostile view, see E. Kedourie, *Nationalism*, London, Hutchinson, revised edn, 1985. Boyd C. Shafer, *Faces of Nationalism: New Realities and Old Myths*, New York,

Harcourt Brace Jovanovich, 1972, is rich and wide-ranging. E. Kamenka, ed., *Nationalism: The Nature and Evolution of an Idea*, London, Arnold, 1976, has interesting essays. H. Kohn, *Nationalism: Its Meaning and History*, Princeton, Van Nostrand, 1955, provides a useful general introduction to short readings. Anthony Smith has made a major contribution to the subject: *Theories of Nationalism*, London, Duckworth, 1971; *Nationalism in the Twentieth Century*, Oxford, Martin Robertson, 1979; *The Ethnic Origins of Nationalism*, Oxford, Blackwell, 1986; and *National Identity*, Harmondsworth, Penguin, 1991. A. Cobban, *The Nation-State and National Self-Determination*, London, Collins/Fontana, 1969, is a classic study of the national question in Europe, and H. Seton-Watson, *Nations and States*, London, Methuen, 1977, is a valuable wide-ranging history. L. Tivey, ed., *The Nation-State: The Formation of Modern Politics*, Oxford, Martin Robertson, 1981, contains a varied collection of essays.

Competing general explanations of the relationship of nationalism to modernity are offered by: E. Gellner, *Nations and Nationalism*, Oxford, Blackwell, 1983; J. Breuilly, *Nationalism and the State*, 2nd edn, Manchester, Manchester University Press, 1985, whose wide-ranging historical survey stresses political rather than socio-economic factors; and B. Anderson, *Imagined Communities*, London, NLB/Verso, 1983, who examines how nationalist leaders come to conceptualise national identity.

For nationalism in the United Kingdom, A.H. Birch, *Political Integration and Disintegration in the British Isles*, London, Allen and Unwin, 1977, provides a useful start. Stimulating are: T. Nairn, *The Break-Up of Britain: Crisis and Neo-Nationalism*, 2nd edn, London, NLB/Verso, 1981; B. Crick, ed., *National Identities*, Oxford, Blackwell, 1991; L. Colley, *Britons*, New Haven, Yale University Press, 1993; D. McCrone, *Understanding Scotland*, London, Routledge, 1992; D.G. Boyce, *Nationalism in Ireland*, London, 1982. For a sympathetic account of modern cultural nationalism, see P. Mayo, *The Roots of Identity*, London, Allen Lane, 1974, and J. Tomlinson, *Cultural Imperialism*, London, Pinter, 1991. For the roots of decolonisation, see R. Emerson, *From Empire to Nation: The Rise to Self-Assertion of Asian and African Peoples*, Cambridge, Mass., Harvard University Press, 1962. Imaginative analyses of the colonial relationship are F. Fanon, *The Wretched of the Earth*, London, MacGibbon and Kee, 1963, and A. Memmi, *The Colonizer and the Colonized*, London, Earthscan, 1990.

Chapter 7

Fascism

Rick Wilford

Fascist theory is not a tightly knit bundle of ideas . . . . It is, in fact, rather untidy and inchoate . . . composed of a large number of diverse ideas, drawn from different cultures.

Paul Hayes, *Fascism*, London, Allen and Unwin, 1973, 19

INTRODUCTION

Despite the final military defeat of the Axis powers in 1945, the obituary for fascism cannot yet be finally written. In the latter part of the twentieth century, the resurgence of parties on the radical right through-out western and eastern Europe, including the former Soviet Union, suggests that the epitaph on fascism penned by an eminent historian – 'it began in 1922–23 . . . came of age in the 1930s . . . ended in 1945' – was somewhat premature.[1] At the end of the 1990s, the lingering appeal of the ideology still stirs a justifiable unease and also poses a problem: why does such a discredited set of ideas still muster support?

Part of the answer to fascism's apparent durability lies in its ability to simplify the complexities of political life. Fascism thrives on simp-listic thinking and sloganising, blaming 'them' – whether Jews, blacks or 'foreigners' in general – for 'our' problems. This feature of the doctrine alerts us to its exclusivity: it is characterised by the disposition to divide peoples and/or nations into two irreconcilable camps, *viz.* 'them' and 'us'. Moreover, such dualism is invested with a hierarchy of value: 'they' are not just different from, but inferior to, 'us'. In turn this conveys the inegalitarian character of fascism. Whether couched in terms of statehood, as in Mussolini's Italy, or race, as was the case in Hitler's Germany, the sense of superiority typifies fascist thinking.

Among other things, the stress on superiority rather than difference distinguishes fascism from nationalism with which it does have an affinity. But, whereas nationalism (see Chapter 6) can both co-exist with other doctrines, whether socialism, conservatism or liberalism, and respect the integrity of other self-governing nations, fascism neither tolerates ideological competitors nor recognises a fundamental equality among nations. This basic intolerance is also signalled by its celebration of aggression. Fascism is a belligerent form of nationalism, contemptuous of the rights of both individuals and other nations, seeking proof of its vitality in the ability to subject others to its thrall. The pursuit of its goals – whether national glory or racial supremacy – is not conducted through the power of argument but rather through the argument of power.

Fascism did flourish in the inter-war period, initially in Italy and subsequently in Germany and thereafter was mimicked by parties and movements elsewhere in Europe, including Britain and the Republic of Ireland. To that extent it appeared as, and according to many of its exponents was, the new doctrine for the new age of the twentieth century, superseding all others. It was represented as a break with the past, consigning other competing doctrines to the dustbin of history. Yet, while extolling its novelty, the ideologues of fascism were also mindful of the past. In that sense, they were backwards-looking, seeking to revivify some imagined, pre-industrial sense of community and belonging – whether it was the equally romanticised Roman Empire or the image of a sylvan medieval Germany. At the same time, fascism was also a counter-revolutionary ideology, seeking to subvert the civilising effects of the Enlightenment which had displaced myth and superstition with rationalism and secularism.

Already we can sense something of the duality of fascism's appeal. While celebrating those aspects of the past that fascist thinkers considered congenial and inspiring, it also rejected other traditions and ideas that encumbered its mission: that of national redemption. Conservatism, while sensitive to the past, was regarded by fascists as being unequal to the task of national reawakening and rebirth. While a hierarchical doctrine, the attachment of conservatism to emergent democratic norms and institutions rendered it powerless to confront the universalising ambitions of competing ideologies. The radical task of national regeneration required the excision of conservative vested interests which acted as a brake on the wheel of history. Moreover, service in the cause of national redemption required not the pursuit of individualism prescribed by liberalism, nor the realisation of an egalitarian society promised by socialism, but the rebirth of the nation as the living community to which all true peoples belonged. A recovered national identity thus transcended the individual and united all classes in a common enterprise.

Beset by liberalism and socialism, fascists believed that the prospect of national solidarity was in imminent danger of collapse, either through the neglect of a people preoccupied with their own selfish interests or via the promotion of class conflict which threatened to set them against one another. To combat these twin dangers fascism sought to reinvent and reinvigorate a common national identity and to expunge any and all ideas that threatened the totalising homogeneity of its beliefs. As Sternhell observes: 'Fascism was a vision of a coherent and reunited people [and] waged an implacable war against anything which stood for diversity or pluralism.'[2]

PROBLEMS OF DEFINITION

Though we inevitably associate fascism with the regimes of Hitler and Mussolini, it did not emerge entirely unannounced with Mussolini's march on Rome in 1922, but from an eclectic range of ideas that long predate the twentieth century. This chapter attempts to trace the lineage of those ideas that were shaped into a relatively coherent perspective on society by the proponents of fascism. This is not a simple task since the ideas themselves are 'untidy and inchoate' and were unscrupulously pillaged from other traditions, cultures and doctrines. Moreover, there is no single classical text akin, say, to the works of Marx, which supplied the inspiration of fascist leaders and thinkers. Its tributaries flowed from a variety of sources, creating pools of thought that surged into the mainstreams of Italian fascism and German national socialism.

To lend some order to the task of plotting the course of fascism the chapter provides a conspectus of organising themes: statism, racialism, imperialism, elitism, and national socialism. These interact and overlap and vary in their significance across the various fascist parties and movements, each of which was influenced by its own national history, traditions, cultures and prejudices. Thus, while acknowledging that there were distinctive national variations, the argument of this chapter is that a recognisably fascist worldview can be apprehended by concentrating upon its intellectual heritage. The exploration of these origins thereby provides a framework within which each of the variations can be accommodated. What the chapter offers is not, therefore, an unambiguous definition of fascism but a rehearsal of its key themes.

Besides the difficulties of tracing these themes, there is another problem confronting the interpretation of fascism. The heavy and fatal emphasis upon racialism by German national socialism that paved the way to the death camps of Europe does, in the view of some scholars, set it apart from other fascist movements. According to such writers the systematic practice of mass genocide renders Nazism as unique, not just an exaggerated variation of fascism. While not diminishing this argument, the purpose here is to identify the ideas that, among other things, supplied the pretext for the 'final solution'. Moreover, to imply that other fascist regimes were not implicated in the holocaust is to turn a blind eye to their complicity in transporting Jews and others to certain death in Auschwitz and elsewhere.

While the exponents of fascism sought to celebrate its modernity, none of the various elements that they fashioned into a body of doctrine was new in itself. The inter-war fascist movements inherited their ideas most immediately from a mood of revolt that was current in Europe towards the end of the nineteenth century and which had developed throughout its course. This mood is, then, our starting point.

ORIGINS AND DERIVATIONS

The temptation to label historical periods in terms of a prevailing mood or climate is a hazardous undertaking, often concealing more than it reveals. With that caveat in mind, one can characterise the European intellectual climate towards the end of the last century as one of revolt. Just as the regimes of Mussolini and Hitler emanated from economic and political crises, the embryonic ideology of fascism was one outcome of an intellectual upheaval that become more apparent as the nineteenth century drew to a close. Initially, this upheaval took the form of an assault upon liberal doctrine.

The birth of liberalism, as Robert Eccleshall indicates (Chapter 2), was associated with Enlightenment optimism, its proponents stressing the importance of individual judgement as the guide to action. Enlightenment thinkers demanded a new political system that would liberate individuals from the shackles of feudalism. Their portrayal of society as an aggregate of rational individuals, possessed with natural rights, challenged conservatism's gloomy and pessimistic view of human nature. The liberal belief that individuals in interaction would produce a natural harmony of interests was opposed to the conservative belief in the necessity for order imposed by a natural hierarchy. Whereas conservatives espoused a paternalistic conception of society, emphasising duty and deference, liberals stressed individual rights and a belief in self-government.

However, the advance of liberalism in Europe was uneven and at first opposition to it tended to be rather sporadic. Yet, by the 1880s and 1890s a generation of thinkers had emerged whose works constituted a challenge to what they perceived as the outmoded character of liberal ideas. It is within the context of this revolt against liberalism that the more immediate precursors of fascism can be located.

The rational individualism of the liberal doctrine, its belief in diversity, pluralism and tolerance led, so these critics argued, to insecurity, instability and mediocrity. The focus of analysis for the architects of this intellectual revolt was not the individual, but the wider inter-connected or organic community. Moreover, the liberal precept that reason was the guide to action was challenged by a preference for non-rational motives – instinct, heredity, race – which were acclaimed as the primary motors of human behaviour.

Such thinkers, some of whom owed their inspiration to a perverse reading of Charles Darwin's (1809–82) *Origin of Species* (1859) and who have been dubbed 'Social Darwinists', tended to portray individuals as unreflective and amoral creatures, spurred by the instinctive fight for survival. Darwin himself did not draw any normative lessons from the theory of natural selection that were applicable to human society. The phrase 'the survival of the fittest' was not Darwin's but was coined by Herbert Spencer (1820–1903), the British philosopher, thereby putting a simplifying and distorting gloss on the theory of evolution.

Such distortions presented a fundamental antithesis to liberalism's emphasis upon deliberate, rational choice as the basis of human action. While Spencer was an arch defender of *laissez-faire* his belief, shared by other Social Darwinists, that society progresses through a harsh struggle for survival and that the weak suffer from their own incompetence, did contribute to the assault upon liberal values. Moreover, the rather muscular philosophy of Social Darwinism helped to foster an intellectual climate within which the myth of racialism began to flourish.

RACE AND STATE

Pseudo-scientific 'theories' of racialism, partly inspired by a wilful misreading of Darwin's ideas, were but one manifestation of a much longer current of thought. For instance, during the late eighteenth and early nineteenth centuries the theme of racial superiority surfaced in Germany with the popularisation of the *Volk*. At a literal level this concept translates as 'the people', but it also has a more abstract connotation: a system of absolute values, an immutable metaphysical ideal of peoplehood. As George Mosse puts it: 'Just as individual men had a soul, so there existed a *Volk* soul which, like man's soul, gave the *Volk* its unique and unchanging character.' The task for Germans was to recover and liberate their collective soul which was 'wild and dynamic, based on emotions rather than on a tortured intellectualizing'.[3]

An early exponent of this abstract interpretation of the *Volk* was Johann Fichte (1762–1814) who, like his contemporary Johann Herder (1744–1803), depicted the German nation as a natural whole united by descent, language and culture. At the beginning of the nineteenth century Fichte propagated the belief that Germany, though disunited and having been militarily humiliated by France, would eventually prevail because of the natural superiority of its people. In his *Addresses to the German Nation* (1807–8), he portrayed the Germans as an archetypal *Volk*, in whom was invested a special mission on behalf of mankind: that of leading a cultural struggle against Western, primarily, French influence.

Such implacable beliefs, allied to a sense of mission, provided a source of brooding consolation – one that was also promoted by Herder. He traced the origins of the *Volk* to medieval Germany which he envisaged as a close-knit rural society wherein the *Volkisch* 'spirit' or 'soul' was freely expressed. In the writings of both thinkers, the *Volk* was presented in romantic terms – a happy, rural idyll – that emphasised the organic wholeness of the national community. Both, moreover, regarded the interests of the individual as subordinate to the national 'spirit', while the German 'spirit' was claimed to be superior to that of other peoples.

This emphasis upon the organic nature of the state was also characteristic of Georg Hegel (1770–1831). Unlike Fichte, however, Hegel did not equate the state with a racial or natural conception of the *Volk*, although he did address the issue of German unification. In

The German Constitution (1803) he lamented the disintegration of the nation into a hotch-potch of rival petty princedoms, thereby depriving it of the collective sentiment he believed to be the foundation of statehood. He elaborated these and other ideas in *Philosophy of Right* (1821), which presented history as a dynamic process whose engine was the conflict or dialectic of ideas. In his view the state was the ultimate idea, the realisation of spirit or reason in history. Unlike Fichte and Herder, Hegel was not preoccupied by the search for German statehood but rather by the 'idea' of the state which he believed to be based upon 'the power of reason actualising itself as will'. Thus, while conceptualising the state as an integrated community, he argued that its basis was rational freedom: within it individuality and collectivity, the particular and the universal, co-existed on the basis of reason.

Such a state was to be neither absolutist nor founded upon arbitrary force. It would secure many of the legal rights championed by liberals: the right to acquire private property and of free expression, for instance. In this way plurality and diversity would be preserved. His intention was not to subordinate the individual to the whole, but to illustrate how the state supplied its inhabitants with a common focus: a set of institutions and values with which all could freely associate. It was through their common membership of the state that individuals could move beyond their own private interests and identify with the common good. Yet Hegel's ideas, like those of Darwin later in the nineteenth century, were to fall prey to the fascists' search for an intellectual tradition.

Hegel's portrayal of the state as the culmination of history was to infatuate Mussolini as well as his leading ideologue and arbiter of cultural policy, Giovanni Gentile (1875–1944). But, whereas Hegel recognised the relationship between civil society and the state to be one of mutual dependence, in fascist Italy state and society were conflated: 'Everything for the State, nothing outside the State.' The quest for a renewed Roman Empire required a cloak of philosophical respectability and this Mussolini and Gentile purported to find in Hegel's perception of the idea of the state as an end in itself. This, however, was a perversion of Hegel's thought: he became another casualty of the avid need for an intellectual pretext for national regeneration. By contrast, as we shall see, German national socialism did not require even a distorted interpretation of Hegel. Unlike Mussolini, Hitler regarded the state not as an end in itself but as a means to assure racial superiority.

It was Fichte who had laid the basis of the *Volkisch* ideology that was to become the central organising principle of Nazism.

The belief in a superior German culture charged with a mission to overcome Western influences, coupled with the growth of intellectual support for the primacy of the state, gathered pace throughout the nineteenth century. In Germany, Friedrich Jahn (1778–1852) furthered the idea of a natural organic community and extolled the superiority of an anti-liberal, authoritarian Germanic political tradition. In *German Nationhood* (1810) Jahn defined the basis of nationhood as racial purity and asserted the uniqueness and superiority of all Germans. His goal was a greater German 'people's democracy', encompassing Austria, Holland, Switzerland and Denmark, from which all foreign influences would be banished.

Jahn prized national sentiment and nationhood above both individual rights and universalism and as such supplied a motive for a struggle against 'the West', i.e. against liberal precepts. It was a message that became increasingly strident at the turn of the nineteenth century as intellectuals from different national backgrounds sought a 'third way' between Enlightenment values and the growing 'threat' of international socialism.

By the mid-nineteenth century the concept of racial superiority was firmly established in European thought and was by no means confined to the works of German thinkers preoccupied with the goal of national reunification. One of the earliest expositions of racial 'theory' was provided by a French diplomat, Count Arthur Gobineau (1816–62), whose *Essay on the Inequality of Races of Man* (1853–5) proclaimed both the superiority of white 'races' over non-whites and Jews as well as the primacy of 'race' above individual and nation. Furthermore, he claimed to identify degrees of racial purity among whites: those possessing the highest levels of purity carried the potential to advance civilisation, whereas those less richly endowed transmitted racial decay. In the former category lay the Teutons, whereas Slavs and Celts were consigned to the latter group.

The attempt to invent a racial hierarchy within which Jews occupied the lowliest position can be placed within a tradition of anti-Semitism that long predates Gobineau. Stereotypes of Jews were commonplace throughout much of European history, assuming the form of religious antagonism towards Judaism during the later eighteenth and the first half of the nineteenth century. This cultural prejudice, which was widely propagated in popular literature, supplied a spurious rationale for anti-Semitism and assisted in creating a receptive climate for the ideas of Gobineau and certain of the Social Darwinists.

It had earlier been contended that the 'Jewish problem' could be solved by resocialising Jews, encouraging them to shed their religious beliefs which served to set them apart from the dominant cultures of their 'host' societies. By engaging in 'honest toil', moreover, Jews would acquire new roots and thus become deserving of assimilation into their adopted countries. However, as the essentially irrational *Volkisch* nationalism began to subvert Enlightenment values, Jews came to be regarded not merely as non-assimilable but as constituting a racial rather than a cultural threat to the German nation.

This transformation from cultural to biological anti-Semitism was stimulated by Social Darwinism whose adherents could be found throughout Europe. One English thinker who contributed to this metamorphosis was Houston Stewart Chamberlain (1855–1927). Asserting that the fittest were those who were racially pure, Chamberlain developed the notion of the 'Aryan folk nation' which, he believed, was 'destined to triumph because of its superior genetic gifts'.[4] On this basis, inter-racial marriage (miscegenation) was scorned as an unnatural evil since it diluted the purity of the blood. Egalitarianism, internationalism and pacifism were dismissed on the ground that they offended the natural order. In their place, war and the struggle for survival by the fittest were extolled as evidence of a race's vitality. Destiny belonged to those confident of their intrinsic superiority, itself bestowed by racial purity.

NATIONAL IMPERIALISM

During much of the nineteenth century, nationalism, through its association with the French Revolution, was understood by many as an agent of emancipation and freedom. However, under the impact of a racially defined conception of statehood, a new European nationalism began to develop: one nourished by the conviction that the unification of both Italy and Germany was the outcome of an intoxicating mixture of 'blood and iron'. The growing belief in a racial state spanning generations and existing frontiers, together with the advocacy of struggle by Social Darwinists of the Spencerite persuasion, fused to provide a rationale for imperialism. This found expression in the principle of *Machtpolitik*: the belief that might was right.

The creed of *Machtpolitik* was succinctly expressed by the German General Friedrich von Bernhardi (1843–1930):

> might gives the right to occupy or conquer. It is at once the supreme right and the dispute as to what is right is decided by the arbitrariment of war. War gives a biologically just decision, since its decisions rest on the very nature of things.[5]

Here lay the pretext for national expansion: racial superiority and the naturalness of conflict provided a perverse normative guide. Power and morality were fused and the interests of the nation displaced any attachment to the rule of international law and the universal rights of man.

The interaction of power politics with nationalism and racialism is equally explicit in the works of Chamberlain and his fellow Englishman, Karl Pearson (1857–1936). Pearson regarded the exercise of might as a moral injunction: 'when wars cease there will be nothing to check the fertility of the inferior stock'.[6] Chamberlain shared this view. Presenting the process of history as a race struggle, and arguing that only the Aryans were capable of creating culture, he proposed that 'the power of might is the destiny of selected races . . . it is their duty to conquer and destroy the impure and inferior'.[7]

The advocacy of war as a moral duty, the growing equation of race with statehood and the primacy of national as opposed to individual interests, began to coalesce towards the later part of the nineteenth century. National greatness, imbued with a spiritual mission, supplied the motive for imperial expansion.

ELITISM AND LEADERSHIP

The growing emphasis upon race and the idea of a universal mission required leadership of a distinctive character: a figure who embodied the claimed virtues of the race. The disdain for egalitarian principles espoused by Social Darwinists led them to mock democratic forms of government. Not only did they postulate a natural hierarchy among 'races', they also asserted the existence of naturally superior individuals within racial groups. Here lay the justification for leadership by an elite.

One exponent of elitism was Friedrich Nietzsche (1844–1900). Some of his ideas and much of his rhetoric were to be appropriated by fascists and yet he too fell foul of their greedy search for a philosophical tradition. Nietzsche affirmed the irrational 'will to power' as the mainspring of personality and the value of life to be measured by perpetual struggle: 'Life itself is essentially appropriation, infringement, the overpowering of the alien and the weaker, oppression, hardness, the imposition of one's own form, assimilation and, at the least and mildest, exploitation'.[8] This virile prescription demanded an elite of the tough and the strong who would lead the 'lower orders' whose instincts were slavishly to defer to their natural leaders and betters.

His portrayal of the leader figure took on heroic proportions: a 'Superman', a 'magnificent blond beast', who would trounce the weak, the decadent and the mediocre. Equality had no place in this vision; in its place was a conception of the naturally superior. This credo was to prove irresistible to later fascist leaders: in Nazi Germany this image of leadership was enshrined as the *Führerprinzip*, and in Italy it was personified in the cult of *Il Duce*.

Yet, as already suggested, Nietzsche's reputation was sullied by fascism. While a proponent of irrationalism, he was not an advocate of the organic society but rather a radical individualist. He did not embrace nationalism and, far from decrying miscegenation, considered it to be the source of great culture. But it was the appeal of his wilder rhetorical flourishes – the imagery of blond beasts animated by the will to power – that proved compelling to the would-be 'Supermen' of Nazi Germany and fascist Italy. As with Hegel and Darwin, the appropriation of Nietzsche as a progenitor of fascism was testimony to the selective looting of ideas engaged in by its ideologues.

The advocacy of elitism was also shared by many of Nietzsche's contemporaries. At a time when the fitful but progressive movement towards mass enfranchisement was occurring, the fear of the implications of democracy encouraged numerous thinkers to devise arguments for the continuation of leadership by the few. The Italian academic Vilfredo Pareto (1848–1923), for instance, in a number of works extolled the virtues of elite leadership (*Les Systèmes socialistes*, 1902, and *The Mind and Society*, 1916–19). He likened society to a pyramid, at the apex of which stood a gifted minority fitted to govern, supported by an acquiescent and mediocre mass below. Such ideas bore the hallmark of Social Darwinism, as did his theory of history which he understood as the story of conflict between warring elites. So popular were his views that in 1922 Mussolini made him a member of the Italian Senate.

Similar ideas were expressed by the French intellectual Roberto

Michels (1876–1936). In *Political Parties* (1911), he argued the need for a dominant social group to ensure the well-being of social and political life. Both he and Pareto feared popular participation and democratic control and were convinced of the unfitness of the people to govern themselves. Each represented their ideas not as theoretical or ideological formulations but as natural laws, thereby seeking to legitimise their anti-liberal and anti-democratic beliefs by asserting their 'scientific' credentials.

Disdain for 'the masses' was shared by another French theorist, Gustave Le Bon (1841–1931). His *Psychology of Crowds* (1865), later cited with approval by Mussolini, offered a justification for elitism and authoritarianism. In Germany, Julius Langbehn's (1851–1907) *Rembrandt as Educator* (1891) echoed Le Bon's contempt for mass democracy. Langbehn postulated race as the determining factor in history: the 'power of blood' was, he claimed, supreme and transcended the nation. His preferred elite was the hereditary aristocracy which he urged to mobilise the masses in order to crush those he considered guilty of propounding liberal, democratic, and socialist ideas: the bourgeoisie and assimilated Jews.

Though their precise roles as progenitors of fascism differed, Nietzsche, Pareto, Michels, Le Bon, and Langbehn did foster the 'baleful creed' of permanent struggle, elitism and unreason. In that respect each contributed to the climate of irrationalism that characterised the intellectual ferment of the later nineteenth century. The cult of elitism, the emphasis on power, struggle and authoritarianism, the stress on feeling and instinct, were pitted against the rational individualism of the liberal world. In the developing mass societies of late nineteenth-century Europe, the portrayal of the individual as an integral part of an organic whole, valued only inasmuch as s/he served that whole, was a direct challenge to liberalism. Moreover, the defiant critique of Enlightenment values supplied by Social Darwinists led them to prize inegalitarianism. The celebrants of unreason regarded the people as an unthinking, irrational and pliable mass, responsive to the appeals of emotion and feeling orchestrated by those Nietzsche had characterised as 'the highest specimens'.

NATIONALIST SOCIALISM

The appeal of the prophets of unreason was not restricted to the realm of ideas, but was enhanced by their explanation of worsening material conditions confronting Europe. The experience of a severe economic depression in the last quarter of the nineteenth century weakened the grip of a belief in both *laissez-faire* economics and free trade: as such liberalism's claim to be the guarantor of economic progress came under increasing strain. Furthermore, the Prussian rise to ascendancy in Germany, the Piedmont ascendancy in Italy and the defeat of France in 1870 by the Prussian army, all appeared to demonstrate the law of the strong advocated by Social Darwinists. The conjunction of these economic and political events underpinned the threat to liberal values. But the shock troops of the doctrinal assault against Enlightenment values, armed with their irrational remedies for national renewal, also had to confront the growth of socialism.

Socialism 'threatened' to divide nations on the basis of class interest and to promote international class solidarity which, to proponents of elite-led *Machtpolitik*, were anathema. In order to confront both liberalism and socialism a 'third way' needed to be fashioned between these competing ideologies. Part of the answer lay in extolling national solidarity and promoting economic self-sufficiency (autarky).

In German thought, the idea that all national resources should be marshalled for the national purpose was well rooted. Fichte, for instance, had advocated a planned economy, reduced imports and the restriction of external trade as the means to cohere the state. His prescriptions amounted to a highly regulated economy which were wholly at odds with the tenets of economic liberalism advanced by Adam Smith (1732–90). Moreover, Fichte proposed the expansion of the German state to its 'natural boundaries', as did another apostle of autarky, Friedrich List (1789–1846). List advanced a plan for expansion which involved the regulation of capital and labour, thereby endorsing a planned economy founded upon a Germany that incorporated both neighbouring states and overseas countries.

In Germany during the course of the nineteenth century, economic self-sufficiency came increasingly to be seen as necessary for the development of the power of the state and that entailed imperial expansion. In an atmosphere suffused with *Machtpolitik*, the espousal of internationalism by socialists was derided as nothing more than cowardice, whereas the exercise of power politics demanded the heroic appropriation of resources. In domestic terms, autarky was deemed to require loyalty, obedience and service in the national interest, not the rights of liberty, equality and fraternity. Liberal political economy was rejected because of its opposition to state intervention and its advocacy of free trade, while socialism was spurned because it was seen to weaken the nation by advocating class conflict, to champion egalitarianism, and promote internationalism.

In Britain the case for autarky was voiced both by Joseph Chamberlain (1836–1914) during the tariff reform campaign and the *fin de siècle* advocates of social imperialism, including George Bernard Shaw (1856–1950). What they shared in common was, as Robert Skidelsky notes, a belief in 'the national community as a value to be defended against free-trade internationalism on the one side and working class internationalism on the other'.[9] The themes of protectionism, imperial preference and a belief in a technocratically managed economy that Shaw and Chamberlain rehearsed were later to be taken up by Oswald Mosley (1896–1974), the leading British fascist of the inter-war period.

While autarky did not, ultimately, take root in Britain it was to flourish in Germany and Italy. In each case economic self-sufficiency was intimately related to the corporate state. Corporatism asserted that the array of social institutions, whether the family, region and, above all, the nation, enjoy a higher value than the individual. Its exponents claimed that the development and security of the individual depended upon the well-being of these institutions and their ability to foster social, economic, emotional and spiritual solidarity. As such their interests took precedence over those of the individual. From this perspective the health of the wider community, represented as a living and dynamic organism, was paramount. All the constituent parts were required to serve this higher purpose.

It was no accident that Mussolini chose an organic metaphor to characterise Italy under fascism: 'A society working with the harmony and precision of the human body. Every interest and every individual is subordinated to the overriding purpose of the nation.'[10] Here lay the third way between liberal capitalism and socialism. 'Liberalism', wrote Mussolini, 'denies the state in the interests of the individual' while 'socialism . . . ignores the unity of classes established in one economic and moral reality in the state'.[11] Through the imposition of functional organisations purporting to represent the interests of workers and employers, the wider national interest would be served.

Keenly aware of the mobilising appeal of nationalism and persuaded of the necessity for conflict to secure change, Mussolini attempted to fuse nationalism and socialism. The means lay through corporatism which exhorted all classes to collaborate in building the fascist state. Instead of fighting among themselves on the basis of misguided class interests or lending primacy to the pursuit of individual interests, Italians were urged to engage in a common external struggle: that between proletarian and bourgeois nations. This would rescue Italy from its status as the poor relation of Europe and thereby restore national greatness.

In devising this corporatist formula, Mussolini appropriated and perverted syndicalist ideas.[12] Originating in France, syndicalism advocated the creation of autonomous worker organisations (syndicates) as the basis for proletarian revolution. Its exponents believed that through direct action at the workplace the revolutionary transformation of capitalism could be achieved. In an earlier incarnation Mussolini had been a leading socialist and was familiar with the syndicalist vision. When he came to power, and especially after 1925 when he consolidated his dictatorship, he began to install a system of corporations loosely modelled upon these ideas. But, whereas revolutionary syndicalists had envisaged their organisations as being composed solely of workers, Mussolini's corporations encompassed both workers and employers. Moreover, though notionally equal, the spokesmen of capitalist interests were relatively unfettered while those of labour were mere puppets of his regime: the authentic voices of the working class were stifled by imprisonment, exile or death.

The exertion of centralised control over these corporations signals a crucial distinction between the syndicalist aspiration and that of Mussolini. The syndicalists were profoundly anti-statist whereas he elevated the state to a position of dominance:

> The keystone of Fascist doctrine is the conception of the State, of its essence, of its tasks, of its ends. For Fascism the State is an absolute before which individuals and groups are relative. Individuals and groups are 'thinkable' only in so far as they are within the State . . . when one says Fascism one says the State.[13]

Here lay the crude attempt to fuse nationalism and socialism. Italian fascism emphasised duty, sacrifice, and obedience in the service of the nation-state. The compelling interest was that of the nation, served by the rigidly organised and hierarchically controlled corporations that were bereft of autonomy. The conflation of nationalism and socialism was allegedly served by a brutally simplistic formula: the nation is the community to which all belong, thus all classes must serve the interests of the nation.

The pursuit of autarky also led to the imposition of a centralised and planned economy in Germany, the purpose of which was primarily rearmament. While corporatism was less fully developed than in Italy, the crushing of independent trade unions and their replacement in 1933 by the 'Labour Front' was couched in organic terms. Workers and employers were exhorted to serve, in Hitler's words, 'only one interest, the interest of the nation; only one view, the bringing of Germany to the point of political and economic self-sufficiency'.[14]

In Nazi Germany, as in Italy, the claim to socialist credentials was baseless. A belief in the common ownership of the means of production or of the abolition of wage slavery, for instance, held no place in Hitler's worldview. In *Mein Kampf* (1925–6) Hitler purported to define the 'socialist' aspects of Nazism in quite vacuous terms such as 'nationalising the masses' or 'giving the broad masses back to their nation'. To be 'social' was to share in a sense of 'feeling and destiny' in the national community.

As Robert Cecil observes, in Hitler's view the only acceptable form of socialism was that of the 'front-line' which had developed in the trenches of the First World War. This was characterised by Alfred Rosenberg (1893–1946), a leading ideologue of Nazism's racial 'theory', in the following terms: 'Out of the battlefield, the men in grey brought back something new: a feeling for the social and national cohesiveness of the different classes.'[15] The camaraderie of soldiers, the common bonds forged in battle, became the spurious metaphor for socialism.

The 'Twenty-Five Point Programme' of the Nationalist Socialist German Workers Party published in 1920[16] included such ostensibly impeccable socialist goals as the nationalisation of large corporations, the abolition of unearned incomes, the confiscation of war profits and the prohibition of land speculation. But the commitment to such an agenda wore increasingly thin, albeit that Hitler was keenly aware of the need to counter the growth of support among workers for socialism, which was portrayed as a 'Jewish Marxist conspiracy'.

By the later 1920s the relative failure of the Nazi Party to secure mass support among the working classes led them to reorientate their appeal to capitalists, small businessmen, farmers and white-collar workers. While there were those in the Nazi Party, like the Strasser brothers, Gregor and Otto, and the leader of the SA (the Brownshirts), Ernst Rohm, who sought to promote more tangible material benefits for the working class, they were progressively marginalised. The persistence of Gregor Strasser and of Rohm in seeking to sustain and develop gains for workers led, ultimately, to their murders in 1934. Their 'purge', on the pretext that they were engaged in a plot against Hitler, also effectively purged the Nazi Party of an already threadbare socialist programme.

Consistent with his unwavering belief in racial hierarchy, egalitarianism was anathema to Hitler, whether within or among peoples. What mattered was the moulding of a common unity among Germans as nationalists, thereby transcending the alternative appeals of class or individual interest. Like Mussolini, Hitler subscribed to an organic conception of society. Individuals mattered only insofar as they served the whole: 'If we consider the question, what in reality are the state-forming or even state-preserving forces, we can sum them up under one single head: the ability and will of the individual to sacrifice himself for the totality.'[17]

Ostensibly a mode of economic organisation, fascist corporatism supplied the means to mobilise and control the working population: it served the purpose of integrating the working class into a national organic whole. The encouragement of improved working conditions through the 'Beauty of Labour' scheme, the organisation of leisure activities by the 'Strength through Joy' movement and the reduction in high levels of unemployment achieved by a massive programme of rearmament were all deployed after Hitler's appointment as Chancellor in 1933 to win over industrial workers.[18]

Yet, while expressing socialist pretensions, corporatism in inspiration and practice was nothing more than state capitalism. Individuals were perceived as expendable means to be used in pursuit of a regenerated national community. The grotesque simplicity of the national socialist dimension of fascism was epitomised by Oswald Mosley: 'If you love our country you are national and if you love our people you are socialist.'

INTERIM SUMMARY

All the various elements of a fascist worldview were apparent in the Europe of the later nineteenth century. The emphasis that each of them received – statism, racialism, elitism, imperialism, and national socialism – varied in accordance with the diverse traditions of those nations that produced fascist regimes, movements, or parties. In Italy, Mussolini stressed statism. It was not until 1938, for instance, that racialism in the form of anti-Semitic laws were introduced. Five years earlier he had praised Italian Jews for their military service in the First World War and their exemplary roles in society and economy.[19] The abrupt about-turn was a cynical move by Mussolini: from being celebrated as 'good citizens', Jews of Italian birth became pawns unscrupulously used as a means of consolidating the axis with Nazi Germany.

Though Mussolini was to adopt biological racialism, proclaiming Italians to be 'Aryans of Mediterranean type', his key preoccupation was the renewal of the Italian state. The introduction of corporatism provided the means of instilling the will and of securing the resources to embark on the imperial regeneration of the fascist state. Portraying Italy as a living organism supplied the rationale for imperialism: just as healthy, individual organisms develop and grow, so too must the state. War and conquest were symptoms of its health: 'For Fascism the tendency to Empire . . . is a manifestation of its [the state's] vitality: its opposite, staying at home, is a sign of decadence . . . . War alone puts the stamp of nobility upon the peoples.'[20] The renewal of empire was testimony to the well-being of the state.

In Nazi Germany, the goal was racial supremacy. Hitler was a racial nationalist, obsessed by a fanatical belief in the redemptive power of blood. History was, in his view, the record of the rise and fall of biologically determined racial groups. Humankind, he asserted, fell into three categories: creators of culture; bearers of culture; and destroyers of culture. The Aryans comprised the first group, Chinese and Japanese the second and Jews the last. To re-establish the primacy of the Aryans their blood had to be repurified – and this required the elimination of 'the Jewish threat'.

Hitler explained the German collapse at the end of the First World War as the outcome of the progressive degeneration of its people's blood which had eroded national resolve and purpose. The responsibility for this degeneracy lay with the Jews. By promoting doctrines – liberalism and Marxism – that celebrated either individualism, egalitarianism or internationalism, they had engineered the cultural acceptability of miscegenation and subverted the national solidarity of Germans. The resulting dilution of the racially pure blood stock not only left Germany enfeebled, but by proscribing mixed marriages 'International Jewry' had kept its own blood pure and was therefore poised to achieve world domination.

Thus, the racial policy was twofold. Aryan blood had to be repurified and those who threatened impurity had to be eradicated: 'There is no making pacts with Jews: there can only be the hard "either-or".' The introduction of racial laws in 1933 and their acceleration thereafter was an early indication of the path destined to lead to mass genocide. The laws were accompanied by an unrelenting propaganda campaign that depicted Jews as the enemy within. In *Mein Kampf*, Hitler had portrayed Jews in terms that resonated with the conception of Germany as a 'national organism': 'virus', 'bacillus', 'parasite' were his preferred metaphors. Such imagery was recycled, whether in official proclamations or popular literature, presenting Jews as carriers of disease. Without the removal of 'the Jewish menace . . . all attempts at German reawakening and resurrection are . . . absolutely senseless and impossible'.

The representation of Jews as the embodiment of evil was one side of the racial policy equation: the other was a whole panoply of measures designed to promote 'racial hygiene'. Thus, while Jews and other 'lesser races' were to be exterminated and the 'hereditarily ill' (the mentally and physically handicapped) and the 'asocial' (certain criminal offenders and homosexuals) either compulsorily sterilised or killed, 'positive' measures were introduced to improve and purify German blood.

Selective breeding programmes were introduced favouring those who personified 'Aryanism', the SS (*Schutzstaffel* or guard squadron). Its members were ordered to 'produce children of good blood' through a union with racially pure women, whether within or outside marriage. Children from countries occupied by Germany who were deemed to exhibit Aryan characteristics were abducted and returned to 'the Fatherland' where they were to be 'Germanised' within 'racially acceptable families'. Such were the means that were adopted to create 'a community of physically and psychically homogeneous creatures'. This task was, moreover, invested with divine mission by Hitler: 'I believe that I am acting in the sense of the Almighty Creator: by warding off the Jews, I am fighting for the Lord's work.'

Such policies were also said to be consistent with what Hitler styled 'the aristocratic principle of Nature' – that the fittest, the strongest, the most racially pure – would always prevail. This 'principle' was also employed to justify dictatorship: 'leadership and the highest influence . . . fall to the best minds [and] builds not upon the idea of the majority, but upon the idea of the personality'. On this basis Hitler erected the *Führerprinzip*: 'absolute responsibility unconditionally combined with absolute authority . . . the one man alone may possess the authority and right to command'. Democracy was rejected as a 'sin' against the 'aristocratic principle – the authority of the individual'.

Whereas in fascist Italy imperialism was the test of the vitality of the state, in Nazi Germany it was a measure of racial superiority. The conquest and occupation of neighbouring countries designed to procure resources and living space (*Lebensraum*) symbolised the restoration of the 'natural order'. 'Nature', declared Hitler, 'knows no political boundaries . . . soil exists for the people which have the force to take it'. In this respect, the two dictators subscribed to opposed theories of the state. Mussolini, as we have seen, regarded the state as an end in itself. By contrast, in *Mein Kampf* Hitler portrayed it as a means to the end of racial supremacy: 'the state must regard as its highest task the preservation and intensification of the race . . . . We, as Aryans, can conceive of the state only as the living organism of a nationality . . . . We must distinguish between the state as a vessel and the race as its content.'

The heavy and fatal emphasis on biological racialism within Nazism does perhaps set it apart from Italian fascism. But rather than trying to draw a contestable distinction between Nazism and fascism on the basis of their ideological priorities, the preferred approach here is to represent the doctrine in fluid rather than solid terms. The argument of this chapter is that while its national varieties may have stressed differing elements, each fascist movement drew upon a common set of ideas that had long been current in European political thought. One such idea exemplifying the inegalitarian core of fascism was its treatment and representation of women.

FASCISM AND WOMEN

In the chapter on feminism we note the pervasive dualism that has underpinned Western political thought. This both assigned women to a different realm from that inhabited by men and put a premium on the activities and attributes of men. The distinction between the private, female 'world' and the public, male sphere was not just implicit in fascism; it was openly promoted. On this issue there was nothing to distinguish the beliefs of Hitler from those of Mussolini.

Both exemplified patriarchal attitudes, asserting that the natural sphere for women was that of home and family. Hitler distinguished between the 'greater world', monopolised by men, in which affairs of state, politics and war were conducted and the 'smaller world' which was the domain of women: 'her world is her husband, her family, her children and her home'. The enfranchisement of women, which had occurred in Weimar Germany, was an 'invention of Jewish intellectuals' that distracted women from 'the duties nature imposes'. Such 'duties' were summarised by Hitler's propaganda chief, Joseph Goebbels (1897–1945): 'The mission of woman is to be beautiful and to bring children into the world . . . the female prettifies herself for her mate and hatches the eggs for him.'[21]

The natural superiority of men was axiomatic within fascist ideology. This was conveyed in the popular Nazi slogan *Kinder, Kirche, Küche*. Respectively, this confined women to bearing children, attending church and working in the kitchen. The clear boundary drawn between the public and private worlds was founded upon the assertion of intrinsic, if complementary, differences between the sexes: 'Man and Woman represent two quite different characteristics: in Man understanding is dominant [which] is more stable than emotion which is the mark of Woman.'[22]

The recurring view peddled by Hitler was of the naturally dependent and submissive woman, prone to passion and outbursts of jealousy. Preserving the public realm for men was represented as a chivalrous act preventing women from making an exhibition of themselves:

> I detest women who dabble in politics . . . . There she is, ready to pull her hair out, with all her claws showing. In short gallantry forbids one to give women an opportunity of putting themselves in situations that do not suit them. Everything that entails combat is exclusively men's business. There are so many other fields in which one must rely upon women. Organising a house, for instance.[23]

In Italy, Mussolini retailed similar attitudes, yet his views on women followed a more serpentine course than those of Hitler. In 1919 the fascist programme advocated female suffrage and three years later endorsed equal rights for women. Mussolini's own support for female enfranchisement seems, though, to have been less than principled. His ambition to institute corporatism led him to favour occupational suffrage rather than the enfranchisement of individuals electing representatives to a democratic assembly. Moreover, from the early 1920s the party's support for female suffrage waned and increasingly patriarchal policies prevailed.

As in Nazi Germany legislation was introduced barring women from certain occupations and exhorting them to produce children.

Echoing Hitler's gendered perception of 'greater' and 'smaller worlds', Mussolini asserted that 'war is the most important thing in a man's life as maternity is in a woman's'. From the mid-1920s, under the slogan 'woman into the home', measures were introduced that encouraged them back into the domestic realm where they would be prized as the pillars of the family. Such measures were welcomed by the Vatican. In 1930 Pius XI issued his encyclical *Casti Connubi* which urged women to perform their natural roles as wives and mothers within the hearth and home.[24]

Mussolini's stated opinions on women were disdainful. He regarded them as a 'charming pastime, when a man has time to pass, a means of changing one's trend of thought . . . but they should never be taken seriously, for they themselves are rarely serious'. In *Talks with Mussolini* published in 1933 the author, Emil Ludwig, reports that the dictator expressed his opposition to feminism, his belief that women should obey and stated that 'while a woman must not be a slave . . . in our state women must not count'.[25]

In one essential respect, of course, women did count in both Nazi Germany and fascist Italy: as producers of children. Women's reproductive role was vital to both regimes. In Hitler's design Aryan women were to be the bearers of the master race while Mussolini needed a growing population to people his planned renewed empire. Incentives were introduced in both countries to increase the birth rate, reducing women to little more than breeding machines. In Germany the laws governing marriage and fitness to reproduce were minutely governed by racialism; in Italy the preoccupation was with the sheer necessity for population growth, itself a signal of the vitality of the state.

Fascism's treatment of women further underlines the exclusivism and inegalitarianism that lay at the heart of the doctrine. Confined to their 'lesser worlds', women were valued only insofar as they submitted to subordination.

BRITISH FASCISM IN THE INTER-WAR YEARS

We have already noted the contribution of two English thinkers – Pearson and Chamberlain – to the evolution of fascist ideas, but the development of the doctrine in Britain is most closely associated with Oswald Mosley.

In 1932 Mosley founded the British Union of Fascists (BUF) having previously been a Conservative, Independent Conservative, Independent and a Labour MP. His transition from the Labour Party – from which he was expelled in 1931 – to fascism was by way of the 'New Party', a short-lived parliamentary-based all party group that was launched primarily to advance protectionist economic policies.

His political career had convinced Mosley of the need for the pursuit of autarky via corporatism which, he believed, had ushered in a new era. On his return from a visit to Italy in 1932 he declared: 'Italy has produced not only a new system of government but a new type of man who differs from politicians of the old world just as men from another planet.'[26] Like Hitler and Mussolini, he presented fascism as a youthful, vigorous movement propounding novel ideas for a new age. Yet, like those he sought to emulate, there was little that was original in his thought. Mosley merely packaged fascist themes into a form he believed acceptable to 'the British character'.

RACIALISM

Initially Mosley denied that the BUF subscribed to racialist ideas or harboured anti-Semitic beliefs, yet both were to become increasingly prominent throughout the 1930s. Indeed, anti-Semitic sentiments were evident from the first even though they were expressed in coded terms. Thus: 'we have within the nation a power, largely controlled by alien elements, which arrogates to itself a power above the State'.[27] In 1933, though claiming that anti-Semitism had been Hitler's 'greatest mistake', he banned Jews from joining the BUF. In the same year the Irishman William Joyce, one of Mosley's chief aides – later to achieve notoriety as 'Lord Haw Haw' – wrote in the movement's journal, *Blackshirt*: 'the low type of foreign Jew together with other aliens who are debasing the life of the nation will be run out of the country in double-quick time under fascism'.

From the mid-1930s the strain of anti-Semitism became more pronounced. The Jews were presented as a subversive 'state within the state' seeking to engineer war with Germany. A signal of the growing virulence of these beliefs was the change in 1936 of the name of his movement to the British Union of Fascists and National Socialists. Anti-Semitism, though couched in oblique terms ('the money power' or 'international finance'), bulked ever larger in Mosley's speeches. Allegations that Jews were manipulating the established political parties became routine. Only his movement would root out 'alien influences' since it alone was not in thrall to their 'money power'.

His rhetoric recalls that of Hitler. In musing on his preferred 'final solution' to 'the Jewish problem', Mosley proposed the creation of an artificial homeland 'in one of the many waste places of the world' where they could languish 'and cease to be the parasite of humanity'. Such an option had been contemplated by Mussolini but, as we noted above, the introduction of racial laws in Italy did lead to the deaths of Italian Jews in Europe's concentration camps. It is not implausible to suggest that Mosley, who shifted his allegiance to Hitler in 1936, would have followed the same genocidal route had a fascist regime secured power in Britain.

CORPORATISM

Mosley's infatuation with the corporate state in his earlier writings matured with his experiences in Italy. His advocacy of this model of economic and political organisation dovetailed the themes of statism and nationalist socialism. In 1932 he argued that Britain's economic crisis was the result of the stubborn attachment of the 'old gangs' of politicians to *laissez-faire* at home and free trade abroad: attachments which reflected the influence and power of 'international finance'. The remedy was the modernisation or 'rationalisation' of the economy by corporate means.

In the place of minimal government and a free-market economy, he prescribed planning and protectionism. In advancing such measures his remarks were virtually indistinguishable from those of Mussolini. Urging the need to introduce corporatism so as to reconcile 'individual initiative with the wider interests of the nation' he verged on plagiarism: 'it means a nation organised as the human body, with each organ performing its individual function but working in harmony with the whole'.[28] The national organism was paramount, its interests superseding the individualism celebrated by liberals and the class interests prized by socialists. Here lay the meshing of nationalism and socialism. Yet his scheme for a 'third way' between competing doctrines extinguished autonomy and freedom for workers' and employers' organisations and quashed democratic party politics. 'There will', he stated ominously, 'be no room in Britain for those who do not accept the principle "All for the State and the State for All".'

Internally, Britain would be run on authoritarian lines with pride of place given to the virtues of obedience, order and discipline: all would be bent to 'the national purpose'. To ensure self-sufficiency he proposed 'insulation'. This entailed a ban on the importation of all goods that could be produced in Britain and a closed imperial economy wherein the colonies would supply resources and markets for British products. Here there are echoes of social imperialism's autarkic design, amplified by a racially inspired argument. The colonies were to be denied independence both because they would be susceptible to 'alien influences' and also because Mosley considered the colonial 'races' to be unfitted for the task of economic development.

ELITISM AND LEADERSHIP

Mosley's apocalyptic vision of impending economic collapse, allied to his conviction that the 'old gangs' had succumbed to the machinations of 'the money power', led him to justify the need for political authoritarianism. In the first edition of *The Greater Britain* (1932) he appeared to favour collective leadership since it was better suited to 'the British character'. Two years later his view had changed:

> Leadership in fascism may be an individual or a team, but single leadership in practice proves the most effective instrument. The leader must be prepared to shoulder absolute responsibility for the functions clearly allocated to him.

Mosley's dictatorial ambitions were clear from his plans to 'reform' Parliament which he portrayed as an assembly of 'do-nothing committees'. The first fascist Parliament would invest the government with the power to impose the corporate state by order, leaving the executive free from scrutiny. While Parliament would, at this stage, possess the authority to dismiss the government through a vote of censure, thereafter that power would be denied. Political parties would be expunged, an occupational franchise introduced, the House of Lords abolished and replaced by a new second chamber composed of a technocratic elite charged to assist in the implementation of the corporate state.

To supplement the occupational franchise Mosley proposed to introduce a series of plebiscites or referendums. The population would be invited to express their support for the fascist programme through this populist device. Party-based democratic politics would cease:

> In such a system there is no place for parties and politicians. We shall ask the people for a mandate to bring to an end the Party system and the Parties. We invite them to enter a new civilisation. Parties and the party game belong to the old civilisation which has failed.[29]

Mosley's blighted vision, his readiness to employ violence to realise it – 'by one road or another we are determined that Fascism will come to Britain' – and his parroting of themes common to Hitler and Mussolini places him firmly in the fascist retinue. His initial enthusiasm for corporatism, though it never waned, was complemented by his later alignment with Hitler: 'the principles of National Socialism are necessary to the solution of Britain'.

CONTEMPORARY BRITISH FASCISM

The election in 1993 of a member of the British National Party (BNP) to the local council in Tower Hamlets, London, provided a disturbing reminder of the resilience of fascist ideas. The east end of London, including Tower Hamlets, was a favoured stamping ground of Mosley and his erstwhile stormtroopers, the Blackshirts. In the 1930s, these uniformed thugs engaged in street fights with the area's Jewish population and others, notably communists and socialists, in the attempt to inflame prejudice against 'outsiders' and 'alien influences'. Mosley's efforts to rekindle fascism in the area following his release from wartime internment proved to be singularly unsuccessful. In his wake other groups emerged to promote fascist ideas, seeking to exploit ill-founded concern over non-white immigration. One such group was the National Front (NF).

The National Front was created in 1967, though it in turn was to split in 1982, one faction of which – led by John Tyndall – was to form the BNP, itself flanked by a number of other British neo-fascist organisations including 'Third Way' and 'Blood and Honour'. The pattern of factionalism and splintering that has characterised neo-fascist organisations appears to be caused by the clash of inflated egos rather than any substantive doctrinal differences. Each has tried to garner support by fomenting anti-immigrant feeling directed against black Britons. Irrespective of ethnic differences, all are lumped together as 'them', an amorphous mass said to represent a fundamental threat to 'the British way of life'.

It is no coincidence that such groups seem to secure support at times of economic insecurity. Britain in the 1980s and 1990s has been char- acterised by recession, massive levels of unemployment, growing evidence of increased deprivation and homelessness – circumstances not wholly unlike those of the 1930s. Pressure on economic resources, coupled with atavistic feelings about British supremacy, are mixed into a potent formula which lays the blame for all social ills on a culturally or physically distinctive community, be they Jewish or black.

The construction of 'them' as folk-devils, responsible for perceived social decline, is a simplistic response to material insecurity and political uncertainty. The experience of recession throughout Europe has contributed to the modest revival of support for neo-fascist parties. The squeeze on economic resources, coupled with the flight of refugees from eastern Europe seeking employment in the more affluent parts of the continent, has been used to scapegoat non-nationals, prompting governments to introduce ever more restrictive controls on immi- gration. The arousal of anti-immigrant feeling has been the stock-in- trade of Tyndall, whose career in fascism leaves little doubt about the lineage of the BNP.

Prior to founding the BNP, Tyndall had been involved with a number of neo-Nazi groups. In 1961 he co-founded the World Union of National Socialists which acknowledged the 'spiritual leadership of Hitler' and included among its objectives 'the promotion of Aryanism'. A year later he joined the National Socialist Movement whose journal, asserting 'the correctness of Nazi ideology', exhorted its readers to 'join a movement which could ideologically and . . . physically smash the Red Front and Jewry'.[30] *En route* to the NF and the BNP, Tyndall co- founded the Greater Britain Movement which advocated racial laws prohibiting inter-marriage between Britons and 'non Aryans' and the compulsory sterilisation of the physically and mentally handicapped. Both measures would guarantee the country's future – 'a pure, strong, healthy race'.

Biological racialism has been a consistent feature of Tyndall's beliefs. The recycling of Hitler's ideas concerning 'racial hygiene' and anti- Semitism have marked all the groups with which he has been associ- ated. Though the anti-Semitic character of these ideas tends, as with the

BUF, to be expressed in euphemistic terms – 'money power', 'loan capitalism', or 'finance capitalism' – it lies at the core of current fascist groups in Britain. While they are associated primarily in the public mind with attacks on black British communities, below the surface the ideologues of fascism also peddle racially inspired attacks on Jews.

As with Hitler, what grips their fevered imagination is a belief that Jews are engaged in a world-wide conspiracy whose aim is to establish a global tyranny. By exercising their 'money power' so as to subvert Britain's economic independence; fostering internationalism through their support for Marxist ideas and the European Community; and 'polluting' the 'race' by promoting both inward migration and miscegenation, 'the British will to resist' will be eroded and Jewish world domination achieved. The remedies, like the analysis, are wearyingly familiar: autarky, corporatism, elite leadership, racialism, the primacy of the nation and the submissiveness of the individual to the state. Naturally, men will monopolise the public realm while women are, in Tyndall's terms, consigned to 'the feminine role – wife, mother, home-maker': if not barefoot then certainly pregnant in the fascist kitchen.

CONCLUSION

Proponents of fascism have proven adept at rummaging around in intellectual history in order to fashion their doctrine. In this undertaking they have been able to draw upon themes and ideas whose longevity is undeniable. Such ideas began to be particularly evident in the later eighteenth century as a reaction against the rational liberalism of the Enlightenment. Fascism's intolerance of difference and its corresponding preference for a monolithic unity, whether defined in national or racial terms, represented a counter-revolution against liberal values. Latterly, its precursors drew upon the same or related sources when faced by the ideological challenge from socialism in the later nineteenth century.

The antithetical character of the doctrine is clear from the following remarks of Mussolini and Goebbels. Referring to the values of liberty, equality and fraternity bestowed by the French Revolution, their target was clear: 'We stand', stated Mussolini, 'for a new principle in the world . . . sheer categorical definitive antithesis to the world which still abides by the fundamental principles laid down in 1789.' In a 1933 radio broadcast Goebbels was more succinct: 'The year 1789 is hereby eradicated from history.'

While fascists asserted the novelty of their ideas, the mainsprings of their beliefs were pre-modern. Lamenting a lost past, whether it was the Roman Empire, the agrarian society of medieval Germany or some other imagined community, fascism proposed a 'barbarous utopia' from which all diversity, individualism and pluralism would be extinguished. Now, as in the past, fascists seek to exploit the emotive simplicities of a national or a racial myth and to impose an unquestioning conformity upon all.

This intolerance of competing ideas and subjugation of individuals generated a way of analysing fascism that focused less upon its ideas, concentrating instead upon its character as a system of rule: totalitarianism. The word 'totalitarian' originated in Italy where it was employed by Mussolini in approving terms to characterise the fascist state (*stato totalitario*). However, the practititioners of fascism secured no monopoly of its usage. Totalitarianism has become both a widely used tool of analysis in the critical literature on fascism and a popular term of abuse levelled at regimes that seek to enforce political order through the systematic use of coercion. It has, for instance, been applied to the former apartheid regime of South Africa, Kampuchea under Pol Pot and Saddam Hussein's Iraq.

An influential representation of totalitarianism is the six-point syndrome formulated by Friedrich and Brzezinski.[31] Such systems of rule are, they argue, typified by an official, monolithic ideology; dictatorship within the context of a single party; the reliance on organised terror; and a state monopoly of mass communications, arms and the economy. Where such attributes are evident, the regime is, by definition, totalitarian.

Inspired by the regimes of Mussolini and Hitler, the syndrome was applied with equal vigour to the Soviet Union and its satellite states within central and eastern Europe. Such a parallel did, of course, serve an ideological purpose during the cold war period. Equating Stalin's Russia with Nazi Germany and fascist Italy was a powerful way of demonising the communist threat to liberal democracy. Totalitarianism became, in Griffin's terms, a 'boo-word', used to distinguish between closed and open societies.[32]

Though it may have been over-used for polemical purposes, totalitarianism does retain value as one means of acquiring an understanding of fascism. Yet, it does not by itself disclose the ideas upon which this system of rule was based: indeed, employed in a cavalier fashion it can even obscure them. It is the nature and lineage of those ideas that this chapter has tried to establish. However its exponents fashion the doctrine, whether in the past or in the contemporary world, at root fascism was, and is, profoundly anti-rational. The theatrical arousal of emotion, whether in the form of hate against 'them' or pride in 'us', represents no less than the attempt to numb the intellect and quell the critical spirit.

NOTES

1 Hugh Trevor-Roper, 'The Phenomenon of Fascism', in S. Woolf, ed., *Fascism in Europe*, London, Methuen, 1981, 19.
2 Zeev Sternhell, 'Fascist Ideology', in W. Laqueur, ed., *Fascism: A Reader's Guide*, Harmondsworth, Penguin, 1979, 368.
3 George Mosse, *Germans and Jews*, London, Orbach and Chambers, 1971, 8.
4 See Paul Hayes, *Fascism*, London, Allen and Unwin, 1973, 23ff.
5 Friedrich von Bernhardi, *Germany and the Next War*, London, Arnold, 1914.
6 Karl Pearson, *National Life from the Standpoint of Science*, London, Black, 1905, 27.
7 Quoted in Hayes, *Fascism*, 115.
8 Quoted in Hayes, *ibid.*, 34.
9 Robert Skidelsky, *Oswald Mosley*, London, Macmillan, 1975, 57.
10 Quoted in Martin Walker, *The National Front*, London, Fontana, 1977, 17.
11 Quoted in Adrian Lyttelton, ed., *Roots of the Right: Italian Fascism from Pareto to Gentile*, London, Cape, 1973, 42.
12 See D. Roberts, *The Syndicalist Tradition and Italian Fascism*, Manchester, Manchester University Press, 1979; A. James Gregor, *Italian Fascism and Developmental Dictatorship*, Princeton, Princeton University Press, 1979.
13 Quoted in Lyttelton, ed., *Roots of the Right*, 53, 55.
14 See Jeremy Noakes and Geoffrey Pridham, eds, *Documents on Nazism, 1919–1945*, London, Cape, 1974, 405.
15 Quoted in Robert Cecil, *The Myth of the Master Race*, London, Batsford, 1972, 57.
16 On the 'Twenty-Five Point Programme', see Noakes and Pridham, eds, *Documents on Nazism*, 37–40.

17 Adolf Hitler, *Mein Kampf*, London, Hutchinson, 1969, trans. by Ralph Mannheim, 140.
18 See Noakes and Pridham, eds, *Documents on Nazism*, 438ff.
19 See Laura Fermi, *Mussolini*, Chicago, University of Chicago Press, 1961, 290–1.
20 See Lyttelton, ed., *Roots of the Right*, 53, 56.
21 See Noakes and Pridham, eds, *Documents on Nazism*, 363.
22 See Norman Baynes, ed., *The Speeches of Adolf Hitler: April 1922 – August 1939*, New York, Howard Fertig, 1969, 531.
23 See *Hitler's Table Talk 1941–1944: His Private Conversations*, introduced by H. Trevor-Roper, trans. Norman Cameron and R.H. Stevens, London, Weidenfeld and Nicolson, 1973, 251–2.
24 See Philip Cannistraro, ed., *Historical Dictionary of Fascist Italy*, London, Greenwood Press, 1982, 203.
25 Quoted in Gregor, *Italian Fascism*, 287.
26 Quoted in Walker, *The National Front*, 23.
27 See Neil Nugent, 'The Ideas of the British Union of Fascists', in Neil Nugent and Roger King, eds, *The British Right*, Farnborough, Saxon House, 1977, 149.
28 Oswald Mosley, *Blackshirt Policy*, London, n.d., 25.
29 Quoted in Skidelsky, *Oswald Mosley*, 315.
30 Quoted in Walker, *The National Front*, 45.
31 Carl Friedrich and Zbigniew Brzezinski, *Totalitarian Dictatorship and Autocracy*, Cambridge, Mass., Harvard University Press, 1956.
32 Roger Griffin, 'Totalitarianism', in William Outhwaite and Tom Bottomore, eds, *The Blackwell Dictionary of Twentieth-Century Social Thought*, Oxford, Blackwell, 1993, 673–4.

FURTHER READING

The texts I found indispensable in plotting the origins of fascism included: Zeev Sternhell's 'Fascist Ideology', in Walter Laqueur, ed., *Fascism: A Reader's Guide*, Harmondsworth, Penguin, 1979; Karl Dietrich Bracher's *The German Dictatorship*, Harmondsworth, Penguin, 1973; Arno Mayer's *The Persistence of the Old Regime*, London, Croom Helm, 1981; George Mosse's *Crisis of German Ideology*, New York, Grosset and Dunlap, 1964; and Eugen Weber's *Varieties of Fascism*, New York, Van Nostrand Reinhold, 1964. All the foregoing are good on the European, and notably German, intellectual heritage of fascism. On Italy see

Adrian Lyttelton's 'Italian Fascism' in Laqueur, ed., *Fascism: A Reader's Guide*; David Roberts's *The Syndicalist Tradition and Italian Fascism*, Manchester, Manchester University Press, 1979; and A. James Gregor's *Italian Fascism and Developmental Dictatorship*, Princeton, Princeton University Press, 1979. The *Historical Dictionary of Fascist Italy*, London, Greenwood Press, 1982, edited by Philip Cannistraro, is a useful source of reference on both the major figures and institutions of Mussolini's regime.

Paul Hayes's *Fascism*, London, Allen and Unwin, 1973, from which the opening quotation is taken, also traces the sources of the doctrine and is especially informative on the role of British thinkers in its development. Hayes also supplies potted notes on key figures. Roger Griffin's *The Nature of Fascism*, London, Routledge, 1993, is a recent recommended study. On the varieties of Social Darwinism see Greta Jones, *Social Darwinism and English Thought: The Interaction Between Biological and Social Theory*, Brighton, Harvester Wheatsheaf, 1980.

There are a host of texts that convey the nature and diversity of fascism. These include three books edited by Stuart Woolf: *European Fascism*, London, Weidenfeld and Nicolson, 1968; *The Nature of Fascism*, London, Weidenfeld and Nicolson, 1968; and *Fascism in Europe*, London, Methuen, 1981; George Mosse, ed., *International Fascism: New Thoughts and Approaches*, London, Sage, 1979; and Ernst Nolte, *Three Faces of Fascism*, New York, Mentor, 1969.

On British fascism see Robert Skidelsky's biography, *Oswald Mosley*, London, Macmillan, 1975; Neil Nugent and Roger King, eds, *The British Right*, Farnborough, Saxon House, 1977; and Robert Benewick's *The Fascist Movement in Britain*, London, Allen Lane, 1972. Two studies of the National Front are Martin Walker's *The National Front*, London, Fontana, 1977, and Stan Taylor's *The National Front in British Politics*, London, Macmillan, 1982. See also Kenneth Lunn and Richard Thurlow, eds, *British Fascism*, London, Croom Helm, 1980. The London-based organisation, 'Searchlight', maintains a watching brief on British and other neo-fascist groups and is a helpful source of information.

Hitler's *Mein Kampf*, London, Hutchinson, 1969, with an introduction by D.C. Watt, is a key primary source, although it is a debilitating read. See also W. Maser's *Mein Kampf: An Analysis*, London, Faber, 1970. The one-volume *Documents on Nazism, 1919–1945*, London, Cape, 1974, edited by Jeremy Noakes and Geoffrey Pridham, is a compelling selection with commentaries by the editors. *Hitler's Table Talk 1941–1944: His Private Conversations*, London, Weidenfeld and Nicolson, 1973, introduced by Hugh Trevor-Roper, provides numerous glimpses into the dictator's obsessions. Norman Baynes has translated and edited *The Speeches of Adolf Hitler: April 1922 – August 1939*, New York, Howard Fertig, 1969. Mussolini's own works are more expansive. Shorter works include *Fascism: Doctrine and Institutions*, Rome, Ardita, 1935, and *The Political and Social Doctrine of Fascism*, London, Leonard and Virginia Woolf, 1933. His autobiography is imaginatively entitled *My Autobiography*, London, Hutchinson, 1939. Key biographies of the dictators are Alan Bullock's *Hitler: A Study in Tyranny*, London, Hamlyn, 1973, and Denis Mack Smith's *Mussolini*, London, Weidenfeld and Nicolson, 1981. Mosley's ideas can be found in *The Greater Britain*, London, BUF, 1934, and *Fascism: 100 Questions Asked and Answered*, London, BUF, 1936. His autobiography is *My Life*, London, Nelson, 1968.

The final works I would like to cite are by Primo Levi. His canon is dedicated almost entirely to an attempt to understand the mentality of those who ran the death camps of Europe. He is an apt choice: an Italian Jew, a chemist by profession, and a partisan, he was captured and sent to Auschwitz which, in one sense, he managed to survive. His *If This Is A Man* and *The Truce*, published in one volume by Abacus, 1993, is an account of, respectively, his incarceration and liberation, made all the more moving by the tone of controlled passion he musters. Another work, *Moments of Reprieve*, London, Abacus, 1989, recounts the resilience of the inmates of Auschwitz and demonstrates that even in the most dire of circumstances common humanity could not be wholly eclipsed. Shortly after completing the work Levi took his own life. His books are a poignant and accessible reminder of the horrors that fascism visited upon so many.

Chapter 8

Ecologism

Michael Kenny

[T]he Green movement lacks its own Machiavellis, Lenins, and Gandhis. Greens need political theory; they need to be clear about both ends and means; they need to think through how we are to get to a Green society.
> Derek Wall, *Getting There*, London, Green Print, 1990, 7

Despite the fact that the changes sought by environmental organisations today amount to a wholesale transformation of contemporary capitalism, the Green movement likes to portray itself as being above politics.
> Jonathon Porritt, *The Guardian*, 7 August 1992

PROBLEMS OF DEFINITION

Attempting a definition of the core principles of any ideology is a hazardous enterprise. This is especially true of ecologism. Commentators have only recently begun to describe the emergence, in the last twenty years, of a distinctively Green outlook. This has been labelled *ecologism* or *environmentalism*.[1]

In this chapter I argue that we are witnessing the slow process of debate and convergence which characterise the formation of a new ideology – *ecologism*. This ideology is concerned primarily with a fundamental shift in the relationship between humans and nature so that humans no longer operate as the 'masters' of the natural world but as partners with other living organisms. This perspective also involves changes in the organisation of the human world. The remainder of this chapter provides a basic definition of some of the key concepts that hold ecologism together, though this is an ideology that has been and will remain characterised by a high level of disagreement about its core principles. *Environmentalism*, on the other hand, involves a different approach to Green politics, attempting to deploy the techniques and ideas of the mainstream to achieve a cleaner and environmentally safer version of contemporary society. It does not therefore constitute a separate ideology.

The term 'ecologism' is unfamiliar to many people, a paradoxical situation given the increasing importance of concern for the environment and the profile accorded to ecological problems in our social and political lives. If it can be demonstrated that such an ideology has come into being, we need to think through the profound implications for our familiar traditions of political thought and examine more sceptically the claim made by many mainstream politicians that the 'solution' to our environmental problems lies in the existing techniques of the political and economic worlds. Proponents of ecologism fundamentally reject such an argument.

APPROACHES TO ECOLOGISM

The environmental movements and Green parties that have come to prominence in the last two decades have sponsored a bewildering range of interpretations of the depth and nature of the ecological crisis we face and how we are to save ourselves from its effects. Indeed some of these differences are so profound that many commentators have found it necessary to divide these ideas into a number of mutually exclusive camps. Fundamental opposition has been proposed between: environmentalists and conservationists; 'dark' and 'light' Greens; deep and shallow ecologists; ecologists and environmentalists; and, finally, 'fundis' (from the German word for political fundamentalists) and 'realos' (from the German word for realists).[2] Not all of these terms match each other neatly. For example, a 'dark' Green may believe that we need a revolution in our relationship with nature and our consequent way of life in a 'Green' society – a 'fundi' position; yet s/he may also believe that these views are best represented through a Green party prepared to behave pragmatically and enter a coalition in a national Parliament – a 'realo' position. In other words, we are not dealing with one division among Greens which has been given different labels by different commentators. Rather, Green political thought, and ecologism in particular, is characterised by *many* conflicts and divisions which cannot be reduced to one simple and neat dualism.

Ecologism, however, is not solely about disagreements and discord. If it were, we would be unable to characterise it as an ideology at all. Most Greens are united by the challenge that ecological principles issue to the dominant values cherished by Western industrialised societies. They reject these societies' commitment to economic growth, citing this as the fundamental cause of many of our environmental problems because finite and non-renewable resources are relentlessly exploited. They also criticise the competitive and individualistic ethos of these societies, which results in social atomisation and, most importantly, a profound alienation from nature. The dominant cultural and intellectual traditions in the West have been subjected to a powerful critique by Greens who find in Western political theory and philosophy the justification of the domineering and exploitative attitude towards nature which these societies have institutionalised. Thus, the blame for the present ecological crisis is firmly laid upon these societies, their political systems and ideological beliefs. Without a fundamental overhaul in all these areas, Greens argue, the profound ecological crisis which we face can only worsen.

In other words, Greens challenge the core premises behind the social images projected by the ideologies of modern industrial society, in particular those that condone the free market. Far from a society made up of rational and self-governing individuals, where the market provides the context of economic abundance for secure and mutually beneficial social relationships, Greens see in the present a 'dystopia' in which we are advancing headlong towards planetary destruction. This situation is reinforced by the unquestioning pursuit of economic growth and complacency about human capacity to rectify the increasingly obvious damage which the modern industrial system has done to the natural environment. The gap between society as it now stands and as it ought to, remains appallingly vast for most Greens, hence their hostility to the technology and belief systems of industrialism, the dominant paradigm in the world today.[3]

These beliefs bind Greens together and provide the central ethical critique at the heart of ecologism. Once we move beyond this critique, however, we encounter far more diversity of thought. In particular, Greens disagree among themselves about three types of question. First, a range of competing ideas claim to provide the most powerful *philosophical* justification for an ecological outlook. Several of these will be examined below. Secondly, Greens differ fundamentally about the *political dimensions of ecology*. Questions of tactics, strategy and political organisation have proved contentious issues within Green parties and environmental organisations. This area of disagreement is connected to a third in which Greens have failed to achieve consensus: the realm of *political theory*. This area, as the quotations that head this chapter indicate, is the 'Achilles heel' of environmental politics. Few attempts have been made to define and disseminate an accessible and rigorous body of Green political ideas and a related set of coherent moral commitments.

The deep hostility many Greens show towards conventional politics arises from the quasi-religious fundamentalism that motivates many within this movement, resulting in a tendency to demonise the contemporary industrial system and eulogise the pre-industrial world. This mind-set helps explain why Greens have failed to develop an adequate body of political ideas to help them resolve some of the problems that beset their agenda. Fundamentalists, of varying political and religious persuasions, tend to view the existing political world in a one-dimensional manner, anticipating the complete overthrow of the values and structures of the present system. This outlook tends to obscure the question of *how* their desired alternative is to be reached and to simplify the nature of the political world. Greens are equally guilty here: they have neglected to think through some central political questions. How are we to move towards a Green society? How are Greens to build a popular movement to shift the balance of power away from the dominant ethos of materialism and productivism? By what principles should Greens be influenced in the course of their political struggles, for instance in choosing whether to enter coalitions with non-Green parties? Should they dilute the less popular aspects of their programmes to secure electoral advantage? Should they operate as a grassroots, locally-based movement or organise as a national body and enter parliaments? Several of these questions have been highlighted in debates about leadership selection in West European Green parties: while 'fundis' have argued that the party's leaders should be replaced on a regular basis to avoid the emergence of a bureaucratic elite or personality cult, 'realos' have rejected such a model as naive and impractical in the tough world of parliamentary politics.

These questions are the stuff of political life and have affected those Green parties that have come to prominence in the last two decades. Yet, these groups have received little guidance from the intellectual and ideological wing of the ecological movement because of the absence of a cogent and clear Green political theory. The definition and development of ecologism as an ideology is important, therefore, because, like all ideologies, it offers a potential source of ethical principles and political ideas. As we shall see, ecologism develops from two overriding normative principles which lead to a number of important political recommendations.

ECOLOGISM AS AN IDEOLOGY

Before we establish the precise content of ecologism, however, it is important to note three problems which arise in the course of defining it as an ideology. Firstly, as Iain MacKenzie points out in the Introduction to this book, the very notion of ideology is essentially an Enlightenment concept. Greens are, in general, extremely sceptical about the Enlightenment and its associated modes of rationalist thought, connecting these to justifications for industrial capitalism and economic growth from the late eighteenth century onwards. Not all Green commentators share this view: John Dryzek, for instance, suggests that ecology is compatible with our capacities as rational beings.[4] Yet, on the whole, ecologism is characterised by an emphasis upon a number of values generally downplayed in liberal rationalist thought: emotions (especially emotional communion with nature); the virtues of community (against the individualism of contemporary capitalism); an emphasis upon spritual and mystical values; and holism – the need to view all life as part of a larger 'environment' (Greens borrow from a number of scientific theories, in physics and biology for example, to justify this axiom).

The ideological status of ecologism is awkward, secondly, because many Greens view themselves as non-ideological in the sense that they reject current political orthodoxies. They argue that the *real* issues which should be debated and resolved within the political realm are marginalised by a consensus among the different political parties and ideologies. This consensus is based upon a commitment to economic growth and to perpetuating the exploitative policies that Western societies have pursued towards nature. Indeed, political ecologists have proved as hostile to state socialist societies as they have to capitalism, though some Greens have explored the possibility of fusing environmentalist concerns and socialist principles, a process outlined below. In general, it is difficult to locate Greens on the conventional political spectrum: many claim to be 'neither left nor right but ahead'. We should not, however, accept such arguments too readily. Certainly we need to understand the novel and distinctive aspects of ecologism, yet its history reveals that at different moments it has 'taken sides' on the political spectrum and, moreover, has been deeply influenced by other ideologies and traditions, in particular socialism, anarchism and conservatism. The Green claim to be 'above politics', therefore, should be treated sceptically.

The third problem regarding the definition of ecologism concerns the content of this ideology. What principles does ecologism include and, thus, exclude? Here it is worth sounding a strong note of caution. As was indicated earlier, this is an ideology in the process of formation. Little agreement exists as yet about the content of ecologism. It is worth remaining openminded about this ideology and regarding sceptically attempts to erect boundaries around 'core' principles. Such rigid definitions are unlikely to characterise this shifting body of ideas in an accurate fashion, though certain key themes are emerging within this ideology's fluid repertoire of ideas.

DEBATES ABOUT ECOLOGISM

Recent academic commentators have opted for two different kinds of definition. Firstly, some emphasise the plurality of ecologism, suggesting that it provides room for more fundamentalist and revolutionary Greens as well as 'lighter' shades of Green thought which stress the value of nature for human well-being and retain a degree of optimism about the capacity of the political systems in the West to respond to the ecological crisis.[5] The virtue of this interpretation is that its advocates refuse to align ecologism with the preferences of one wing of the ecological movement, for instance the philosophical ideas of the deep ecology movement (outlined below). From this perspective we need to understand the different positions within the Green movement as equally valuable, even if these conflict with other perspectives within this movement. The problem with this eclectic interpretation is that it tends to dissolve the notion of an ideology altogether, obscuring the central beliefs of political ecologists.

Secondly, some critics have offered more strict definitions of Green political thought, distinguishing between *ecologism*, which emerges as a coherent challenge to conventional political life, and *environmentalism*, which involves deploying the ideas and arguments of the mainstream in the pursuit of Green reform. This perspective welcomes the advent of environmental consumerism, celebrates the achievements of lobbying groups (such as Greenpeace and Friends of the Earth) and advocates the education of the public about the dangers *for humans* that arise from harming our natural environment. However important these goals may be, environmentalist commitments do not fundamentally challenge pre-existing ideologies. Ecologism, on the contrary,

> argues that care for the environment … presupposes radical changes in our relationship with it, and thus in our mode of social and political life. *Environmentalism*, on the other hand, would argue for a 'managerial' approach to environmental problems, secure in the belief that they can be solved without fundamental changes in present values or patterns of production and consumption.[6]

This interpretation is also problematic. Defining ecologism around the more revolutionary or fundamentalist agenda of 'dark' Greens who propose radical changes in our living habits and political system possibly allows too much licence to this perspective. To compare with another ideology – socialism – we would not wish to argue that the revolutionary tradition associated with Leninism is the only legitimate heir to the title of socialism. Most Greens, in practice, accept the importance of compromising their ideals by entering the conventional political system, viewing the changes heralded by more fundamentalist Greens as suitable for some point in the distant future only. In addition, there is a danger that if ecologism is defined too rigidly, we may regard those who diverge from this 'dark' Green agenda as straying from the ideological path of ecologism. As we shall see, political ecology has been interpreted in different ways by different ideologues in the Green movement.

It is important, however, to comprehend the increasingly consensual agenda at the heart of ecologism which motivates many Greens. For this reason, the more strict interpretation of ecologism will be deployed in this chapter (the second definition described above) though it is important to think of ecologism as incorporating a spectrum of beliefs as well as an agreed set of principles. In fact, the specific composition of ecologism varies according to the time and place within which its general principles are developed.

THE HISTORY OF ECOLOGISM

The sources of industrialism and ecologism

The origins of ecologism lie in the history of ecology as a biological science in Europe. In the 1860s the German biologist Ernst Haeckel advocated the development of a new science concerned with the relationship between organisms and their natural environments. Once ecology was established as a branch of the natural sciences increasing attention was paid, in both theory and practice, to the interconnections between living entities and their habitats. The application of such ideas to humans occurred with increasing sophistication from the late nineteenth century onwards, as Anna Bramwell, a historian of the ecology movement, has revealed.[7] The principal legacy of the birth of ecology and the development of ecological thinking in the mid-nineteenth century was the belief that nature could be deployed as a model for human relations. Indeed, key principles which were seen as ordering nature, including species diversity, interrelatedness and harmony, were applied to the social world of humans.

Such views stood in stark opposition to the hostile and domineering attitude towards nature that emerged as a by-product of the growth of mechanistic science from the sixteenth century. Francis Bacon, writing in England at the beginning of the seventeenth century, interpreted nature as a dead organism, to be appropriated for human benefit. The discipline of natural science was increasingly motivated by the belief that technological development was directly connected to the domination of nature. These ideas helped shape the intellectual and cultural environment within which capitalist social relations came into being in western Europe. These relations were determined by the imperative to perpetuate the rapid accumulation of capital, a process enormously enabled by technological invention and the increasingly widespread use of machines. In philosophical terms, the growth of human productive capacity was accompanied by the dissemination of rationalist explanations of the world, which had their origins in the Renaissance and earlier traditions of thought. Reason was deployed to open up the mysteries of the world for human comprehension and offered the possibility of human harmony and perfectibility. Nature, by contrast, was increasingly viewed as the site of irrational and uncontrollable forces which needed to be 'tamed'. According to the seventeenth-century philosopher René

Descartes, humans should 'render themselves the masters and possess-ors of nature'.[8] Not surprisingly, many Greens interpret the growth of mechanistic science and the rationalist schemes of thought of this period as the source of modern industrial practices which ravage the natural environment and now threaten planetary extinction. Consequently, some ecologists have revived interest in the cultures that preceded this era, celebrating primal, hunter-gatherer societies. These are applauded for their proximity to nature and development of environmentally friendly living patterns, in stark contrast to modern industrial society.

Yet the story of human relations with nature is more complex than this suggests. First, the representation of these primal societies has been seriously questioned by historians and anthropologists who warn against romanticising the cultures of pre-modern peoples. Secondly, some commentators have located the origins of the domineering attitude humans have tended to adopt towards nature even further back in time, specifying the emergence of the Judeo-Christian religious traditions as the source of these attitudes. Lynn White, in an influential interpretation of the Christian tradition, has read the Old Testament as a justification for human exploitation of nature.[9] Third, human attitudes towards nature in a given historical period cannot be reduced to one strand or interpretation. Dominant views have always been checked by countertraditions. Thus, Robin Attfield has challenged White's inter-pretation of the Christian tradition, highlighting the importance of human 'stewardship' over nature as an alternative to outright domina-tion in the Old Testament.[10] In fact, concern about the relationship between humans and nature long precedes the ecological outlook of the nineteenth century, constituting a central theme within political and theological debate for centuries. Philosophers have found the concept of nature a rich resource in attempting to justify their accounts of human nature. Additionally, the need to draw a boundary between humans and nature and, indeed, to establish moral rules of conduct governing human behaviour towards the natural world, have an equally long heritage. In this sense, contemporary concern for nature is not new at all.

The question of humanity's relations with nature, however, gained a new sense of urgency with the experience of rapid industrialisation, urbanisation and the shift to a factory system which occurred in the most developed economies of western Europe in the late eighteenth and early nineteenth centuries. Concern for nature provided a powerful motif in protests against the practices and values of industrialised

society in Britain and Germany especially. The location of this opposition is no surprise. Both countries had experienced the fastest pace of
industrialisation and associated social and economic dislocation. In
Britain, for instance, the Romantic movement of artists, intellectuals and
critics, which emerged in the early nineteenth century, lamented the
disappearance of traditional, rural communities. They highlighted the
disruption of customary relationships between humans and the dis-
appearance of a proximity with the natural world for many who now
lived in cities and worked in factories.[11] Many of these ideas drew
strength both from an idealisation of nature and from the invention of
a happy, harmonious past which may have never actually existed.

These ideas influenced a wider intellectual audience too. The
nineteenth-century liberal philosopher John Stuart Mill reflected these
sentiments in his discussion of the 'stationary state', a society of nil
economic growth, as a counterpoint to the relentlessly acquisitive and
competitive drives at the heart of entrepreneurial capitalism. His
critique of this system was argued in terms of its effects upon nature
and alienation of humans from the natural world, and anticipated later
Green ideas:

> Nor is there much satisfaction in contemplating the world with
> nothing left to the spontaneous activity of nature; with every rood
> of land brought into cultivation, which is capable of growing food
> for human beings; every flower waste or natural pasture ploughed
> up, all quadrupeds or birds which are not domesticated for man's
> use exterminated as his rivals for food, every hedgerow or
> superfluous tree rooted out, and scarcely a place left where a wild
> shrub or flower could grow without being eradicated as a weed
> in the name of improved agriculture. If the earth must lose that
> great portion of its pleasantness which it owes to things that the
> unlimited increase of wealth and population would extirpate from
> it, for the mere purpose of enabling it to support a larger, but not
> a better or a happier population, I sincerely hope, for the sake of
> posterity, that they will be content to be stationary, long before
> necessity compels them to it.[12]

This critique was echoed by many conservative opponents of the
changes associated with industrial progress. The first decades of the
twentieth century witnessed the emergence of a number of conservative
'back to the land' movements in Britain and Germany. Further to the

right, several historians have pointed out the ecological commitments of Nazi ideologues in the 1920s and 1930s. Such associations have led commentators to wonder whether ecologism was an essentially conservative and reactionary creed, most comfortably located on the right of the political spectrum. Certainly, there is evidence that ecology as a science and the values that emanate from an ecological perspective are compatible with authoritarian and conservative hostility to modern, cosmopolitan culture. Others have argued that the left can also stake a claim to be the 'natural' home of ecological awareness. Examples abound of socialist concern for the impact of capitalist industrialisation upon the urban environment in the late nineteenth century, for instance in the ideas of the Owenite movement in England. Additionally, the alienated relationship between humans and the environment, engendered by capitalism, was rigorously denounced by Marx himself. For socialists such as William Morris, writing in late nineteenth-century England, the re-establishment of a system of self-governing communities in which humans lived in harmony with nature, not as parasites upon it, was imperative.[13]

The emergence of ecologism: from the 1960s to the present day

Where, then, does ecology lie on the political spectrum? The answer to this question became clearer in the late 1960s and early 1970s when ecologism as a systematic and self-contained ideology began to emerge out of the radical, libertarian politics of this era. The New Left movements which appeared in the United States and western Europe were particularly important in this context. They combined their concern for the effects of modern industrial practices upon human living conditions with a denunication of the artificiality of capitalist culture and the inability of the 'system' to satisfy basic human needs. The New Left highlighted environmental degradation and floated the notion of a counterculture, a space away from capitalist values where a new life based on co-operative ethics might be discovered. The Green movement of the next decade was inspired by the notion of escaping from the imperatives of modern industrial life, and developing a more self-sufficient, rural and harmonious context for living with other humans and nature.

Such concerns did not, by themselves, cause the re-emergence of ecological ideas on the political agenda in the 1970s. As the decade wore on, information about the damage being wrought to the natural environment inflamed public concern, especially in the United States. The publication of Rachel Carson's bestselling *Silent Spring* (1962), which dramatised the dangers of pesticides and chemical defoliants for the human food chain, marked the arrival of environmental concern at a popular level in post-war North America. Additionally a series of hysterical studies concerning population levels had a marked impact upon public debate, in particular Paul Ehrlich's controversial (and occasionally racist) book, *The Population Bomb* (1968). Yet the key moment in the transformation of disparate anxiety about environmental problems into more focused discussion of an alternative to present-day society occurred with the publication of *Limits to Growth* (1972), a computer simulated assessment of the dangers to human survival resulting from the maintenance of present levels of resource extraction, population growth and usage of non-renewable resources, such as gas, coal and oil. Despite the melodramatic nature of its claims and its dubious methodology, this study caught the imagination of many. The need to challenge economic growth was placed on the political agenda by this report which had emerged from an apparently respectable quarter, a group of Italian industrialists. For some commentators, *Limits to Growth* marks the birth of ecologism as a distinctive and separate ideological perspective. This novel outlook received a tremendous boost from several sources in the 1980s: the electoral success of Green political parties throughout western Europe and Australasia; the efforts of environmentalist lobbying and campaigning groups, in North America especially; the high profile accorded to environmental issues in the mid-1980s, following a series of ecological catastrophes; and the 'greening' of a number of mainstream political parties in response to the increased concern about the environment manifested by their electorates.

All of these factors have played an important role in popularising the distinctive interpretation of ecological disasters and environmental issues that Green politics offers. It is, nevertheless, important to separate the emergence of ecologism as a political ideology from these developments. This ideology has been in its infancy throughout the 'greening' of mainstream political life and has remained relatively marginal within Western societies. Many Green parties and individuals are not fully Green in the sense demanded by ecologism; instead they subscribe to environmentalist beliefs. Moreover, the penetration of concern for the environment into the media, education and popular habits (the growth of vegetarianism and awareness of animal rights, for instance) of some Western countries, does not necessarily prove that ecologism is a growing, well-understood force. In fact Greens remain highly suspicious of developments such as the arrival of environmentally friendly products for the individual consumer. They view this process, somewhat puritanically, as the deliberate creation of new market niches under the guise of a designer Green lifestyle. Whatever their limitations, these trends do suggest that an explicitly ecological perspective is operating in a context far better suited to its ideals than ever before, rendering it unlikely that it will disappear from view within the political systems of the West.

THE PRINCIPLES OF ECOLOGISM

The centre of gravity within ecologism is held by two ideals. Firstly, the commitment to revolutionising the relationship between humans and the rest of nature is common to all who share this perspective. Secondly, Greens believe in the fundamental overhaul of the social and political lives of humans.

Modern industrial societies depend upon the exploitation of natural resources and have sundered humans geographically and spiritually from nature. Only when humans learn a degree of 'humility' with regard to their environment and to the plurality of species on earth, will a more harmonious relationship be re-established. Greens view the principles of economic growth, centralisation, bureaucratisation and materialism as central to the modern industrial world. They argue that alternative principles need to order post-industrial societies: sustainability, the virtues of small-scale/local organisation, the limiting of population levels, individual responsibility, and a spiritual reawakening, placing humans back in touch with nature. The implications of these principles are profound.

Before we briefly assess them, it is important to stress the degree of variation which characterises interpretation of these principles by Greens. Depending upon national context, the influence of rival ideologies and political culture, each of these ideas has been understood in various ways and is emphasised to a lesser or greater extent. Taken together, however, they provide an indication of the range of themes that sustain contemporary ecological discourse.

Sustainability

Greens believe that the exploitation of non-renewable resources is endemic within the industrial systems which have come into being over the last two centuries. The model of economic development, which since the Second World War has been exported to the 'underde-veloped' world, involves the relentless extraction of natural minerals and resources to feed an increasingly greedy manufacturing system. This, in turn, pours pollutants into the atmosphere, causing a number of now familiar environmental problems, for instance the greenhouse effect and ozone depletion.[14] This system is sustained by the creation of artificial desires which are satisfied only through wasteful and unnecessary levels of human consumption. Ecologism therefore proposes the principle of sustainability: humans have to be educated to consume less and to produce more self-sufficiently to satisfy their basic needs. Simultaneously, the industrial system will have to be dismantled and replaced by a smaller-scale system of manufacture which is sustained by a number of self-governing, local communities. In other words, a new set of social and ecological ethics will override the priority of economic values. This commitment has inspired a number of Green economists to challenge the conventional calculations of mainstream economics, arguing, for instance, that estimates of the Gross National Product of a particular nation exclude the costs incurred when environmental resources are systematically destroyed by the industrial system.[15]

The notion of sustainable economic development also leads to the common Green belief that economic growth needs to be reversed if these new priorities are to take precedence. Here Greens issue a strong challenge to the belief that economic growth is an essential goal, an assumption common to all other ideological perspectives. For Greens, a 'steady-state' economy will be organised around essential human needs and remain subordinated to the collective interests of the community. It will use 'the lowest possible levels of materials and energy in the production phase and emit the least possible amount of pollution in the consumption phase'.[16] Conventional economic growth cannot be relied upon to alleviate present economic ills and inequalities. In fact sustainability places a more just distribution of resources firmly on the political agenda because a fairer spread of existing resources is central to Green preferences for self-reliant communities in which humans live according to their basic needs. In this sense Greens are social and economic radicals. It is important though to recognise the arguments of more conservative elements within this movement who suggest that self-interest determines human behaviour, particularly in a situation of scarcity, a position dramatised by Garrett Hardin's 'lifeboat ethics'.[17]

What this commitment to sustainability will mean in concrete terms varies widely across the Green movement. For some fundamentalist ecologists, in North America for instance, it involves a frugal pattern of living as part of a return to pre-industrial society. Other Greens, however, suggest that sustainability means reordering the priorities of contemporary society so that genuine human needs will take precedence over more frivolous wants. The latter will not be abolished entirely as the diversity of human taste and expression is an important countervailing principle to heed.

Small is beautiful

This phrase was first coined by the 'Buddhist' economist Ernst Schumacher in an influential book which was published in the 1970s.[18] He pointed to the need to return to 'human-scale' dimensions, celebrating the virtues of smaller, more decentralised human communities within which harmonious and fulfilling relationships could be restored. Many Greens support this view, arguing that production should be geared to satisfying genuine human needs. A return to 'human-scale' would also allow for a more democratic culture based upon a system of decentralised and self-governing communities, entering only voluntarily into larger systems of organisation and regulation. The inspiration for this vision also comes from a rich variety of political and religious sources. Anarchism, in particular, has persistently experimented with models of self-governing communal living as alternatives to the 'indirect' model of representative democracy evident in the parliamentary systems of the West. For many Greens, the 'small is beautiful' principle is an essential axiom governing the future organisation of post-industrial society.

Indeed, a number of political ecologists suggest that this commitment is best expressed by the radical principle of *bioregionalism*. In essence bioregionalism involves the belief that human communities should be situated within natural, topographical and geographical boundaries, not the artificial borders of nation-states or cities. Communities might therefore be located within a valley or on land divided naturally by rivers or mountains. These communities would be self-sufficient in terms of production and consumption, operating in harmony with the rhythms of nature and the particular agricultural characteristics of the given bioregion.[19] Not all Greens are so militant in their opposition to centralism; some have remained more agnostic, suggesting that for certain functions some degree of centralisation and regulation from above remains vital. The principle articulated here is 'small is beautiful', wherever practically possible.

Reducing the human population

While a reduction in population levels remains an important principle for many Greens, this has become one of the more controversial elements within ecologism as an ideology. The rapidly increasing size of the human population has concerned critics of industrialisation for over two centuries. The most important forerunner of contemporary anxieties was Robert Malthus, a late eighteenth-century British economist who predicted that rising population levels would be naturally 'rectified' by the occurrence of cyclical famines and outbreaks of disease. Human society, he concluded, operated within strict natural limits.[20] Contemporary Green advocates of population controls have been commonly referred to as neo-Malthusians. Appalled by a number of predictions concerning levels of population by the year 2000, Greens advocate a reduction in the size of the human population. Such beliefs have engendered tremendous controversy. The implication of some Green writing, especially in the 1970s, was that the backward Third World was 'teeming' with unnecessary lives and that population reduction through sterilisation programmes and contraceptive education should take place within these countries. A similar programme was controversially implemented in India in the 1970s. More recently, such ideas have been criticised both within the ecological movement and by representatives of these countries. Given the vastly higher rates of consumption and pollution associated with the developed West, it has been suggested that population control remains as important an issue in western Europe and North America as in Africa or Asia.

Greens differ greatly about this principle. Advocating a reduction in population levels has proved electorally damaging for some Green parties. This emphasis upon the evils of overpopulation has also been challenged by development specialists who argue that rising levels of population in the 'Third World' are not the causes of environmental degradation and social squalor but the consequences of these factors. In many countries, producing a large family has become a rational, economic strategy to increase the familial income. Rather than proposing a reduction in population levels, Greens should campaign against the vast inequalities which predominate between the developed and non-developed worlds and within developing nations. Despite these debates, the historical connection between Green politics and the belief in population reduction remains strong, engendering great divisions between the developed and developing worlds at the Earth Summit in Rio in 1992.

Individual responsibility

The slogan 'think globally, act locally' neatly expresses this part of the Green outlook. Green politics implicitly challenges the assumption that politics should take place solely at the level of the nation-state. Indeed, central to Green perceptions of the environmental crisis lies the belief that change for the better will occur on a number of fronts and at different levels of social behaviour. Clearly it is important to devise tough environmental laws at an international level; issues such as toxic emissions into the biosphere and the commercial hunting of whales cannot be resolved within the boundaries of one nation-state. Simultaneously Greens suggest that individuals need to be 'recharged' as responsible agents who can make morally informed choices about the environment in which they live and the social system which they support.

In particular, many Greens have explored alternative lifestyles as part of their rejection of conventional, materialist values, in order to prefigure the collective adoption of more sustainable living patterns. The expansion of organic farming, the adoption of non-monetary exchange economies in certain localities and the growth in greener lifestyle choices all suggest that the notion of the counterculture, which first appeared in the 1960s, remains central to contemporary Green politics. Here the moral commitments of many Greens find expression in their refusal to engage in the corrupt and damaging systems that surround them. Simultaneously such movements highlight the radical belief, shared with many feminists, that politics spills into the social lives of all, on an everyday basis; choices about consumption, transport and education, for instance, have all been politicised by this aspect of Green politics. The emphasis upon 'lifestyle' politics has, nevertheless, proved problematic for Greens. It has tended to encourage a retreat from the realm of orthodox politics. Despite the environmentalist veneer adopted by mainstream political parties since the mid-1980s, the nature of the polluting and exploitative industrial system remains largely untouched. Altering the priorities of this system must involve profound political change. Greens have come to recognise this only slowly, being reluctant to compromise their doctrinal purity and engage with the messy and complex world of orthodox politics. At present explaining ecological issues in the public sphere is frequently left to more conventional environmentalist organisations which are often campaigning solely on single issues. Moreover these lifestyle choices have been associated with one of the most unconventional aspects of contemporary Green politics – the celebration of a number of spiritual values, from the Chinese philosophy of Taoism to New Age mysticism.

Spiritual reawakening

Many Greens do not subscribe to these beliefs and regard them as a fringe element within political ecology. Yet the stress upon spiritual reawakening which some Greens enunciate follows from several core ecological ideas, not least the fundamentalist mind-set described earlier in this chapter. The repeatedly enunciated belief that industrial society cannot meet essential human needs also encourages spiritualism within the movement. Only by manufacturing artificial desires and a corrupt set of ethical values can this system win the consent of its subjects, according to Greens. Thus, the social agenda of these societies is rigged so that, for instance, status is accorded to individual ownership of a particular brand of car rather than the social provision of a cheap and environmentally friendly transport system. Any fundamental reordering of modern society will, therefore, depend upon a radical transformation in 'consciousness' of human potential and the depth of our interrelations with nature. The various spiritual movements that have found favour within the Green movement function, like religion in other contexts, as a constant reminder of an unsullied ethical tradition in human history, pointing to a golden age beyond the confines of the present world. Perhaps the most significant impact made by spiritual thinking upon Green ideas can be found in the potency of *Gaia* philosophy among ecological activists. Gaia (the Greek word for Earth) theory was developed in the late 1970s by a British scientist working for NASA – James Lovelock. He argued that the planet's biosphere is a self-regulating system. This means that the enormous diversity of living and inorganic elements of planetary life function as part of a larger being, or life-force, which holds them in a complex equilibrium. In fact life plays an active role in perpetuating the conditions necessary for its own survival, generating the necessary balance of land masses, air, oceans and atmospheric gases. The principles that sustain Gaia, the living earth, include holism, which means that every element connects with another as part of a larger whole, and balance, meaning that each element is held in equilibrium with others. These principles are fundamental to Green approaches to environmental and social issues.

Not only has this thesis influenced the approach of many natural scientists, it has also appealed to Greens as a means of fusing their 'scientific' assertion that all life is sustained by relationships with environments with the desire to discover alternative values and meaning in the world in which they live. For some Greens there is now a new God to worship – nature itself. Many others, probably the majority, remain unconvinced by Gaia philosophy, yet welcome Gaia as a metaphor to encourage a more holistic attitude to life – for instance the practice of holistic medicine – and to appreciate the interrelationships and balance between different elements in the world, of which humans are merely one part. While Gaia, like other spiritual and religious traditions, has proved significant as a means of sustaining an alternative perspective on the world, these beliefs have helped Greens precious little in the task of constructing a rigorous theory of politics.

Transition to a Green society

This theme, in particular, has received little systematic treatment by ecologists. While ecologism sustains a powerful critique of existing social practices and values, and advocates the need to shift to a cleaner, more sustainable future, it provides little guidance for the transition from one society to another. Belief in wholesale spiritual conversion and the advocacy of alternative lifestyles have proved unhelpful for Greens and environmental organisations engaged in the messy and complex world of political struggle. Here the absence of a body of theory that relates to a number of key questions is most evident. How are Greens to tackle vast and influential centres of vested interest, such as multinational companies? Do Greens need the state or the market to regulate their sustainable society? Is there a distinctively Green view of the state? With whom and under what conditions should Greens forge alliances? All these questions, and others, have pressed upon small and electorally disadvantaged Green parties whose responses have been little helped by ecological theory. This is not to suggest that Green theorists have ignored such questions altogether. In fact, as we shall see, a number of competing outlooks jostle for position as the philosophical source of influence upon Greens and have a direct bearing upon some of these political issues. These perspectives remain problematic when applied to the political sphere, however, and have failed to generate consensus within the Green movement. In philosophical terms therefore, ecologism remains a fragmented ideology, beset by a number of competing paradigms.

ECO-PHILOSOPHY

Deep ecology

Deep Ecology goes beyond the transformation of technology and politics to a transformation of humanity. Taking a holistic, total-field view, it denies any boundaries between man and nature.
Grover Foley, 'Deep Ecology and Subjectivity', *The Ecologist*,
18 (4–5), 1988, 119

Deep ecology constitutes the most influential of these perspectives, both in terms of its philosophical outlook and its claim to provide the normative core of ecologism as an ideology. For deep ecologists, ecologism involves a break from all traditions of thought that view human welfare as more important than the fate of other species and organisms. These traditions which elevate humans above other species (a perspective entitled *anthropocentrism*) are unable to comprehend the importance of living in harmony with nature and the imperative that humans actually learn and adopt principles of organisation from the natural world (a perspective entitled *ecocentrism*). This ideal lies at the heart of the work of the most renowned and influential deep ecological thinker, the Norwegian philosopher Arne Naess. Naess has argued since the 1970s that concern for the environment ultimately leads to a novel philosophical outlook, incorporating a number of principles eschewed by anthropocentric (people-centred) analyses. First, the individual 'self' and our capacity for freedom depend upon as wide a process of identification with external forces as possible, in particular with the natural world. In addition, an ecocentric perspective involves the recognition that life on earth is shared by a number of different species and organisms, all of which possess a potential for development. Humans are therefore merely one element of a larger biospherical community and need to rethink their position less as masters of the natural world and more as willing partners within this larger community. This principle, biospherical egalitarianism, carries a number of ethical implications. Most obviously it commits humans to as little intervention as possible within the non-human world, except in cases where the survival of the human species may be at stake. More generally, this ethic involves the contentious notion that it is possible to apply moral arguments not just to humans and animals but also to the inorganic world. Here deep ecology has generated its own internal divisions. While some ecologists welcome the opportunity to extend notions such as 'rights' to inorganic nature, others reject such arguments as anthropocentric. According to a second group of thinkers, we need to move beyond the application of human norms to nature and build into our outlook a recognition of the limits of human knowledge and thought in comprehending the complexity of the biospherical world of which we are only a small part. This has led Naess and other deep ecologists to formulate a more recent principle in defence of biospherical equality – the notion of *intrinsic value*. This involves the recognition that some objective value lies within each species on earth, beyond the particular moral calculations of one of these species, in this case humans. As a number of commentators have pointed out, it is not clear that this concept involves a break with anthropocentrism, nor is it evident that complex questions about conflicts between different species and the right to kill members of other species in certain circumstances can be satisfactorily answered by the notion of instrinsic value.[21] Controversy has arisen, for instance, over organisms that are inherently destructive or dangerous to other species, such as the HIV virus for humans: does this possess an intrinsic value which we have to weigh in our moral calculations?

In political terms, deep ecology has become increasingly influential in recent years, though it remains a minority commitment within the Green movement. It has provided inspiration for a controversial grouping in North America, Earth First!, who came to prominence in the 1980s due to their deployment of direct action tactics against the exploitation of natural resources in wilderness and conservation areas. While their aims are nearly always non-violent, critics view them as the unacceptable and logical consequence of the misanthropy which they argue lies at the heart of deep ecology. Earth First! have been accused of advocating injuring humans to protect nature, while much publicity was given to arguments that appeared in the group's journal opposing aid to Ethiopians during the famine in the mid-1980s and suggesting that the HIV virus represented nature's revenge on human overpopulation. In fact these arguments emanated from the movement's outer fringes and were swiftly challenged within Earth First! This image of crazed misanthropists is a caricature. Earth First! have proved influential as the militant, direct action wing of a larger coaliton of environmental groups in the United States and have drawn support from across the political spectrum. Significantly, their direct action approach has influenced groups in other countries; in Britain, for instance, a number of similar groups came to national prominence in the campaign to obstruct the construction of a motorway at Twyford Down in the early part of 1993.

This is the most militant, contemporary face of ecologism. Yet deep ecology remains ambivalent about more orthodox political interventions and indeed about political struggle at all. It characterises politics as essentially a conflict between two outlooks – anthropocentrism versus ecocentrism. This is, however, too simplistic a reading of the political terrain to aid environmental groups and Green parties. The central principles of ecologism, as defined in this chapter, do not necessarily depend upon an ecocentric outlook. Indeed, as some commentators have pointed out, a 'weak' form of anthropocentrism may be conceptually inescapable.

Social ecology

The most important philosophical challenge to deep ecology has emerged from this rival school of thought. Social ecologists reject the emphasis upon the anthropocentrism/ecocentrism divide which motivates deep ecology. Inspired by the anarchist-influenced American theorist Murray Bookchin, social ecology has developed a pertinent and attractive alternative. Bookchin was one of the first intellectuals of the late 1960s to recognise the significance of the environment as a key issue in the modern world. His definition of social ecology draws upon the 'natural' principles of balance, wholeness, spontaneity and freedom. These principles were recognised in many primal societies but were supplanted by the spread of hierarchy and domination as a result of male dominance, the increasing role of elders, the scarcity of resources and the prevalence of warfare. Thus, he argues that human society is now characterised by hierarchical modes of behaviour and thought which are often expressed in dualisms, for instance between the intellectual and the physical aspects of life or between care and self-interest. In philosophical terms, Bookchin draws upon the belief of the nineteenth-century German philosopher Hegel that a dialectical move-ment towards total freedom lies at the heart of history. Freedom, according to Bookchin, will be achieved when intellectual and cultural progress are harnessed to environmental awareness and used to abolish human inequalites. This will mean the reconciliation of humans with nature. In this scenario all organisms must be allowed to develop spontaneously so that they can contribute in diverse ways to the greater unity of human and natural freedom. Unity in diversity is a key principle for social ecologists, embodying their commitment to the interdependence of human life and inorganic nature. Human life has evolved in a complex web of ties with the natural world. Humans may play the role of 'managers' of natural processes as long as they act only to enable the natural and diverse evolution of organisms within the biospherical community.

Politically, social ecologists are as commited to the abolition of human inequalities, of class, gender and race, as they are to the reorientation of human relationships with nature. Not surprisingly their perspective has come into conflict with the ideas of deep ecology, culminating in a celebrated confrontation between Bookchin and his critics at the National Greens Conference, in Massachusetts in 1987. For Bookchin, deep ecology obscures and possibly reinforces existing inequalities within society with its tendency to retreat into mystical 'ecolala' (Bookchin's own phrase) and occasional eco-fascism. His critique of deep ecology probably constitutes his most distinctive contribution to ecologism; his own political preferences for a system of decentralised, quasi-anarchist communities correlate with many of the political instincts of ecological activists.

Eco-feminism and eco-socialism

Deep and social ecology do not exhaust the range of philosophical positions vying for influence over Greens. Some feminists have been concerned to connect their ideas with an environmentalist outlook, developing the perspective of *eco-feminism*. They are especially interested in the connection between gender inequality and the domination of nature, celebrating the role of women as 'earth mothers'. For many eco-feminists, women should play a leading role in the Green movement for two reasons. Firstly, women are closer to nature than men, by virtue of their biological roles and historically subordinate position. They argue that the domination of women is organically connected to the domination of nature, suggesting that feminists must expand their concept of patriarchy to account also for the control men exercise over the natural world. They point especially to the frequency of representations of nature as female in contemporary culture. Secondly, the Green movement shares with feminism a suspicion about the processes and institutions of the conventional political world. Eco-feminists suggest that women will find it far easier to participate in the grassroots and direct action wing of the Green movement. Significantly some feminists remain uneasy about this school of thought, suspecting the role of 'earth mother' as a variation of the roles that patriarchy has all too often allotted to women rather than a liberation from them.

Certainly eco-feminism has challenged many of the assumptions of deep ecology. So too has a long tradition of attempting to fuse socialist beliefs with an ecological outlook (*eco-socialism*). This has been developed in the work of a number of influential, contemporary European thinkers, such as André Gorz, Rudolf Bahro and the recently deceased British writer Raymond Williams. There are substantial variations within this outlook, yet eco-socialists agree that socialism cannot provide sufficient ideological vision for a post-capitalist society. Drawing upon many of the insights of the environmentalist movement, eco-socialism offers a programme of abolishing inequality and ending human exploitation of nature. These writers have tended to analyse contemporary society in a more theoretically sophisticated way than many Greens, drawing upon the rich intellectual heritage offered by the Marxist tradition especially. They have accordingly raised the awareness of Greens about specific features of contemporary society such as the operations of the labour process in advanced capitalism. Gorz, for instance, has influenced the thinking of several Green parties through his advocacy of the abolition of work and the need to liberate the time of individuals in a post-industrial world for the pursuit of their own self-expression and development.

As with eco-feminism, these ideas have proved relatively controversial. Eco-socialists have encountered hostility from the socialist camp for jettisoning Marxist and socialist ideas too readily in their shift to ecology. They have been criticised from the Green camp too for appearing to synthesise Red and Green goals, while perpetuating the socialist belief that the liberation of nature is secondary to the prior goal of human freedom. Significantly one of the thinkers cited above, Bahro, has found these tensions too difficult to bear, shifting rapidly from eco-socialism towards a 'deep Green' outlook. These ideas have made a significant impact upon the thinking of leading figures in the parties of the European left, however, and have begun to break into the realm of policy formation, for instance the increasing environmentalist rhetoric evident in the British Labour Party's election manifestos since 1983.[22]

EVALUATING ECOLOGISM

The philosophical dimension behind this ideology remains disparate. Ecologism lacks an agreed philosophical core and has failed to develop a lucid body of political theory. As we have seen, however, a number of political principles have emerged as the distinctive concerns of this ideological perspective. While it would be wrong to claim that these constitute the coherent basis of a fully developed ideology, a particular outlook is gradually emerging around the themes of sustainability, the return to human-scale, population reduction, individual responsibility and a critique of the values celebrated in modern industrial society.

Yet a number of problems beset the further development of eco-logism. As a distinct ideological outlook it has been heavily influenced by other ideological traditions, some of which still claim to provide the answers to environmental problems. Some commentators are led to observe that ecologism can become the home for conservative, if not fascistic, ideas about the re-creation of homogenous, pre-industrial communities, untainted by the cosmopolitan influences associated with cities. Others point to the congruence between nineteenth-century anarchist and socialist visions of self-governing communities living in harmony with nature and contemporary Green preferences. At which political pole does ecologism lie? The answer to this question is further complicated by the peculiar combination of libertarian and authoritarian ideas embedded within the ecological outlook. As we have seen, Greens were strongly influenced by the countercultural ideas of the 1960s, developing a commitment to individual freedom of expression and autonomy. Simultaneously it is clear that the emphasis of some Greens upon human harmony with nature downplays the importance of securing more equitable and just social arrangements. Accordingly some Greens have been prepared to countenance the establishment of highly authoritarian social and political structures as the only means of developing more ecologically secure societies. This was evident, for instance, in the programme for environmental renewal put forward in 1972 by *The Ecologist* magazine in Britain – *Blueprint for Survival*. In addition the suspicion remains that the absence of any serious theory of transition from present conditions to a sustainable society within Green circles stems from an implicit reliance upon the coercive power of the state to enforce sustainability and sound ecological practices.

These are complex and difficult problems for ecologism. Both the libertarian and authoritarian impulses remain within this outlook. We can suggest, however, that the general commitment to the transformation of human society necessitated by ecologism involves a shift towards a set of social arrangements that allow for greater, not less, human autonomy and freedom, and enshrine diversity, not simple, repressive homogeneity. These arguments can be supported by the first general commitment at the heart of ecologism: the need to revolutionise human relationships with nature involves the application to human society of principles that are said to order nature, such as autonomy and diversity. Thus, Greens can furnish ideological arguments to disqualify or marginalise more authoritarian tendencies in the movement. They would be greatly helped in this task, however, by the construction of a serious body of Green political theory.

A second problem persists for ecologism in terms of its attitude towards the natural world. Appeal to the non-human realm lies at the heart of this outlook. Yet Greens have been criticised for adopting an attitude that sometimes parodies the natural world (as, for instance, harmonious) and on occasion presents nature as a coherent and autonomous 'actor' which stands in opposition to human life. This fetishistic attitude towards the natural world is clear from Green phrases such as 'Nature teaches us that . . . '. Critics point out that such thinking fails to incorporate human life within the biosphere (a central tenet of deep ecology) and obscures the sense in which our (human) understanding and knowledge of nature occurs through a number of longstanding traditions and categories. These range from the tradition of mechanistic science developed from the Renaissance, which leads us to view nature as irrational and dangerous, to the pastoral tradition, which suggests that nature is a benign or harmonious realm in which a more spiritual dimension to life can be re-created. However close we get to nature geographically, our contact with it is mediated through such traditions. Greens, however, tend to downplay the potency of these mediations between us and nature, suggesting simplistically that we can easily and swiftly remove these 'barriers' and get closer to the natural world. This point has been reinforced by radical critics who question the interpretation of the environment that Greens deploy. In contemporary debate the environment is too readily taken to mean rural areas. Consequently political ecology has been slow to highlight the pressing issues of urban environmental degradation and reluctant to redefine the environment as an entity that includes substantive, economic and social issues such as poverty, housing and conditions of employment. Certainly if Greens are to take seriously their own commitment to fundamental social and political change, such issues need to be the starting points for, not supplements to, their analysis of the ecological crisis that faces us.

The third major problem that persists for ecologism concerns the absence of a developed theory of the agency of Green change. Who is to carry out the ecological revolution? Two different kinds of answer have been offered to this question by Greens. The first is the simple, yet highly problematic, response that ecological issues have a global impact, therefore everyone is a potential constituent for the Green message. A number of objections can be made to this claim. Environmental degradation does not affect everyone in society equally. Indeed such universal thinking ignores real differences of interest and power within contemporary Western societies. Greens therefore need to come to terms with the different social and political identities that have been generated by modern society. The second answer to the above question concerns the specific groups in Western industrial societies who might be more sympathetic to ecological ideas. In particular, a lively debate has taken place among academic commentators about the 'new class' of white-collar professionals and public-sector workers whose size and influence have expanded since the 1950s in many countries in western Europe. It has been suggested that this class is motivated by particular kinds of political and social questions and is especially sensitive to issues such as the quality of life and the state of its environment. This has been termed the advent of 'post-materialist' politics, a paradigm closely associated with the work of Ronald Inglehart.

Certainly ecologism does seem to have gained a foothold among this social grouping, proving especially attractive to its younger members. Greens, though, are reluctant to limit their attentions to one class in modern society, firstly because political ecology claims to cut across the class antagonisms institutionalised within industrial societies and, secondly, because the commitment to fundamental change in human society cannot be channelled through the social aspirations of one group alone. The fortunes of this ideological perspective depend upon the ability of Greens to develop a more diverse social and electoral base, a goal they will achieve only if universal ecological ideals can be rendered more appealing to specific groups in society.

CONCLUSIONS

Ecologism remains a relatively unfamiliar ideology for many people. Some sceptics have claimed that it represents a number of ideas that came into fashion in the late 1980s and have now disappeared; others refuse to believe that ecologism is an ideology at all. Yet a case can be made that we are witnessing only the beginning of a slow process of convergence in which disparate ideas, diffuse philosophical perspectives and various political preferences are gradually coalescing around a shared ideological agenda. This agenda involves the beliefs that the relationship between humans and nature needs fundamental reorientation and that human society, in turn, should be profoundly restructured. A number of political preferences follow from these commitments, as we have seen. At this more concrete level, consensus is harder to find. Certain themes, such as sustainability, can be commonly found in ecological discourse, yet their precise meaning remains unclear and provides grounds for substantial disagreement within the Green movement.

It has been suggested in this chapter that the next stage in the development of ecologism lies in the articulation of a body of hard-headed political ideas, developed from a Green perspective. This is especially important given the redistribution of resources that Green and environmentalist politics require. Proposals for carbon taxes and financial penalties for polluters, which are being seriously entertained

by mainstream political parties, involve questions about the just allocation of resources in contemporary societies. More fundamental economic and resource redistribution, upon which Green politics depends,
will only be carried by a popular mandate which is won through
vigorous political and ideological debate. In this area Green politics
remains relatively weak. The future development of the principles of
ecologism will therefore substantially affect the chances of achieving
the sustainable society of which Greens dream.

NOTES

1 This conflicting terminology is evident in A. Dobson, *Green Political
Thought: An Introduction*, London, Unwin Hyman, 1990; and R.
Eckersley, *Environmentalism and Political Theory: Towards an Ecocentric Approach*, London, UCL Press, 1992.
2 These divisions are discussed in Dobson, *Green Political Thought*,
1–12; J. Porritt and D. Winner, *The Coming of the Greens*, London,
Fontana, 1984, 9; and Eckersley, *Environmentalism and Political
Theory*, 33–47.
3 See J. Porritt, 'Updating Industrialism', *Resurgence*, 112, 1985, 36.
4 J. Dryzek, *Rational Ecology, Environment and Political Ecology*, Oxford,
Blackwell, 1987.
5 This view can be found in A. Vincent, 'Ecologism', in *Modern Political
Ideologies*, Oxford, Blackwell, 1992, 208–37; and B. Norton, *Towards
Unity Among Environmentalists*, Oxford, Oxford University Press,
1992.
6 Dobson, *Green Political Thought*, 13.
7 *Ecology in the Twentieth Century*, New Haven and London, Yale
University Press, 1991.
8 Cited in C. Merchant, *Radical Ecology: The Search for a Livable World*,
London and New York, Routledge, 1992, 47.
9 L. White, 'The Historical Roots of our Ecologic Crisis', *Science*, 155
(37), 10 March 1967, 1203–7.
10 See R. Attfield, *The Ethics of Environmental Concern*, Oxford, Blackwell, 1983.
11 See R. Bourke, 'Places of Retreat: Lakes, Vales and Borders', in
*Romantic Discourse and Political Modernity: Wordsworth, the Intellectual
and Cultural Critique*, Hemel Hempstead, Harvester Wheatsheaf,
1993, 92–105.

12 J.S. Mill, 'Principles of Political Economy with some of their Applications to Social Philosophy (1848)', in E. Jay and R. Jay, eds, *Critics of Capitalism: Victorian Reactions to 'Political Economy'*, Cambridge, Cambridge University Press, 1986, 118.

13 For an account of these ideas, see E.P. Thompson, *William Morris: Romantic to Revolutionary*, London, Merlin, 1977.

14 For an accessible scientific discussion of these issues, see E.G. Nisbet, *Leaving Eden: To Protect and Manage the Earth*, Cambridge, Cambridge University Press, 1991.

15 See HRH The Prince of Wales, 'First Unshackle the Spirit: The Brundtland Speech, April 1992', in G. Prins, ed., *Threats Without Enemies: Facing Environmental Security*, London, Earthscan, 1993, 3–14.

16 Herman Daly, cited in Merchant, *Radical Ecology*, 37.

17 G. Hardin, 'Living in a Lifeboat', *Bioscience*, 24, 1974.

18 *Small is Beautiful: Economics as if People Mattered*, London, Blond and Briggs, 1973.

19 See K. Sale, *Dwellers in the Land: The Bioregional Vision*, San Francisco, Calif., Sierra Club Books, 1985.

20 For an account of Malthusian ideas, see D. Winch, *Malthus*, Oxford, Oxford University Press, 1987.

21 See A. Dobson, 'Deep Ecology', *Cogito*, 3 (1), 1989, 41–6; R. Attfield, 'Deep Ecology and Intrinsic Value: A Reply to Andrew Dobson', *Cogito*, 4 (1), 1990, 61–6; and R. Sylvan, 'A Critique of Deep Ecology', *Radical Philosophy*, 40, 1985, 2–12, and 41, 1985, 10–22.

22 See M. Robinson, *The Greening of British Party Politics*, Manchester, Manchester University Press, 1992, 197–8.

FURTHER READING

General

A. Dobson, *Green Political Thought: An Introduction*, London, Unwin Hyman, 1990, provides the clearest and most accessible introduction to many of the themes in this chapter, while C. Merchant, *Radical Ecology: The Search for a Livable World*, London and New York, Routledge, 1992, is also useful for those less familiar with these debates. While less academic in tone, the work of Jonathon Porritt is a lively starting point for approaching Green ideas: J. Porritt, *Seeing Green: The Politics of Ecology Explained*, Oxford, Blackwell, 1984; and J. Porritt and D. Winner, *The Coming of the Greens*, London, Fontana, 1984.

Analysis of Green political theory can be found in some of the thoughtful essays collected in A. Dobson and P. Lucardie, eds, *The Politics of Nature: Explorations in Green Political Theory*, London, Routledge, 1993. More sustained evaluation of Green political ideas is provided by R. Goodin, *Green Political Theory*, Cambridge, Polity Press, 1992; and R. Eckersley, *Environmentalism and Political Theory: Towards an Ecocentric Approach*, London, UCL, 1992, though these authors present differing theses. Many Green ideas are discussed, in a highly critical, yet valuable, assessment by M. Lewis, *Green Delusions: An Environmentalist Critique of Radical Environmentalism*, Durham and London, Duke University Press, 1992. For the spectrum of Green beliefs see T. O'Riordan, *Environmentalism*, London, Pion Press, 1981.

A. Bramwell, *Ecology in the Twentieth Century*, New Haven and London, Yale University Press, 1989, provides a stimulating, if controversial, history of ecological thinking. For a consideration of the contemporary significance of Malthusian ideas, see T. Benton, 'The Malthusian Challenge: Ecology, Natural Limits and Human Emancipation', in P. Osborne, ed., *Socialism and the Limits of Liberalism*, London, Verso, 1991, 241–69. The significance of the concept of nature in earlier eras has inspired the work of a number of historians; see especially C. Merchant, *The Death of Nature: Women, Ecology, and the Scientific Revolution*, San Francisco, Calif., Harper and Row, 1980; J. Passmore, *Man's Responsibility for Nature: Ecological Problems and Western Traditions*, London, Duckworth, 1980; and K. Thomas, *Man and the Natural World: Changing Attitudes in England 1500–1800*, London, Allen Lane, 1983.

A vast literature exists about the non-theoretical dimensions of Green politics. Some of this is relevant to the understanding of Green ideas; the German Green Party has played an especially important role, for instance, as the forum for a number of divisive political debates: see W. Hülsberg, *The German Greens: A Social and Political Profile*, London, Verso, 1988; and the work of the late Petra Kelly, a key figure within this party's history and ideological development: P. Kelly, *Fighting for Hope*, London, Chatto and Windus and The Hogarth Press, 1984. In the British context, the recent history of the Greens and the appearance of environmental issues within mainstream politics are covered in M. Robinson, *The Greening of British Party Politics*, Manchester, Manchester University Press, 1992. The activities of radical environmentalist groups in North America, in particular Earth First!, are presented in the lively, but hagiographic, C. Manes, *Green Rage: Radical Environmentalism and the Unmaking of Civilization*, Boston, Toronto and London, Little, Brown, 1990.

For the post-industrial thesis, see R. Inglehart, *The Silent Revolution: Changing Values and Political Styles Among Western Publics*, Princeton, N.J., Princeton University Press, 1977; and R. Eckersley, 'Green Politics and the New Class: Selfishness or Virtue?', *Political Studies*, 37 (2), 1989, 205–23. The importance of conflicts concerning the reallocation of resources, which Green politics demands, is dealt with in A. Schnaiberg, N. Watts and K. Zimmerman, eds, *Distributional Conflicts in Environmental Resource Policy*, Aldershot, WZB Publications, 1986.

Texts

Selections from many important Green thinkers can be found in A. Dobson, ed., *The Green Reader*, London, André Deutsch, 1991, with a useful commentary by the editor. The work of all of the thinkers cited in this chapter is easily available. The 'founding texts' of political ecology are R. Carson, *Silent Spring*, Boston, Mass., Houghton and Mifflin, 1962; P. Ehrlich, *The Population Bomb*, New York, Ballantine Books, 1968; D.H. Meadows, D.L. Meadows, J. Randers and W. Behrens, *The Limits to Growth*, London, Earth Island, 1972; E. Goldsmith, *A Blueprint for Survival*, London, Tom Stacey, 1972; and J. Lovelock, *Gaia: A New Look at Life on Earth*, New York, Open University Press, 1979.

Exposition of some of the political and economic themes discussed in this chapter is available in W. Schwarz and D. Schwarz, *Breaking Through*, Bideford, Green Books, 1987; W. Ophuls, 'The Politics of the Sustainable Society', in D. Pirages, ed., *The Sustainable Society: Implications for Limited Growth*, New York and London, Prager, 1977, 164–70; E. Schumacher, *Small is Beautiful: Economics as if People Mattered*, London, Blond and Briggs, 1973; H. Daly, 'The Steady-State Economy: What, Why and How?', in Pirages, ed., *The Sustainable Society*, 107–14; P. Elkins, ed., *The Living Economy: A New Economics in the Making*, London, Routledge and Kegan Paul, 1986; B. Tokar, *The Green Alternative*, San Pedro, Calif., R. and E. Miles, 1987; and R. Eckersley, 'Green Versus Ecosocialist Economic Programmes: The Market Rules OK?', *Political Studies*, 40 (2), 1992, 315–33.

On deep ecology, see A. Naess, *Ecology, Community and Lifestyle:*

Outline of an Ecosophy, Cambridge, Cambridge University Press, 1989; W. Fox, 'Deep Ecology: A New Philosophy of Our Time?', *The Ecologist,* 14 (5–6), 1984, 194–200; B. Devall and G. Sessions, *Deep Ecology,* Salt Lake City, Ut., Peregrine Smith Books, 1985; K. Sale, *Dwellers in the Land: The Bioregional Vision,* San Francisco, Calif., Sierra Club Books, 1985; R. Sylvan and D. Bennett, 'Taoism and Deep Ecology', *The Ecologist,* 18 (4–5), 1988, 148–59; and the articles collected in M. Tobias, ed., *Deep Ecology,* San Diego, Calif., 1985. On social ecology, see M. Bookchin, *Towards an Ecological Society,* Montreal, Black Rose, 1980; *The Ecology of Freedom,* Palo Alto, Calif., Cheshire Books, 1982, and *Remaking Society: Pathways to a Green Future,* Boston, Mass., South End Press, 1990. The work of writers in the eco-socialist tradition can be considered in R. Bahro, *From Red to Green: Interviews with New Left Review,* London, Verso, 1984; A. Gorz, *Ecology as Politics,* London, Pluto, 1987; and R. Williams, *Socialism and Ecology,* London, SERA, n.d. For eco-feminism, see P.J. Mills, 'Feminism and Ecology: On the Domination of Nature', *Hypatia,* 6 (1), 1991, 162–78; H. Henderson, 'The Warp and the Weft: The Coming Synthesis of Eco-Philosophy and Eco-Feminism', in I. Caldecott and S. Leland, eds, *Reclaim the Earth,* London, Women's Press, 1983, 203–14; S. Lahar, 'Eco-feminist Theory and Grassroots Politics', *Hypatia,* 6 (1), 1991, 28–45; and Y. King, 'Towards an Ecological Feminism and a Feminist Ecology', in J. Rothschild, ed., *Machina Ex Dea,* New York, Pergamon Press, 1983, 118–29.

Commentary

There is an abundance of material concerned with the philosophical and ethical dimensions of ecology. R. Attfield, *The Ethics of Environmental Concern,* Oxford, Blackwell, 1983, critically examines the argument that an ecological outlook necessitates a distinctive ethic. Also, see the essays collected in E. Partridge, ed., *Responsibilities to Future Generations: Environmental Ethics,* New York, Prometheus, 1980; and L.E. Johnson, *A Morally Deep World: An Essay on Moral Significance and Environmental Ethics,* Cambridge, Cambridge University Press, 1991. More generally, the journal *Environmental Ethics* carries much material of significance here.

Deep ecology has been subjected to some searching critical evaluation. See especially H.M. Enzensberger, 'A Critique of Deep Ecology', *New Left Review,* 84, 1974, 3–31; and the complex, but important, R.

Sylvan, 'A Critique of Deep Ecology', *Radical Philosophy*, 40, 1985, 2–12 and 41, 1985, 10–22. Specifically on the Gaia thesis, see C.J. Hughes, 'Gaia: A Natural Scientist's Ethic for the Future', *The Ecologist*, 15 (3), 1985, 92–4; and A. Weston, 'Forms of Gaian Ethics', *Environmental Ethics*, 9, 1987, 217–30. The spiritual side of Green politics is introduced in F. Capra, *The Tao of Physics*, Berkeley, Calif., Shambala, 1975. Two insightful evaluations of social ecology can be found in R. Eckersley, 'Divining Evolution: The Ecological Ethics of Murray Bookchin', *Environmental Ethics*, 11, 1989, 99–116; and B. Tokar, 'Social Ecology, Deep Ecology and the Future of Green Political Thought', *The Ecologist*, 18 (4–5), 1988, 132–41.

The relationship between socialism and ecology has been intelligently examined by M. Ryle, *Ecology and Socialism*, London, Radius, 1988; and D. Wall, *Getting There: Steps Towards a Green Society*, London, Green Print, 1990. More polemical and less useful analyses can be found in J. Weston, ed., *Red and Green: A New Politics of the Environment*, London, Pluto, 1986; and M. Simons, 'The Red and the Green: Socialists and the Ecology Movement', *International Socialism*, 2 (37), 1988, 49–91. Some commentators have approached this question via the work of Marx: P. Dickens, *Society and Nature: Towards a Green Social Theory*, Hemel Hempstead, Harvester Wheatsheaf, 1992; and R. Grundmann, *Marxism and Ecology*, Oxford, Clarendon Press, 1991.

Chapter 9

Feminism

Rick Wilford

I myself have never been able to find out precisely what feminism is: I only know that people call me a feminist whenever I express sentiments that differentiate me from a doormat or a prostitute.
Rebecca West, 'Mr Chesterton in Hysterics: A Study in Prejudice', quoted in Maggie Humm, ed., *Feminisms: A Reader*, Hemel Hempstead, Harvester Wheatsheaf, 1992, 34

It is hardly possible to specify a core of beliefs that would not be contested by at least some of those who call themselves feminists.
Vicky Randall, 'Feminism and Political Analysis', *Political Studies*, XXXIX, 3, 1991, 516

PROBLEMS OF DEFINITION

Few now accept that the terms 'feminism' and 'feminist' are self-evident. One symptom of this uncertainty is a tendency to employ the plural term *feminisms* in order to capture the diversity of views expressed by feminists. Another is the preference for a minimalist or, as Rosalind Delmar styles it, a base-line definition:

at the very least a feminist is someone who holds that women suffer discrimination because of their sex, that they have specific needs which remain negated and unsatisfied, and that the satisfaction of these needs would require a radical change in the social, economic and political order.

Beyond that, she concludes, 'things immediately become more complicated'.[1]

This is not to suggest that contemporary feminists are unable to act together over issues of common concern to women, although as we shall see they do approach such issues as equal pay, discrimination or the domestic division of labour from differing standpoints. Moreover, the complexities that Delmar signals are not novel in themselves. 'First-wave' feminists during the nineteenth and early twentieth centuries who were associated primarily with female suffrage, also disagreed about how to right the wrongs afflicting women and where to affix responsibility for the source of those wrongs. However, while all ideologies will attract adherents who differ over the means to achieve an ostensibly agreed end – revolutionary vs. reformist socialists, dark vs. light green ecologists, organic vs. libertarian conservatives – the extent of current disagreement among 'second-wave' feminists is said by Vicky Randall to amount to nothing short of 'a crisis of identity'.[2]

Such uncertainty is explained in large measure by the fact that feminism evolved within the context of existing or emerging doctrinal traditions, whether liberalism, socialism or Marxism. This had two effects. Firstly, as exponents of new and radical thinking, feminists had to negotiate space for their ideas within each of these traditions. Secondly, in the process of this negotiation, they became aligned with the basic and exclusive premises adopted by each of these 'isms'. Thus, the dividing lines among feminists were derived from their association with one or another of these ideologies. It therefore makes sense to discuss the evolution of a distinctively liberal, socialist or Marxist feminism.

Yet feminist ideas are not merely derivative. Feminists not only negotiated with existing ideologies; they also interrogated them. In doing so they challenged a number of key assumptions which have underpinned the development of political thought since the time of Plato and Aristotle: not least its 'pervasive dualism'.[3]

Feminists observe that the history of Western political thought is invested with a series of 'binary oppositions', each pole of which is accorded either a positive or negative value.[4] Key dualities included: culture–nature; reason–emotion; public–private; and male–female. The first of each pairing were arranged together, such that maleness was associated with cultural activity and rationality, both of which were enacted in the public sphere. By contrast, femaleness was equated with nature, that is reproduction, and passion, which belonged in the private sphere of home and family. Moreover, such associations were not presented as equivalent or co-equal, but in terms of a simple hierarchy: male characteristics were superior, female inferior. Much of the wider feminist project has been concerned to undermine these dualities, thereby lending it a distinctively subversive character.

Such subversion has, though, taken different forms. Some feminists have adopted an androcentric (male-centred) strategy, encouraging women to adopt the characteristics traditionally ascribed to men. Others have sought not to emulate men, but rather to prescribe an androgynous (male and female) solution, whereby the qualities ascribed to women and men are integrated in a common and non-hierarchical human identity. Yet others have sought to reverse the polarities by adopting a gynocentric (female-centred) strategy which places a posit- ive value on the attributes conventionally ascribed to women, while some feminists have insisted that though women and men are different they are, nevertheless, equal and that such differences should be celebrated, not denied or fused together.

These differing strategies are influenced in large measure by the significance attached by feminists to either sex or gender. Some femin- ists insist upon the primacy of biological sex, that is the distinction between female and male, as the explanation for the oppression of women – that the fundamentally different experiences of women and men in reproducing the species has been used as the motive for perpetuating inequalities between the sexes: on this view, unless these experiences are transformed, women will continue to be subordinate to men. This perspective, as we shall see, has been characteristic of those generally described as 'radical feminists' who have been concerned largely with the politics of sexuality and reproduction.

Other feminists focus not upon biological sex but rather upon the ways in which societies construct gendered, i.e. feminine and mas- culine, roles to explain differences in the life-chances of women and men. Here the focus is on the cultural meanings attached to the roles learned by children of either sex and which society considers appro- priate for women and men. This distinction between the political significance of sex and gender informs much of the debate among feminists. Those favouring the former insist that a woman's social identity is determined by her sex, whereas those stressing culturally induced differences emphasise the gendered character of woman's identity. The relative weight attached to the variables of sex and gender and the ways in which they are understood to interact, critically influence the question of whether women should be regarded as being essentially the same as, or fundamentally different from, men.

What one might describe as 'the man problem' has become in-creasingly prominent within feminist debate. For instance, there are feminists who cast men as the implacable enemies of women and who prescribe a separatist and autonomous route to the fulfilment of their needs: from this perspective men become wholly redundant in women's lives. Conversely, there are feminists who regard men as potential, if not actual, allies in the struggle for genuine equality between the sexes. They regard the active support of men as not merely politically expedient, because men currently enjoy a virtual monopoly of political power, but also as crucial to the achievement of a just society. This latter position, unlike the former, also allows that men can lay claim to a feminist identity.

While not an entirely novel issue, the portrayal of men as either the friends or foes of women is an item of intense debate among feminists. The prominence of 'the man question' was assured by the emergence of radical feminists who rejuvenated the concept of patriarchy to explain the subordination of women.

PATRIARCHY

In its most radical formulation patriarchy is understood in ahistoric terms: that men are, always have been and always will be, motivated to dominate women and will use all means, fair and foul, to achieve that end. Furthermore, this expansive definition does not restrict the exercise of male power to the 'public' worlds of politics and work: patriarchy is also understood to extend into the 'private' sphere of the family and the intimate realm of sexual relations. It is this belief in the pervasiveness of patriarchy that led to the coining of the phrase 'the personal is political' in order to convey its seamless reach.

In a more dilute form, patriarchy is deployed as shorthand for the conditions of inequality women experience, whether in the public or private realms. In this 'weaker' sense, patriarchy is understood to be socially constructed through the respective meanings imparted to masculinity and femininity: in short, it is gendered. By contrast, the more radical interpretation of patriarchy rests on the essentialism of biological difference and perceives men to be naturally driven by their need to exert power over women. Whereas the former, gendered, interpretation allows the possibility for change to occur in relationships between women and men, the latter implies an immutable character to relations between the sexes: men have no interest, perhaps even choice, in relinquishing their control of women. Pushed to its logical conclusion, this interpretation of patriarchy presents women as enduring victims of male oppression, thereby offending other feminists who both see women in more active terms and regard joint efforts by women and men as necessary to overcome gendered inequalities.

One consequence of representing men as the enemy, in effect as *the* problem confronting women, is the belief that the solution lies with women themselves. Exponents of an undiluted patriarchy believe that women must liberate themselves from their condition of oppression. The task of feminism on this view is to encourage women to recognise that they share a submerged unity, a potential sisterhood, which has to be realised in order to overcome their subordination.

The centrality of patriarchy to contemporary debate has compounded the diversity of feminism. But the issue of sameness/difference that it addresses has reverberated throughout its history.

HISTORICAL DIVERSITY

Diversity is not unique to second wave feminism. Indeed, to talk in terms of a second wave itself implies that there was a first wave of feminism distinct from that which gained momentum in the 1960s. Viewed historically the evolution of the feminist movement falls, conveniently enough, into two broad phases: The first from the early nineteenth century until shortly after the First World War and the second from the early to mid-1960s until the present.

This metaphor of waves of activity suggests flows and ebbs in the feminist tide, and implies that it is associated primarily with organised activities designed to achieve equality for women. Yet, feminist ideas existed before the creation of social and political movements agitating for change. Both in terms of the first and second waves it is difficult to point to a decisive moment when each emerged. Though the terms 'feminist/feminism' did not enter the vocabulary until the later nineteenth century, historians of feminist ideas have, for instance, discovered women writing about women's rights as early as the fourteenth century, while Mary Astell (1666–1731) has been described recently as 'an early' or, in one case, 'the first English feminist'.[5]

Astell, a conservative and a monarchist, did not advocate the extension of political rights to women nor indeed to the majority of men, but rather insisted upon women's capacity for rational thought which was stunted by their socially induced concern to become pretty and feminine in order to capture a husband. She advised women to avoid marriage, to improve their minds and enjoy a life free from dependence upon men, a set of prescriptions that, as Valerie Bryson observes, prefigure a number of the key ideas of contemporary radical feminism.[6]

Besides the somewhat isolated voice of an individual like Astell, the longevity of feminist ideas can also be associated with organised activities intended to secure equal rights for women. For instance the roots of feminism as a movement can plausibly be traced to the creation of women's clubs during the French Revolution, or the activities of women involved in the movements to abolish slavery and to promote temperance during the nineteenth century. In the case of abolition, this led to the meeting at Seneca Falls in July 1848 and the publication of the 'Declaration of Resolutions and Sentiments', the opening line of which extended the Declaration of Independence: 'We hold these truths to be self-evident: that all men *and women* are created equal.' That statement is generally taken to be the catalyst for the emergence of the suffrage movement which came to dominate the agenda of first-wave feminists.

The point here is not to insist that any one individual, event or text has a prior claim on another, but to suggest that the history of feminist ideas and activity is typified by unevenness rather than a smooth and linear progression. If anything, the emergence of second-wave feminism is even more difficult to pin down, not least because much of the early activity took place in informal settings where women engaged in 'consciousness-raising' sessions as much, if not more, than publicly visible, mass meetings.[7] The somewhat haphazard nature of these sessions itself contributed to the diversity that has always characterised the feminist project. While it would be misleading to claim that their predecessors were only concerned with the vote, more recent feminists have fostered a wider agenda of discussion. In particular, the priority given to sexual politics has tended to sharpen the divisions within the women's movement.

SUFFRAGE: A FRAGILE UNITY

The date of the achievement of female suffrage varied from country to country although 1920, when women in the United States secured the right to vote in national elections via the Nineteenth Amendment, is usually understood to mark the high tide of the first wave. The legacy of that achievement, won by women of all races and religions, the young and the old, the rich and the poor, imparted an apparent unity to feminism. Here, it seemed, was an object lesson in the capacity of women to act in sisterly solidarity for a shared goal. True, the suffrage movement brought together many women, and some men, in a common pursuit, but it also masked underlying tensions. The motives and the tactics of the campaign were varied, no more so than those that distinguished equal rights from evangelical feminists.[8]

What differentiated these feminists was precisely the question of whether women should be treated the same as, or differently from, men in matters of public policy. Inspired by the doctrine of natural rights, equal rights feminists insisted that women be treated as human, not sexual, beings since they were equally capable as men of governing themselves by reason. The application of such ideas to women was first given wide currency by Mary Wollstonecraft (1759–1797) in *A Vindication of the Rights of Woman* (1792). Inspired by Enlightenment principles, Wollstonecraft based her plea for women to be treated as free and independent individuals upon the premiss that the mind had no sex: that the opponents of civil rights for women were, in effect, denying that women enjoyed the same capacity as men to engage in rational thought and action.

Here lay the seeds of the 'sameness' argument that was to inform many early proponents of female enfranchisement. But apart from one teasing reference – 'women ought to have representatives, instead of being arbitrarily governed without having any direct share allowed them in the deliberations of government' – Wollstonecraft was muted on the question of votes for women. Yet her ideas were quickly adopted by equal rights feminists in Britain and the United States where her book was regarded as 'the Bible' of the early suffrage movement.

The equal rights tradition of feminism advocated the removal of legal obstacles to the fulfilment of women's autonomy as individuals thereby ending their dependence upon, and hence subjection by, men. During the nineteenth century campaigns to reform divorce laws, to provide married women with property rights and to open up educational institutions and the professions to women, as well as the suffrage issue, represented the pursuit of gender equality. In effect, the insistence upon eradicating legal constraints upon women took as its measure the rights accorded to men: the male citizen became the prototype for the rights of women.

More recently, the proposition that men should be the yardstick for women has been ridiculed by some feminists who reject its effective denial of women's uniqueness. But earlier, both before and shortly after the enfranchisement of women, 'evangelical feminists' chose not to emphasise sameness but rather to celebrate differences between the sexes.

This current of ideas was neither radical nor liberal but socially conservative. Associated with efforts to reform prostitutes and promote the virtues of temperance, these women saw themselves as exemplars of characteristically womanly virtues that derived from their roles as wives and mothers. Thus, women were perceived as co-operative where men were competitive; pacific as opposed to aggressive; selfless rather than selfish; and, perhaps most distinctively, were believed to be morally superior to men. The assertion of such differences justified the extension of the vote to women not on the grounds of equal rights, but in the belief that these natural qualities would enhance the public realm of politics by supplying a necessary corrective to the excesses of men.

The co-existence of the ideas of equal rights and evangelical feminists throughout the nineteenth and into the twentieth century, while logically opposed, did not prevent their respective advocates from combining to press for female suffrage. However, in the immediate aftermath of votes for women in both the United States and Britain, the tension between these variants of feminism could no longer be contained.

In America the campaign for the Equal Rights Amendment (ERA), spearheaded by the National Women's Party in 1923, broke the strategic coalition that had come together in pursuit of suffrage. The ERA sought, via constitutional amendment, to eliminate all legal inequalities between women and men, including those laws affording special protection to women, especially in the field of employment. Having fought hard for protective legislation designed to prevent the exploitation of women (and children), evangelical feminists rushed to defend, and extend, those gains, reasserting the special needs of women and the characteristics attendant upon maternity that distinguished them from men.

In Britain during the 1920s, the campaign led by self-styled 'new feminists' for a state-funded family allowance payable to wives rather than their husbands, offended equal rights or 'old' feminists because of its assumption that women's maternal role naturally anchored them to the home. Whereas equal rights feminists sought to challenge conventional beliefs about the sexual division of labour within the family, those who increasingly espoused state welfare for married women endorsed marriage and maternity as means of fulfilment for women. A self-defined 'old' feminist drew the distinction thus: 'The "New Feminism" emphasizes the importance of the "women's point of view", the "Old Feminism" believes in the primary importance of the human being.'9 That distinction between 'sameness' – the essential humanness of women – and 'difference' – the woman's point of view – which had been accommodated in pursuit of the vote, ruptured the tenuous unity effected over suffrage.

The roots of such a distinction are, as has already been suggested, rather lengthy and are exemplified by a brief discussion of the emergence of modern feminist ideas.

EARLY LIBERAL FEMINISM

As already indicated, Wollstonecraft's *Vindication* was an early plea for equal rights for women. She insisted upon the common capacity of women to engage in rational thought, voicing the demand for equal educational opportunities as the means through which women could realise their independence. Having benefited from the same education, marriage would be freely entered into by rational individuals capable of fulfilling their respective duties within the context of a companionate relationship. Such a union would displace the common pattern of marriage – especially among the middle classes to whom she primarily directed her arguments – wherein 'emotional' women, their intellects stunted by being trained for domestic docility, sought security and a slavish dependence upon 'rational' men.

Here Wollstonecraft anticipates an understanding of the gendered character of the roles deemed appropriate for men and women. In so doing, she rejected the representation of femininity as a natural attribute, insisting that it was an artificial construct, made by men in their own interests, so devised as to deny the essential humanness of women. In debunking femininity, she levelled her sights at her near contemporary, Jean Jacques Rousseau (1712–78).

His educational tract, *Emile*, had asserted innate differences between the sexes which led him to consign women to natural dependence upon men. Rousseau represented women as lacking the attributes required for citizenship – reason, strength, autonomy – characteristics which he contended were naturally male. Women, on the other hand, were portrayed by him as being naturally emotional, weak and obedient. These mooted differences led Rousseau to extol wholly different educational philosophies for girls and boys: the latter were to be educated to become rational, moral and self-governing individuals whereas girls were to be trained for domestic submission and to acquire the skills required to please their future husbands.

Wollstonecraft disdained the 'natural' distinction drawn by Rousseau, insisting upon the common ability of both sexes to engage in reasoned thought and action. In so doing she rejected the proposition that women were possessed of any singular qualities rooted in their sex, although she did acknowledge that the 'peculiar destination' for most women was marriage and motherhood. Framing her prescriptions in somewhat utilitarian terms, she envisaged women as enacting the independence gained from a common education within the private or domestic sphere, where they would exercise the tasks of household management rationally and efficiently: 'Make women rational creatures and free citizens, and they will quickly become good wives and mothers.'[10]

The idea that the sexual division of labour within the family should be transformed did not enter her calculus, nor did the conception that the family itself was the site of female oppression. This latter view was common to socialist and Marxist feminists, and was reinvigorated by radical feminists almost two hundred years later. Moreover, the notion of the working woman was restricted by Wollstonecraft to those who chose not to marry.

Stressing equal rights, early liberal feminism was wedded to the achievement of formal legal equality for women and, in the work of Harriet Taylor (1807–58) and her second husband, John Stuart Mill (1806–73), was to encompass suffrage and widening opportunities for employment. A utilitarian liberal, rather than an exponent of natural rights like Wollstonecraft, Mill's advocacy was framed largely in terms of the benefits that would accrue to society from the implementation of equal rights. A wider array of talents would be available and moral progress be more swiftly advanced if relations between men and women were placed upon an equal footing: in consequence, the sum total of human happiness would be increased.

Allowing the possibility that married women could enter paid employment, Mill considered this to be the destination only of 'exceptional' women. It was more important, in his view, that women were educated to the point where they could, rather than should, seek work outside the marital setting. Like Wollstonecraft, he envisaged married women as choosing to assume the duties of wife and mother. Harriet Taylor, however, held decidedly different views. She positively encouraged women, single or married, to seek employment, not simply as a means of assuring financial but, more importantly, psychological independence. Employment would buttress self-respect and facilitate a genuine and equal partnership among wives and husbands.

Though Taylor's ideas on this matter were more advanced than Mill's she, like him and Wollstonecraft before, operated with a number of unreflective assumptions concerning the sexual division of labour. None proposed an equitable distribution of domestic tasks, assuming that wives would supervise the running of the home. Even Taylor, the advocate of woman's employment, presumed that the working wife and mother would juggle an occupation with domestic management. Here one encounters another problematic assumption shared by all three early liberal feminists. They took for granted that the women they were addressing, drawn from the middle classes, would employ domestic servants, working-class women, who would undertake the drudgery of housework.

This shared perspective reflected existing class divisions among women and as such represented an exclusive rather than an inclusive vision of emancipated womanhood. Moreover, none acknowledged that there might be structural causes of women's oppression rooted in the economic bases of early and developing capitalism. A more robust critique not only of capitalism but also of the family emerged from the utopian socialists of the early nineteenth century.

UTOPIAN SOCIALIST FEMINISM

At its root, socialism offers a vision of an egalitarian and co-operative society, thereby describing an alternative to the competitive individualism that lies at the heart of liberal doctrine. While the early liberals couched their feminist ideas in formal and rather abstract terms, encouraging men to perceive the injustice and unhappiness caused by excluding women from the enjoyment of equal rights, the utopian socialists focused more upon the material inequalities intrinsic to a class-based society.

Historically, utopian socialism emerged between the natural rights philosophy of Wollstonecraft and the utilitarianism of Mill. However, while the early liberal feminists saw no contradiction between women achieving civil and political rights while remaining within the private sphere, utopian socialists – such as William Thompson (1775–1833), Anna Wheeler, alias 'Concordia' (1785-?), and Robert Owen (1771–1858) in Ireland and Britain, and Charles Fourier (1772–1837) and Henri St Simon (1760–1825) in France – understood women to be doubly oppressed: within not only the polity and the economy but also in the family, where they were treated as domestic slaves by their husbands. Here is an early anticipation of patriarchy: the perception that women were subjected in both the public and private spheres to exploitation by men. Further, while liberal feminists sought to extinguish difference by adopting an androcentric perspective, utopian socialists emphasised what they believed were the distinctive qualities of women.

The institution of marriage was understood by utopian socialists to stultify the moral, cultural and psychological development of both women and men and also to foster both selfishness and inefficiency. The solution lay in open, authentic relationships founded upon co-operation, itself nourished by the disposition towards sympathy and benevolence intrinsic to human nature. For Thompson and Wheeler, the achievement of civil and political equality for women was not enough: arrangements whereby women remained economically dependent upon men had to be broken. This meant the abolition of private property, the communal provision of those services normally provided in the home and an economy that redistributed resources on the basis of equality: all would thereby contribute to the maximisation of human happiness.

The implications of this project for men and, particularly, women were profound. Freed from the economic motive for monogamous marriage, liberated from the drudgery and hardship of running a household and enabled to engage in fulfilling and creative labour, both sexes would appreciate the benefits of mutual support within a society where collective ownership meant none was advantaged by material possessions.

The utopian socialists differed from the early liberals in two important respects. Firstly, they stressed the economic dimensions of equality; and secondly, they drew a distinction between women's and men's natures. Here is a clear prefiguring of the sameness/difference polarity that was to be renewed in the wake of suffrage. A belief in the moral superiority of women underlay much of their writing, as did the conviction that the feminine virtues of caring, patience and fortitude endowed women with a capacity to promote benevolence and sympathy within the context of mutually supportive communities.

Besides seeking to establish the affinity between such virtues and communal socialism, utopian socialists also expressed uninhibited and, for their time, controversial views about the joys of sexual fulfilment. For them in general it was not a case of sensibility triumphing over sense, but rather a harmony between emotional needs and rationality that led to individual happiness and co-operative endeavour. Indeed, their advocacy of free sexual expression offered a marked alternative to the rather passionless companionate relationships preferred both by Wollstonecraft and Mill.

Certain of the ideas of the utopian socialists were given practical application in the communal experiments initiated by Owen and followers of Fourier (see Chapter 4). The attempted eradication of the sexual division of labour, the disavowal of marriage, coupled with the collective provision of childcare and housework by both sexes – all demonstrated that the utopian socialists understood the rights of women to be integral and not marginal to the realisation of a genuinely egalitarian society.

MARXIST FEMINISM

The place of utopian socialism in the development of feminism is an important one. However, its reformist and experimental path to an egalitarian society was dismissed by both Karl Marx (1818–83) and Friedrich Engels (1820–95). Wedded to a theory of history founded upon class conflict and a revolutionary transition to a socialist, and ultimately communist, society, feminist ideas were subordinated by them to the primacy of class struggle. As such, the relationship between Marxism and feminism has been characterised as 'an unhappy marriage'.

This perception rests in part upon the virtual absence from Marx's own works of what socialists came to style the 'woman question'. Marx paid scant attention to gender relations, believing that the emancipation of women would be a by-product of the creation of socialism. As such the position of women, and of men, was taken for granted: the transition to communism would provide the context in which sexual equality would prevail.

While Marx understood, as did liberals and the utopians, that human nature was shaped by environmental conditions, he rejected the idea that it could be realised within capitalism or in the communal margins of co-operative association perched at the fringes of capitalist society. He insisted that free, self-determined human nature would flourish and sexual egalitarianism exist only with the transformation of capitalism. That change required revolution by class-conscious workers, with all energies directed towards its achievement. All else was a mere distraction: hence women and men must engage in the fomentation of class politics, effectively setting aside 'the woman question' until capitalism was overthrown.

Marx's wholly inadequate treatment of relations between the sexes was fleshed out by his friend and collaborator Friedrich Engels and the German Social Democrat August Bebel (1840–1913). Both exhorted women to throw in their lot with men in the common struggle to achieve a classless society, free of the exploitative relations intrinsic to capitalism.

Private property would disappear and with it the materialist motive for marriage which enslaved women. Neither Marx, Engels nor Bebel was opposed to marriage, but contended that only in a socialist society would this relationship be based upon love and be free of male domination that was expressed both in the economy and through the inequitable division of labour within the family.

They viewed the subordination of women as an endemic feature of capitalist societies which would disappear under socialism. Of course, the 1917 Bolshevik Revolution seemed to create the opportunity for what Lenin (1870–1924) termed 'the real emancipation of women'. An exponent of equal rights for women, Lenin believed the path to emancipation lay through the full participation of women in economic and political life. Much energy was directed by the new regime into making public provision for tasks formerly undertaken by women in the private home: nurseries, kindergartens and public dining rooms were established as means of enabling women to play a full part in the economic and political mission to build socialism. Additionally, divorce was made easy, as was access to abortion facilities. Such systems of support, coupled with the mass entry of women into the workforce, were seen as essential to ending domestic slavery.

The promise of revolutionary socialism was enticing: in the event it was to be broken. After an initial flurry of activity and reform in the 1920s designed to secure an 'equality of life' as well as equality of rights, the 'woman question' was to be neglected and the earlier reforms reversed with the accession of Stalin (1879–1953). By 1930, just thirteen years after the Revolution, Stalin was to declare the woman question solved. Only with the demise of the Soviet Union has the full extent of women's subordination under communism been appreciated. Despite the advent of women into the public sphere, notably into paid employment, patriarchy, far from having withered away, was seen to have been deeply entrenched in Soviet society.

For later Marxist and socialist feminists, the legacy of Marxism has been discomfiting. While arguing that women were subject to material oppression within capitalism by being treated as a reserve army of labour, hired and fired at will and receiving only low wages, Marxists neglected the possibility that women were also vulnerable to other forms of oppression. The premium that Marxism placed upon class solidarity thereby glossed over relations between men and women. The portrayal of them as class allies could not allow that patriarchy would endure once capitalism had been superseded.

This attempt to associate patriarchy with a particular economic system did not, however, persuade other feminists. Convinced of its universal character as a system of oppression, and underscored by the treatment of women in the Soviet Union and on the revolutionary left outside the USSR, radical feminists accused Marxism of sex-blindness. This charge left socialist feminists in the second wave struggling to reconcile both the sex- and class-based systems of women's oppression.

THE 'OTHER' WOMAN

The achievement of female suffrage was a milestone in the evolution of feminist ideas, representing the acquisition by women of a basic political right. Yet, by the 1920s there were alternative approaches to the means of consolidating that fundamental equality. As we have noted, in both Britain and the United States debate was joined between the exponents of the 'old' equal rights tradition of feminism and the 'new' evangelical or welfare feminists, revolving around the issue of sameness and difference between women and men.

The idea of women's difference is in part explained by the metaphorical association of women with nature (see Chapter 8). Traceable to the origins of Western political thought, this association also characterised the emergence of modern science. As Coole points out, Francis Bacon employed quite explicit sexual imagery to portray the character of scientific enquiry.[11] Knowledge (male) was used to comprehend and control nature (female), thereby conveying a relationship of domination and subordination between the sexes. Man became the active, enquiring, rational subject, woman the object of study, pliant and submissive. Embedded in such a view was the perception of man as 'self' and of woman as 'other', understood only in her relation to man.

The 'otherness' of women was explored in detail by the French philosopher Simone de Beauvoir (1908–86), whose *The Second Sex* appeared in 1949, bridging the gap between the first and second waves of the feminist movement. It is a vast work, informed by Marxism, psychoanalytic theories concerned with the study of the subconscious and existential philosophy's preoccupation with the ability of individuals to realise themselves. The work posed the question 'what is a woman?': in so doing it anticipated the woman-centredness that was to become a hallmark of radical feminism.

While recognising the economic subordination of women, as well as the constraints imposed upon them both by the biological function of reproduction and the denial of equal civil and political rights, de Beauvoir was not satisfied by structural or biological explanations of women's inferior status. Nor was she wholly convinced that either Marxist or liberal projects were sufficient means through which women could be liberated. Rather, she argued that the project for woman was woman herself. Here was the influence of existentialism, a philosophy that insists upon the unique capacity that human beings enjoy for self-awareness and the ability that they possess to make self-conscious choices to realise their existence.

Women, de Beauvoir argued, are required to understand not only that their secondary status as the 'other' has been imposed upon them by men, but that they have internalised this status themselves. This signifies the psychoanalytic aspect of her ideas. She contested Freudian theory which explained the female psyche in terms of penis envy – that women regard themselves as incomplete and, hence, imperfect men – and rejected the proposition that women's anatomy defined their destiny. Women, she insisted, were not fated to become submissive others whose existence was given meaning only in relation to, and by, men. Rather, they must realise their own capacity for self-awareness, make their own choices and celebrate their own needs.

This vision of women shedding their internalised sense of inferiority and transcending their subordinate status did not mean that differences between the sexes would disappear. But while biological distinctions would persist, the availability of contraception and abortion meant that women would be able to take control over their bodies rather than be enslaved by them: anatomy offered opportunity, not a destiny cast in stone. However, while assaulting the dualisms that had created the stifling condition of otherness among women, she did appear to assign a higher value to characteristics – notably reason and culture – traditionally associated with men. In that important respect, there is a current of androcentrism present in *The Second Sex* which lends a certain ambiguity to its legacy.

Observing the social construction of womanhood – 'One is not born but rather becomes a woman' – de Beauvoir was to appeal to a subsequent generation of liberal feminists, concerned to erase gendered rationalisations of the inequalities confronting women. Equally, she was to strike a chord among later Marxist feminists because of her insistence that the material inequalities confronting women would only be resolved in a socialist society. At the same time, her encouragement to women to take control of their bodies was consistent with radical feminism's later concern with the politics of sexuality and reproduction. In addition, her injunction that women should embark on an interior exploration of their selfhood was to commend itself to postmodern feminists more overtly concerned with the psychoanaltyic aspects of women's identities.

THE SECOND WAVE

The period between the first and second waves was not marked by feminist inactivity, although there was a certain ebbing of its tide. Following the Second World War, and within the context of the emergence of the welfare state, campaigns to ensure publicly funded support for wives and mothers reflected the fact that feminism was becoming increasingly 'domesticated'. Far from generating a sense of fulfilment, however, the experience of being decanted back into home and family following their mobilisation into the armed forces and industry during the war, created a sense of loss among women. It was that sense of loss and disquiet that the American writer Betty Friedan (1921-) was to identify in what has come to be regarded as a seminal text in second-wave feminism.

In 1963 Friedan published *The Feminine Mystique*, a work firmly located in the liberal tradition of equal rights feminism. Set within a cultural climate that prized the domestic role for women, it exposed the image of the happy, contented housewife as a disabling myth. Hemmed in by fashionable theories about maternal deprivation, sociological works that endorsed a traditional division of sexual labour and a popular culture that portrayed married women as 'brainless, fluffy kittens' (and single women as dedicated to catching a husband), Friedan argued that women were ensnared in a lifestyle that allowed them no independent identity or sense of achievement. She exhorted them to achieve educational qualifications and to re-enter employment as the means of escape from the less than gilded cage of domestic entrapment.

In 1966, frustrated by the timidity of the US government in implementing the newly won equal rights for women enshrined in the 1964 Civil Rights Act, Friedan and a number of other women established the National Organisation for Women (NOW). Its remit was: 'To take action to bring women into full participation in the mainstream of American society now, exercising all the privileges and responsibilities thereof in truly equal partnership with men.' Within a year, NOW had published a bill of rights for women which endorsed the Equal Rights Amendment, urged the full enforcement of laws against sex discrimination and demanded equal educational opportunities for women, childcare centres and, most controversially, the right of women 'to control their reproductive lives'.

With the exception of the latter, which embraced abortion, NOW's agenda was fully consistent with mainstream American thought. It was no more, nor no less, than a set of liberal demands which argued for the removal of all legislative and economic barriers impeding women from participating in the full range of social, political and economic activities. It assumed no structural inequalities within society, unlike Marxist and socialist feminism, appealing in large measure to well-educated and largely middle-class, white heterosexual women. Moreover, while challenging the prevailing gendered image of woman as the dutiful wife preoccupied with pleasing her man and children, it assumed that women would be enabled to pursue a career while supported by their sweetly reasonable partners who were prepared to share in the tasks of domestic labour.

This reformist and rational view echoed the ideas of early liberals, though in exhorting legions of women to enter the labour market it seemed to owe more to Harriet Taylor than either Wollstonecraft or Mill. But it was nevertheless reformist, believing that legislative change and enhanced educational opportunities would facilitate the entry of women into the public realm. Moreover, it accepted the family as a basic social institution, believing that marriage could become an alliance of rational, co-equal individuals.

Friedan's renewal of liberal feminism was of course at odds with the socialist tradition of feminism which stressed the material basis of women's oppression. However, an emerging radical feminism rejected liberal and socialist feminism alike.

RADICAL CRITIQUES

In the United States, radical feminism grew out of the campaign for black civil rights and the 'New Left' in the 1960s. While ostensibly egalitarian, these groups were discovered by women to be no less discriminatory and sexist than mainstream, or as they became styled, 'malestream', organisations: 'we make the policy, you make the coffee' was a common attitude confronting women. When in 1967 some 200 radical groups met in Chicago at the 'National Conference for a New Politics', delegates refused to allow a motion to debate the problems of women, dismissing it as 'trivial'.[12]

This experience confirmed a growing belief among a number of women of the necessity of developing new groups from which men would be excluded. Marginalised on the left and unattracted to the liberal reformism of NOW, what was styled 'the women's liberation movement' began to crystallise around the issue of male power and privilege. An early statement of the centrality of patriarchy to radical feminism appeared in a 1969 'Manifesto' issued by the New York group, 'Redstockings'.

> Women are an oppressed class. Our oppression is total .... We identify the agents of our oppression as men. Male supremacy is the most basic form of domination .... All men receive economic, sexual and psychological benefits from male supremacy. All men have oppressed women ... we will always take the side of women against their oppressors. We will not ask what is 'revolutionary' or 'reformist', only what is good for women ... .[13]

The concept of women as a universal 'sex-class' was fully articulated by the co-author of the Redstockings 'Manifesto', Shulamith Firestone (1945-), in *The Dialectic of Sex* (1970). Both the title of the book and the phrase 'sex-class' imply something of an intellectual debt to Marxism.

But, in place of the centrality of struggle between economic classes, Firestone depicted the driving force of history as struggle between the biological classes. What was required to secure the liberation of women was, therefore, a biological not an economic revolution, achieved through women seizing control of the means of reproduction.

Firestone, who dedicated her book to de Beauvoir, envisaged that new and developing technologies would liberate women by enabling fertilisation to take place without intercourse, embryos to gestate and be born outside the womb and children raised outside the context of the nuclear family. In the process, the family as a reproductive and economic unit would disappear and a society freed from sexually assigned roles flourish. In its stead she, like her contemporary Kate Millett (1934–), proferred a vision of an androgynous society within which the virtues of men and women would be fused in a common identity.

Millett's *Sexual Politics* (1970) was the first text to elaborate the concept of patriarchy whose principles she believed to be twofold: 'male shall dominate female, elder male shall dominate young'. According to Millett, the family is the patriarchal institution *par excellence*, indoctrinating women to accept the power of men in both the public and private worlds. By representing male power as endemic to domestic as well as public life she underwrote the idea of the personal as political.

Unlike Firestone, however, Millett understood the oppression of women to be based upon the gendered construction of femininity rather than being determined by biological difference. As such, she insisted upon the necessity of a sexual revolution rather than the hi-tech solution favoured by Firestone. This entailed an end to monogamous marriage and the ideology of motherhood: the privatised family would be supplanted by collectively provided childcare. But it was her endorsement of the free expression of sexual practices, whether heterosexual, homosexual or lesbian, that distinguished her prescriptions. Only through such a transformation in consciousness and sexual activity would male supremacy be ended and both men and women evolve towards an androgynous future in which their positive qualities would be integrated in a common humanity.

These visions of an androgynous society did not, however, appeal to radical lesbian feminists in the United States. Accepting fully the pervasiveness of patriarchy, they understood the heterosexual relationship to be primarily a political one. Thus, women in such relationships were accused by them of collaborating in the oppression of women: of, in effect, sleeping with the enemy. This alternative expression of sexual politics was captured in the slogan 'feminism is the theory, lesbianism the practice'.

THE RESPONSE OF MARXIST AND SOCIALIST FEMINISM

The debate about the political correctness of lesbianism was not confined to the United States. In Britain the 'separatist' issue dominated the feminist debates in the later 1970s and was to be the cause of a major split between a vocal minority of radical lesbian and other feminists. The latter, while not deprecating lesbianism as a freely chosen expression of sexuality, argued that political separatism offered nothing by way of engagement with the overwhelming majority of women who chose heterosexuality. Moreover, socialist feminists objected to the separatist strategy because it isolated women from their potential male allies to whom they were ideologically wedded. However, the centrality of patriarchy to the renewal of feminist debate encouraged socialist feminists to respond to the charge that their ideological tradition made them sex-blind.

Some responded to the primacy accorded to patriarchy by promoting a 'Wages for Housework' campaign.[14] This and the accompanying 'domestic labour debate' of the early 1970s stressed the material contribution made by women to the economy through their unpaid work within the home. It was, however, a debate that took a largely theoretical and somewhat abstract form among socialists, rather than engaging the attention of other feminists or indeed women in general. Moreover, many socialist and non-socialist feminists also objected to the idea of paying women for domestic work on the ground that it legitimised rather than confronted the prevailing division of labour within the family, thereby institutionalising patriarchy. Another response among socialists was to develop 'dual-systems' theory, one version of which is associated with Heidi Hartmann. She argued that it was in the material interests of men, of whatever class, to perpetuate the sexual division of labour within both the public and private realms.[15]

From this perspective, men are seen to gain material advantages both from occupational segregation within the economy – the division of jobs into women's and men's work – and the unequal division of labour within the family. This produced a mutually reinforcing system of exploitation that was termed 'patriarchal capitalism'. Thus, it was inadequate to focus on the subordination of women within the economy; battle also had to be joined on the home front. Unless women struggled to make their partners aware of the double burden to which they were subjected, patriarchy would prove to be resilient even with the transition to socialism.

While wedded to a material explanation of oppression, Hartmann sought to identify the functional interaction between the home and the capitalist economy in maintaining women's subordination, rather than focusing solely upon the wider economy. Without such a twin strategy, men would not relinquish their vested material interests in maintaining both patriarchy and capitalism. An alternative dual-systems theory sought to fuse the Marxist analysis of women's subordination with the insights offered by psychoanalysis.

A leading exponent of this approach is Juliet Mitchell (1940–).[16] She has argued that women's oppression cannot be explained solely in material terms, but also has to be understood in its psychological and cultural dimensions. To accomplish this she focused on the family's role in transmitting to individuals their respective social identities as members of either the male or female sex. In essence, Mitchell was seeking to accommodate patriarchal analysis by underlining the ways in which the family engendered women's and men's roles and, in the process, placed a higher valuation on the latter. Thus, while understanding the appeal of patriarchy as a means of explaining the subordination of women, Mitchell rejected its apparent determinism. She presented patriarchy as a socially constructed value system, not as a fixed and universal 'law' based upon biological identity. As such, patriarchy could be successfully challenged and changed.

This marked another departure from orthodox Marxism. Rather than accepting that women were only materially oppressed in the home and the economy, she contended that they were also psychologically oppressed. The site of that oppression was the family. Visualising it as an agency that reproduced patriarchy by conditioning women to accept their subordination, she prescribed an ideological struggle within its confines. This meant that women should realise how they were subordinated in three 'structures of oppression': reproduction, the socialisation of children and the expression of sexuality. Unless these were transformed, patriarchy would not automatically wither away with the demise of capitalism, while the material oppression of women within the 'structure of production' would be sustained. A psycho-cultural revolution, led by women, was therefore crucial to the elimination of patriarchy.

The ideas of Hartmann and Mitchell, in responding to the critiques of radical feminists, represented a departure from the monocausal explanation of women's oppression characteristic of orthodox Marxism. Both allowed patriarchy an independent existence, but dismissed the separatist solution preferred by some radical feminists as well as the reformist strategies of liberal feminists which, even if successful, would leave intact the structural inequalities endemic to capitalism.

The primacy of sexual politics in radical feminist analyses of women's oppression has left a profound mark upon feminist debate. By seeking to integrate patriarchy into their ideas, both liberal and socialist feminists have had to acknowlege its usefulness in explaining the continuing inequalities that beset women. However, rather than interpreting patriarchy in terms of biological essentialism, liberals in particular have sought to stress its gendered character by emphasising the cultural and psychological construction of women's roles. In the case of socialist feminists, the experience has been rather more painful, involving some intellectually athletic attempts to reconcile patriarchy with the enduring attachment to materialist explanations of women's oppression.

PRO-FAMILY AND PRO-WOMAN FEMINISM

The significance of sexual politics has not been accepted by all feminists, notably those who have perceived motherhood as a means of empowerment for women. From the later 1970s and throughout the 1980s these women generated a literature of pro-family feminism which has been characterised as 'maternal revivalism'.[17] Rejecting androcentrism, androgyny and lesbian separatism, Betty Friedan, Germaine Greer (1939–) and Jean Bethke Elshtain among others have, in different ways, contested the argument that mothering is incompatible with feminism.

Greer's *The Female Eunuch* (1971) established her reputation as a prominent (hetero)sexual radical of the formative stages of second-wave feminism. Opposed to monogamous marriage and conventional patterns of child rearing within the nuclear family, she advocated plural childcare within a trans-generational 'stem-family' and, critically, the recovery of sexual energy by women. The unalloyed pursuit of sexual passion would, she believed, turn women from their pitiable feminine condition of passivity, dependence and sexlessness – engineered by the patriarchal motives of men – into dynamic, energetic and self-fulfilled individuals, especially in the bedroom. Through these means all differences, bar that of the physiological, would be eradicated.

By 1984, however, in *Sex and Destiny*, Greer came to expound a version of pro-family feminism that emphasised essential sexual differences between women and men. Continuing to reject the numbing isolationism and lovelessness of the suburban nuclear family, she identified the extended 'family' common to peasant communities as a realm within which mother–child relationships and sisterhood – 'a word we constantly use without any idea of what it is' – can flourish. Her book portrayed a somewhat sentimentalised image of women, communing together and creating a matriarchal and child-centred oasis within a patriarchal desert.

Three years earlier Friedan had published *The Second Stage*, in which she accused the women's movement of creating a 'feminist mystique' which 'denied the profound, complex human reality of the . . . biological relationship between woman and man . . . the reality of woman's own sexuality, her childbearing, her roots and life connection within the family'.[18] Sexual politics had, in her revised view, generated an adversarial relationship between the sexes and alienated women who sought fulfilment through motherhood. Having previously stylised the nuclear family as a 'comfortable concentration camp' for suburban women, she now presented it as one form of relationship within which women could satisfy their emotional needs.

Decrying the 'extremist rhetoric' and 'ludicrous fulminations' of radical feminists, she defined the family as the new frontier of feminism whose appeals could be reconciled with individual fulfilment through work. Moreover, veering close to a view of essential difference between women and men, she adopted two gendered styles of leadership and thinking. The feminine style ('Beta') was intuitive, qualitative and holistic; the masculine (or 'Alpha') analytical, quantitative and abstract. She did not perceive the former, preferred style as the monopoly of women, but as being equally accessible to men. Men, she argued, should embrace this mode of thinking as a means of promoting tolerance, diversity and consensus.

While neither Greer nor Friedan equated the family only with its nuclear form, this is not true of Elshtain. In *Public Man, Private Woman* (1981) she assaults the politicisation of personal life promoted by radical feminists, defends the privacy of a child-centred family life and celebrated mothering as 'a complicated, rich, ambivalent, vexing, joyous activity which is biological, natural, social, symbolic and emotional'.[19]

Embedded in these arguments is a recognition of biological differ-ence and an acceptance of the compatibility of motherhood with feminism. A related perspective is also present in the development of 'pro-woman' or 'cultural feminism', one expression of which is eco-feminism (see Chapter 8). Like ecologism, pro-womanism encompasses a variety of views but tends to represent women as being essentially different from, and superior to, men. As such its exponents reject androcentrism and regard androgyny as suspect on the ground that, at best, it produces bland uniformity.

Pro-womanism is essentialist. It claims that women possess qualities superior to men because of their innate closeness to nature, to their bodies and to nurture. Hand in hand with these claims comes a rejection of rationality and instrumentality which are seen to be characteristically male attributes. Pro-womanism thereby asserts a biologically based, universal and established female character which transcends race, ethnicity and class. Such essentialism is most fervently expressed by eco-feminists who both equate man's rape and despoilation of the earth with their treatment of women and insist that the future of both can only be assured through the diffusion and acceptance of womanly values. A more radical expression of pro-womanism is found in the work of Mary Daly (1928-). She advocates withdrawal into a woman-only culture untainted by patriarchal constructions of femininity. Only in such a context can 'wild' and 'lusty women' express their natural and unrequited passions.[20]

The celebration of motherhood and essentialism has, of course, provoked criticisms from other feminists. Pro-family feminists are regarded as having fallen into a patriarchal snare by internalising a value system that has been insinuated by men into Western political thought. As such, they are accused of providing ammunition to anti-feminists who perceive women's natural place to be the home. Similarly, the advocates of cultural/lesbian separatism, retailing beliefs founded upon the essential superiority of women, have been criticised on the ground that patriarchy can only be undermined if it is critically engaged, not shunned.

THE POLITICS OF IDENTITIES

Whether through the experience of patriarchal oppression or the assertion that all women share values in common, the sub-text of much feminist debate is that women share in a potential and universal sisterhood. Indeed, in the early stages of second-wave feminism, such bold claims about global sisterhood were not uncommon. However, in the renewed rush to demarcate differences between women and men and also to assert an underlying unity among all women, many feminists neglected the needs and agendas of ethnic minority women in the First World and of women generally in the 'Third World'. Western feminism thereby came to be regarded by non-white women as ethnocentric.

Bell Hooks (1952-) is an eloquent critic of the colour-blindness of mainstream feminism in the United States and its effective complicity in perpetuating racial oppression:

> despite all the rhetoric about sisterhood and bonding, white women were not sincerely committed to bonding with black and other groups of women to fight sexism. They were primarily interested in drawing attention to their lot as white upper and middle class women.[21]

Similar views were expressed by ethnic minority women in Britain as early as 1978:

> The women's movement has never taken up the question of racism in any real way . . . [this] has ensured and will continue to ensure that the women's movement as a whole is irrelevant to the needs and demands of most black women.[22]

Such alienation fostered the growth of separate black feminist groups seeking to explore their own histories and identities, leading to a further organisational fragmentation of the feminist movement. The proliferation of such ethnically distinct groups, each celebrating its own identity, not only challenges an unreflective presumption of universal sisterhood but also deconstructs the concept of a unified 'black womanhood'. Thus, the politics of difference between the sexes has been complemented by a growing concern among feminist women to pursue the politics of their own different identities and experiences. An even more profound development has been the growing debate sparked by postmodernism.[23]

The emergence of postmodernism has unsettled feminism by posing fundamental questions about the meaning of woman's identity.

Although postmodern thought contains a variety of perspectives, what its exponents share in common is a rejection of received ideas that claim to explain the realities of existence. They do not accept that there is an ultimate truth or objectivity that can be apprehended by the application of modernist concepts like reason or knowledge which characterised the Enlightenment.

From this perspective, any doctrine purporting to comprehend reality in a unified and integrated way – whether it is liberalism or Marxism, socialism or conservatism, ecologism or nationalism – is both misguided and pretentious. The pretension of such claims is said to be rooted in ways of thinking that seek to impose unitary order on the social (and natural) world. Such a pursuit is misguided because, postmodernists insist, reality is too complex to be grasped by any single 'right' way of seeing the world. The same criticisms are levelled at feminism.

Postmodernists reject attempts to establish one specifically feminist doctrine on the ground that the ways in which women perceive themselves are multiple and diverse. The identities of individual women are understood to be mediated by a host of interacting factors – age, ethnicity, class, race, culture, sexuality, experience – which defy any and all attempts to dragoon them into a single ideological camp. Rather, these intrinsic differences among individual women should be explored by them as individuals. By crafting a new language and ways of thinking about their identities women will be freed from the oppressive meanings imposed by men.

This critique of feminism, depending on one's own view, either threatens or promises to usher in a bewildering multiplicity of under-standings about what it is to be a woman. It scorns essentialism, arguing that women's experiences are plural and diverse, both across time and space. 'Woman' is not understood as a fixed or given category but rather as a fluid and contingent one. It advocates subjectivity and an interior exploration by women of their own, individual identities, making no claim that any one such discovered identity is more authentic or true than another – or that it will remain static.

The injunction of postmodernism to women is that it really is better to travel than arrive. The journey is an internal one and has no destination other than the realisation that 'identity' is protean and transitory. In that sense postmodernism echoes de Beauvoir's concept of otherness: but here this is understood as an opportunity rather than a constraint. By standing back and exploring that condition women will engage in their own critiques of the meanings that men have imposed upon them.

CONCLUSION

Virginia Woolf considered that each woman needed a room of her own in order to realise her autonomy. Postmodernism appears to carry this advice to extreme. Its encouragement to all women to explore their own internal rooms or spaces involves clearing away all the clutter bestowed by modern ideologies so that each individual's shifting identity can be analysed. Such a strategy encourages subjectivity and relativism. There is no designer model of feminism that can be imposed upon all women, but rather each is customised to suit every individual: this implies that there are as many feminisms as there are women.

The dizzying relativism of the postmodern approach does challenge those attached to each of the other intellectual traditions of feminism: it effectively puts a plague on each of their houses by arguing that they are based on flawed doctrinal foundations. As such, it ridicules each of their respective futures and denies the validity of their utopias. But, despite their ideological differences, feminists have always placed a premium on improving the actual conditions confronting women. Whether it is in securing legal and political rights, challenging discrimination, exposing the forms and incidence of violence against women, insisting upon their rights to control their own bodies or express their sexuality, the feminist movement has exhibited a capacity to act in unison on a wide range of issues of practical concern to women.

This is not to gloss over the strategic nature of some expressions of unity, or the differences that exist among feminists. For instance, the issues of abortion and pornography do not command an overwhelming consensus. Some contend that support for freely available terminations is a definitive test of one's feminist credentials whereas others find such a position morally repugnant. Equally, there are feminists who perceive pornography as symptomatic of men's violence towards women, whereas others endorse its availability as an increased expression of freedom. To personify such a controversy, some feminists interpret Madonna's uninhibited celebration of her sexuality as a confident assertion of womanhood, whereas others see it as merely perpetuating men's view of women as sex objects.

Such contrasting opinions are seized upon by anti-feminists as conclusive evidence that feminism is a house divided against itself. It would be more accurate to portray feminism as a house within which there really are many mansions. Rosemarie Tong captures this interpretation of feminism thus:

> We need a home in which everyone has a room of her own, but one in which the walls are thin enough to permit a conversation, a community of friends in virtue, and partners in action. Only such a community can make feminist ethics and politics possible.[24]

The appearance of radical feminism, or rather feminisms, signified a frustration with existing strategies and ideas. The revival of patriarchy, a renewed concern with the politics of sexuality and reproduction and the painful, if necessary, appreciation that differences among women had previously been somewhat neglected, all challenge any assumption that it is possible to construct an integrated feminist movement centred upon an agreed ideology.

Such diversity should not, however, be perceived as a sign of weakness and immaturity. To the contrary, the renewed debate among feminists represents a strong and mature body of thought concerned to interrogate itself, rather than submit to the dead-weight of any particular orthodoxy. Its vitality challenges the belief that there is a definitive answer to the continuing inequalities that confront women. Feminism is not then a settled doctrine, but a dynamic and engaged discourse.

NOTES

1 Rosalind Delmar, 'What is Feminism?', in Juliet Mitchell and Ann Oakley, eds, *What is Feminism?*, Oxford, Blackwell, 1986, 8.
2 Vicky Randall, 'Feminism and Political Analysis', *Political Studies*, XXXIX. 3, 1991 515.
3 Diana Coole, *Women in Political Theory: From Ancient Misogyny to Contemporary Feminism*, Brighton, Harvester Wheatsheaf, 1988, 4.
4 Coole, *ibid.*, 2.
5 Ruth Perry, *The Celebrated Mary Astell: An Early English Feminist*, London, 1986; Bridget Hill, *The First English Feminist: Reflections Upon Marriage and Other Writings by Mary Astell*, Aldershot, 1986.

6 Valerie Bryson, *Feminist Political Theory: An Introduction*, Basing-stoke, Macmillan, 1992, 11ff.

7 Leslie Tanner, ed., *Voices from Women's Liberation*, New York, Signet, 1971, 231–54.

8 Olive Banks, *Faces of Feminism*, Oxford, Martin Robertson, 1981.

9 Quoted in Maggie Humm, ed., *Feminism: A Reader*, Hemel Hempstead, Harvester Wheatsheaf, 1992, 43.

10 Mary Wollstonecraft, *The Rights of Woman*, London, Dent, 1974, 197.

11 See Coole, *Women in Political Theory*, 269–270.

12 See David Bouchier, *The Feminist Challenge: The Movement for Women's Liberation in Britain and the USA*, London, Macmillan, 1983, 52–53.

13 See Tanner, ed., *Voices from Women's Liberation*, 109–11.

14 Maria Rosa Dalla Costa and Selma James, *The Power of Women and the Subversion of the Community*, Bristol, 1972. See too Hilary Rose, 'Women's Work: Women's Knowledge', in Mitchell and Oakley, eds, *What is Feminism?*, 161–83.

15 Heidi Hartmann, 'The Unhappy Marriage of Marxism and Feminism: Towards a More Progressive Union', in Lydia Sargent, ed., *The Unhappy Marriage of Marxism and Feminism: A Debate on Class and Patriarchy*, London, Pluto, 1986, 1–41.

16 Juliet Mitchell, *Psychoanalysis and Feminism*, Harmondsworth, Penguin, 1974.

17 Lynne Segal, *Is the Future Female? Troubled Thoughts on Contemporary Feminism*, London, Virago, 1987.

18 Betty Friedan, *The Second Stage*, London, Abacus, 1983, 51.

19 Jean Bethke Elshtain, *Public Man, Private Woman: Woman in Social and Political Thought*, Princeton, Princeton University press, 1981, 243.

20 Mary Daly, *Pure Lust: Elemental Feminist Philosophy*, Boston, Beacon Press, 1984.

21 Bell Hooks, *Ain't I a Woman: Black Women and Feminism*, Boston, South End Press, 1981, 142.

22 Kum-Kum Bhavnani and Pratibha Parmar, quoted in Joni Lovenduski and Vicky Randall, *Contemporary Feminist Politics: Women and Power in Britain*, Oxford, Oxford University Press, 1993, 81.

23 See Linda Nicholson, ed., *Feminism/Postmodernism*, London, Rout-ledge, 1990.

24 Rosemarie Tong, *Feminist Thought: A Comprehensive Introduction*, London, Unwin Hyman, 1989, 7.

FURTHER READING

Histories of the feminist movement abound, as do treatments of specific campaigns including suffrage. Equally, there are a multitude of books that discuss varieties of feminist thought and the ways in which women have been portrayed by thinkers throughout the development of political thought. What follows merely hints at the rich array of relevant literature and, where applicable, should complement those works cited in the chapter some of which are reiterated here.

Accessible discussions of the variety of ideological perspectives within feminism that I found particularly helpful were Rosemarie Tong's *Feminist Thought: A Comprehensive Introduction*, London, Unwin Hyman, 1989; Josephine Donovan's *Feminist Theory*, New York, Ungar, 1985; and Valerie Bryson's *Feminist Political Theory: An Introduction*, Basingstoke, Macmillan, 1992. A recent collection of extracts that reflect the diversity of feminist ideas is Maggie Humm's *Feminisms: A Reader*, Hemel Hempstead, Harvester Wheatsheaf, 1992, while Juliet Mitchell's and Ann Oakley's edited collection, *What is Feminism?*, Oxford, Blackwell, 1986, contains a number of thought provoking essays. This was a 'sequel' to the equally rewarding *The Rights and Wrongs of Women*, Harmondsworth, Penguin, 1979, also edited by Mitchell and Oakley. Terry Lovell's *British Feminist Thought: A Reader*, Oxford, Blackwell, 1990, is a useful collection of writings by prominent second-wave feminists.

Diana Coole's *Women in Political Theory: from Ancient Misogyny to Contemporary Feminism*, 2nd edn, Brighton, Harvester Wheatsheaf, 1993, is a scintillating critique of the treatment of women within the tradition of Western political thought. A more narrative account of women in history which can usefully be read alongside Coole is the two-volume study *A History of Their Own*, London, Penguin, 1990, by Bonnie Andersen and Judith Zinsser. A briefer and British-based survey written from a socialist perspective during the ferment of early second-wave feminism is Sheila Rowbotham's *Hidden from History*, London, Pluto, 1973. That tumult is also conveyed in Leslie Tanner's *Voices from Women's Liberation*, New York, Signet, 1971, a compilation of extracts by American women covering both the first and second waves of feminism. A comparable British focus on the early phase of second-wave feminism is provided by Micheline Wandor's *The Body Politic: Writings from the Women's Liberation Movement in Britain 1969–1970*, London, Stage 1, 1972.

A good comparative account of the politics and ideas of the women's movements in Britain and the United States is David Bouchier's *The Feminist Challenge*, London, Macmillan, 1983. Martin Pugh's *Women and the Women's Movement in Britain 1914–1959*, London, Macmillan, 1992, is recommended for its overview of the period between the two waves of feminism. On suffrage in Britain see Ray Strachey's *The Cause*, London, Virago, 1978; *One Hand Tied Behind Us*, London, Virago, 1978, by Jill Liddington and Jill Norris; and Sylvia Pankhurst's *The Suffrage Movement*, London, Virago, 1977.

Classic primary sources include Mary Wollstonecraft's *The Rights of Woman* and John Stuart Mill's *The Subjection of Women* available in one volume with an introduction by Pamela Frankau, London, Dent, 1974; August Bebel, *Woman Under Socialism*, New York, Schocken Books, 1971; Friedrich Engels, *The Origin of the Family, Private Property and the State*, New York, Pathfinder Press, 1972; William Thompson, *Appeal of One-Half of the Human Race, Women*, London, Virago, 1983; Simone de Beauvoir, *The Second Sex*, Harmondsworth, Penguin, 1972; Betty Friedan, *The Feminine Mystique*, Harmondsworth, Penguin, 1965; and Shulamith Firestone, *The Dialectic of Sex*, New York, Bantam Books, 1971.

A sense of the vitality of the continuing debates within feminism and of the politics of the women's movement are conveyed in the following: Joni Lovenduski and Vicky Randall, *Contemporary Feminist Politics: Women and Power in Britain*, Oxford, Oxford University Press, 1993; Gisela Kaplan, *Contemporary Western European Feminism*, London, Allen and Unwin, 1992, which also assesses the relative achievements of various national women's movements; and *Introducing Women's Studies*, London, Macmillan, 1993, edited by Diane Richardson and Victoria Robinson. An assertive radical feminist survey of the ubiquity of patriarchy can be found in Marilyn French's *The War Against Women*, London, Penguin, 1992, while patriarchy itself is explored in Sylvia Walby's *Theorising Patriarchy*, Oxford, Blackwell, 1990. Susan Faludi's *Backlash: The Undeclared War Against Women*, London, Vintage, 1992, supplies a readable, if picaresque, overview of the counter-attack against feminism. Among her targets is the controversial figure of Camille Paglia. Paglia's iconoclastic views about feminism are apparent in both *Sexual Personae: Art and Culture from Nefertiti to Emily Dickinson*, New Haven, Yale University Press, 1990, and *Sex, Art and American Culture*, London, Penguin, 1994.

Index

Note: Sub entries are in alphabetical order, except where chronological order is more significant